PRAISE FOR THE COMICS OF JEFFREY BROWN

"Usually reliable."
– The Onion

"emotionally about six years old."
– Warren Ellis

"Mildly confusing."
– Metro Toronto

"Pathetic losers nerd-pornas illustrated by a five year old."
– Portland Mercury

"Jeffrey Brown's work is not precious."
– Rain Taxi

"How poignant."
– The Comics Journal

"... eone ... ill."
... nder

"... ike they've been executed left-handed."
– Portland Tribune

"adds little to... previous observations on relationships."
– Publisher's Weekly

"Utter piece of shit."
– Proper Gander

DEDICATED TO MY PARENTS, WHO DON'T
ALWAYS GET MY HUMOR, BUT HAVE ALWAYS
LAUGHED POLITELY. OR MAYBE NERVOUSLY.

SOME OF THIS MATERIAL HAS PREVIOUSLY
APPEARED IN THE SELF-PUBLISHED MINI-COMIC
ALSO TITLED "I AM GOING TO BE SMALL"

I AM GOING TO BE SMALL

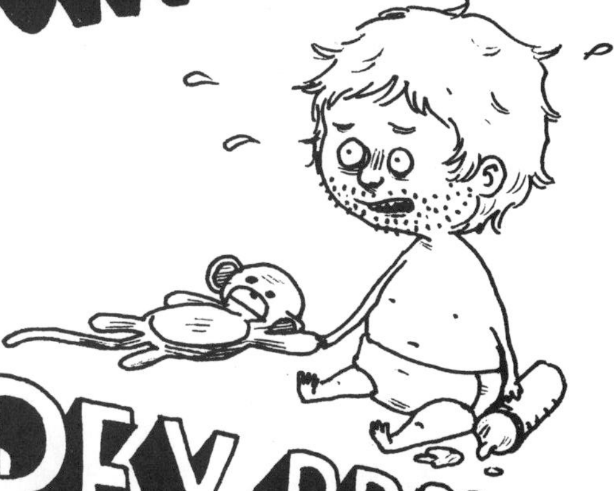

JEFFREY BROWN

ISBN 1-891830-86-4
PUBLISHED BY TOP SHELF PRODUCTIONS INC
PO BOX 1282 MARIETTA GA 30061-1282 USA
www.topshelfcomix.com
TOP SHELF AND THE TOP SHELF LOGO ARE © 2006
BY TOP SHELF PRODUCTIONS INC.

PRODUCTION BY BRETT WARNOCK

PRINTED IN CANADA
FIRST PRINTING. OCTOBER 2006.

I AM GOING TO BE small

A collection of gag and humour cartoons
1997 - 2006

THANK YOU:

AARON, ADRIAN, AGATHE, AHN, AL, ALISON, ALLISON, ALVIN, AMANDA, AMY, ANDERS, ANDREW, ANNA, ANNE, ANNIE, ANNEMARIE, ARCHER, ARTHUR, BABS, BECKY, BEKAH, BEN, BILL, BOB, BRAD, BRANDON, BRETT, BRIAN, BRYAN, CAITLIN, CAL, CARLY, CARSON, CHAD, CHARLES, CHERYL, CHESTER, CHIP, CHONDA, CHRIS, CHRISTA, CHRISTIAN, CHRISTINA, CHRISTINE, CHRISTOPHER, CINDY, CLAUS, COLIN, CRAIG, DAN, DANIEL, DANIELLE, DAVE, DAVID, DEAN, DEIHL, DIANA, DOLORES, DONNA, DOROTHY, DOUG, ED, ELI, ELIZA, ERIC, ERICA, ERIN, FRÉDÉRIC, GABRIELLE, GAIL, GARY, GEORGE, GRANT, GREG, HANNAH, HARRI, HARRIET, HEIDI, IAN, IRA, IVAN, JACKIE, JAMES, JAMIE, JANICE, JASON, JAY, JEAN-LOUIS, JEFF, JENNI, JENNIFER, JEREMY, JESSE, JESSICA, JILL, JIM, JIMMY, JOE, JOEL, JOHN, JONATHAN, JOANNA, JOSE, JOSEF, JOSH, JULIE, JULIEN, JUSTIN, KAROLYN, KATHY, KATIE, KEVIN, KIM, KIP, KRISTI, KRISTYN, LARK, LAURA, LAUREN, LAURIE, LIL, LILLI, LINDSAY, LIZ, LOIC, LORI, LUDOVIC, MAGGIE, MARC, MARIE, MARK, MATT, MEGAN, MERV, MICHAEL, MICHELLE, MICKAEL, MIKE, MIRKKA, MORGAN, NANCY, NAOMI, NATE, NICK, NICOLAS, NICOLE, OUTI, PAUL, PEGGY, PETER, PHIL, PHILIP, PHILLIP, PHYLLIS, PHOEBE, RACHEL, RALPH, REBECCA, REENE, RENEE, ROB, ROBIN, RON, ROSE, RUBY, RYAN, SALLY-ANNE, SAMANTHA, SAMMY, SANDRA, SARAH, SCOTT, SEAN, SETH, SHANNON, SHARON, SOPHIE, SOUTHER, STEPHEN, STEVE, SYLVIA, SYLVIE TARDY, TED, THERESA, THOMAS, THU, TIM, TINA, TOM, TOMMI, TRACEY, TYSON, VANESSA, WAYNE, WES, WILL, WILLA, WILLIAM AND ZAK. AND ALEJANDRA. AND KATHRYN.

AND IF I HAVE MISTAKENLY FORGOTTEN YOUR NAME, I WOULD LIKE TO THANK YOU HERE: _____

MY MOST SINCERE APOLOGIES FOR THIS UNINTENDED INSULT. I WILL COMMIT SEPUKU LATER TO ATONE FOR THIS.

CONTENTS

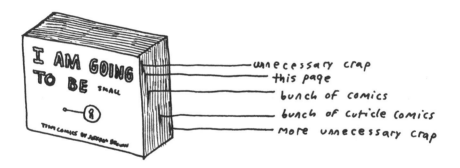

unnecessary crap

this page

bunch of comics

bunch of cuticle comics

more unnecessary crap

READ COMICS!

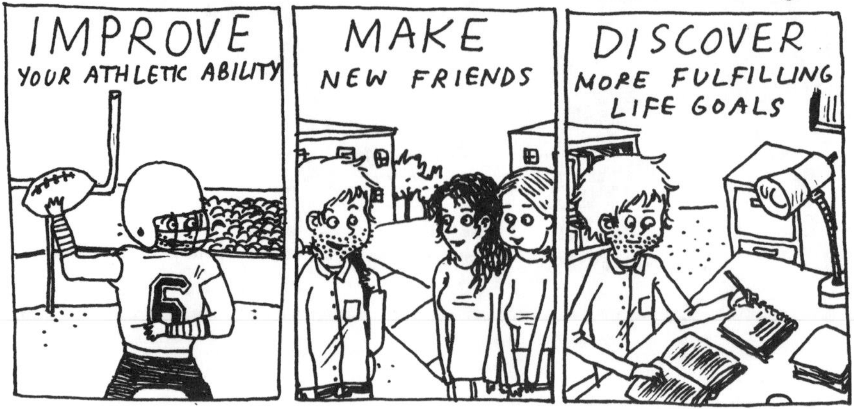
IMPROVE
YOUR ATHLETIC ABILITY
MAKE
NEW FRIENDS
DISCOVER
MORE FULFILLING
LIFE GOALS

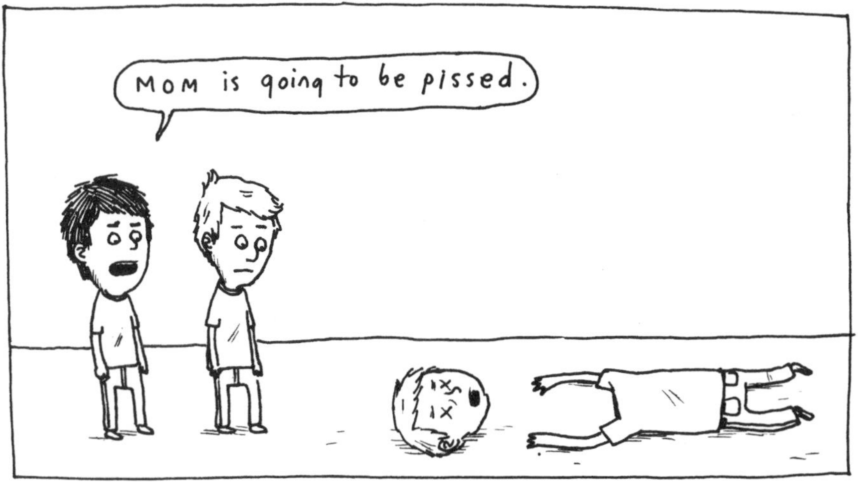
MOM is going to be pissed.

"MOVIE" IS THE MOST EXCITING FILM OF THE SUMMER! STARRING ACTORS AND ACTRESSES! FEATURING CINEMATOGRAPHY! FILMED BY CAMERAS! BOLSTERED BY MERCHANDISING!

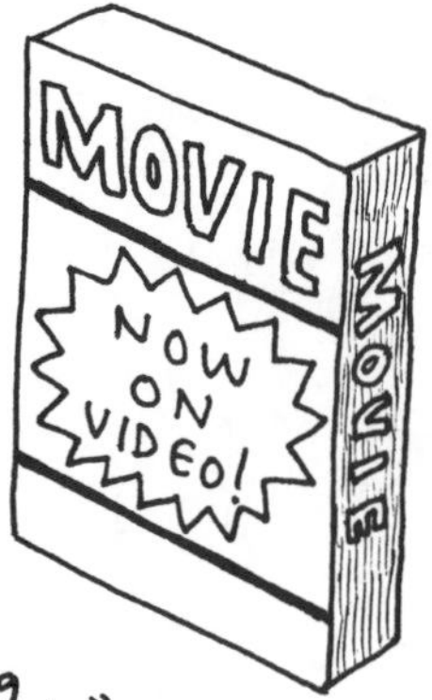
MOVIE
NOW ON VIDEO!
MOVIE

"The lead actor is cute"
— Some Female Film Critic

"The shower scene with the supporting actress made me want to masturbate"
— Some Male Newspaper Columnist

"Photons were bounced off the movie screen to create an image in my mind when the photons subsequently collided with photoreceptors in my eyes."
— some television personality

"I loved the part where one guy jumped in the air and shot the other guy and then the car blew up."
— Some Film Academy Guy

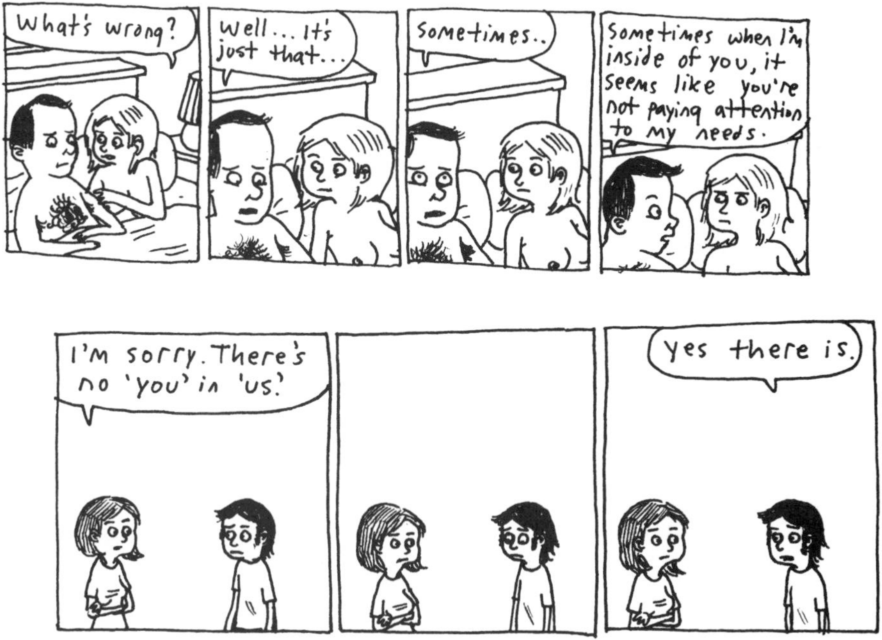
What's wrong?
Well... It's just that...
Sometimes..
Sometimes when I'm inside of you, it seems like you're not paying attention to my needs.
I'm sorry. There's no 'you' in 'us.'
yes there is.

INTERVIEWS

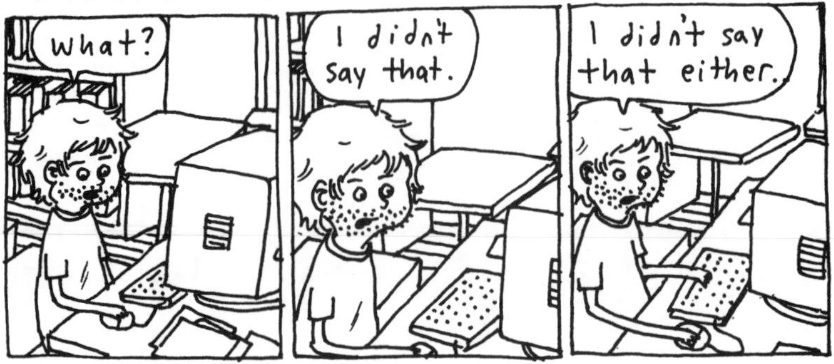
what?
I didn't say that.
I didn't say that either.

CREATE YOUR OWN

NEW!

PHOTON - ZOO!

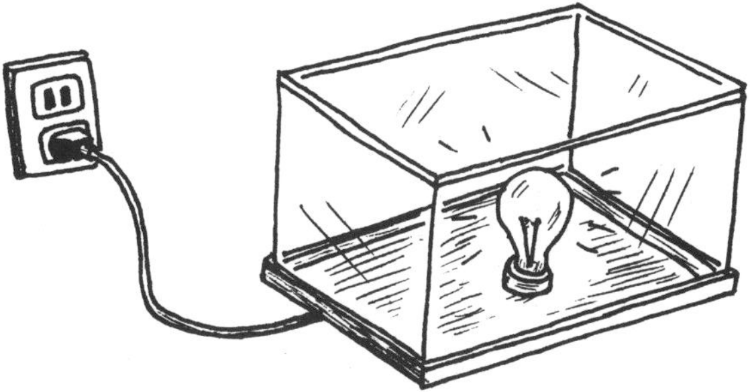

Watch your little photons at play in this easy to assemble Photon-Zoo! Made amazingly enough from every day items. Send $14.95 for blueprints and instructions on how to build your own Photon-Zoo.

HE WAS RIGHT. I LOVED BOXES.

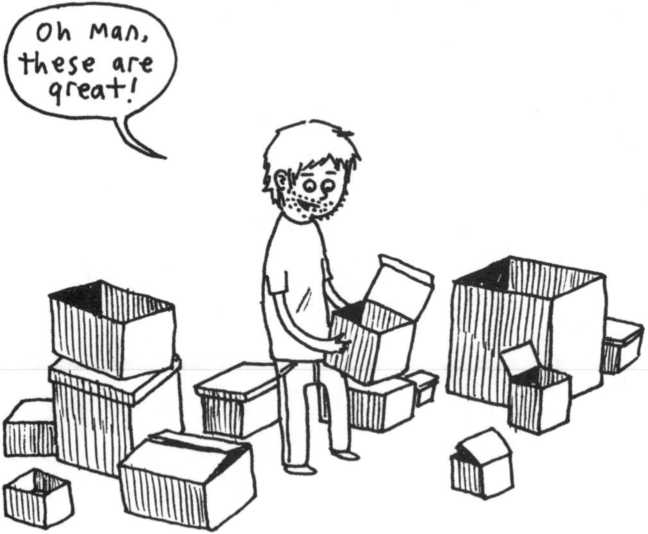
Oh man, these are great!

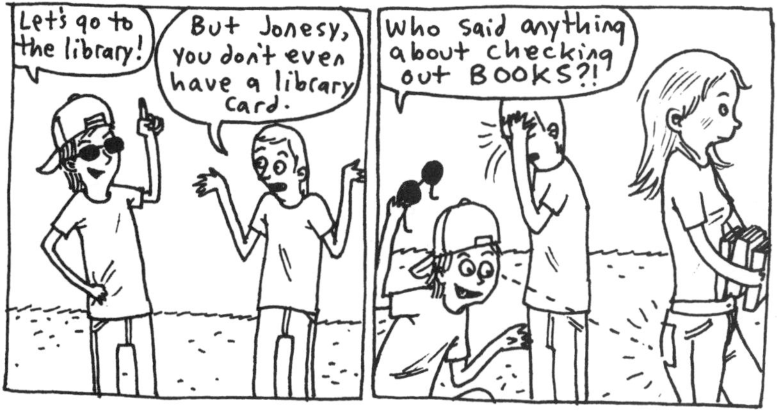
Let's go to the library!
But Jonesy, you don't even have a library card.
Who said anything about checking out BOOKS?!

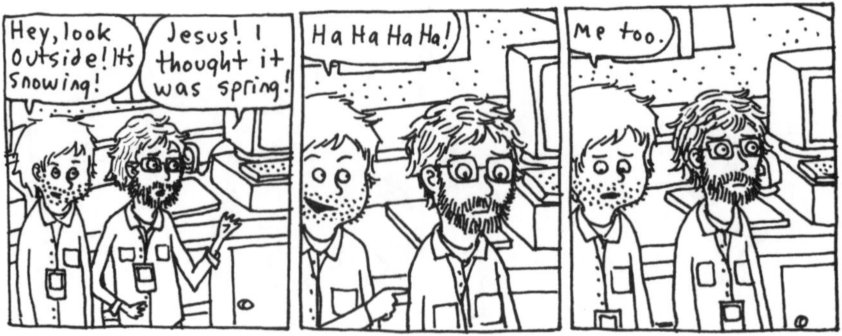
Hey, look outside! It's snowing!
Jesus! I thought it was spring!
Ha Ha Ha Ha!
Me too.

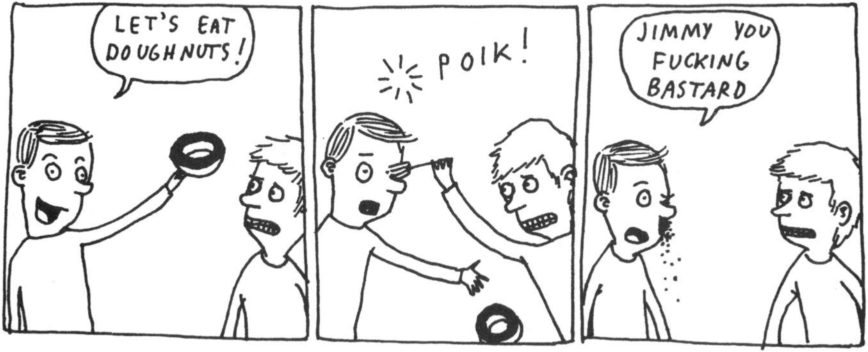
LET'S EAT DOUGHNUTS!
POIK!
JIMMY YOU FUCKING BASTARD

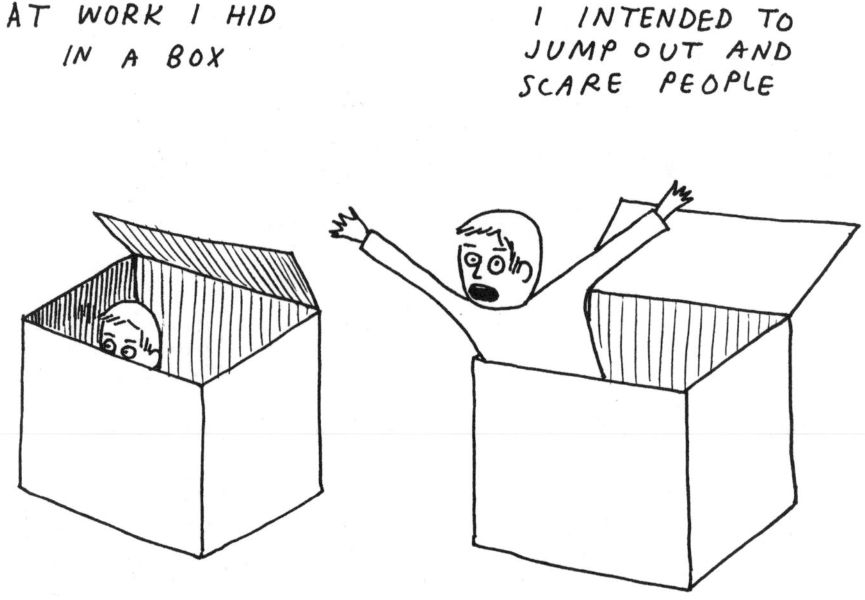
AT WORK I HID IN A BOX
I INTENDED TO JUMP OUT AND SCARE PEOPLE

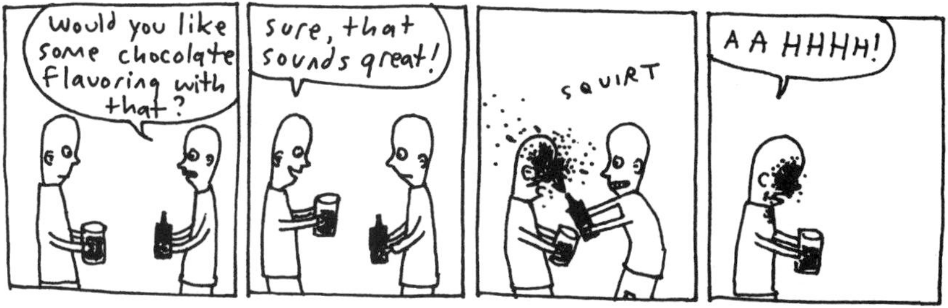
Would you like some chocolate flavoring with that?
Sure, that sounds great!
SQUIRT
AAHHHH!

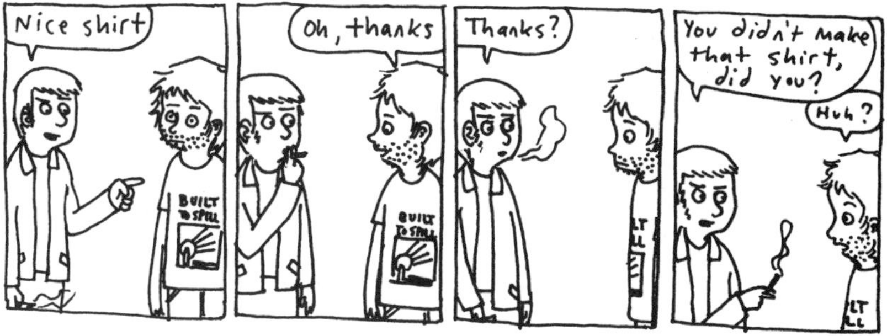
Nice shirt
BUILT TO SPILL
Oh, thanks
Thanks?
You didn't make that shirt, did you?
Huh?

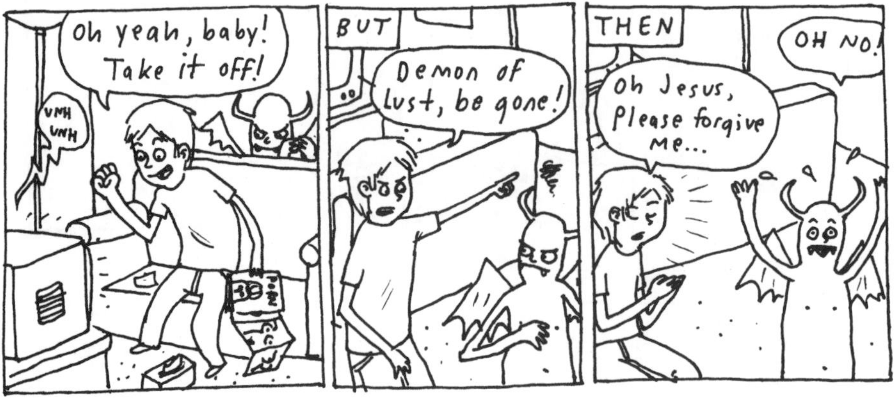
Oh yeah, baby! Take it off!
UNH UNH
PORN
BUT
Demon of Lust, be gone!
THEN
Oh Jesus, Please forgive me...
OH NO!

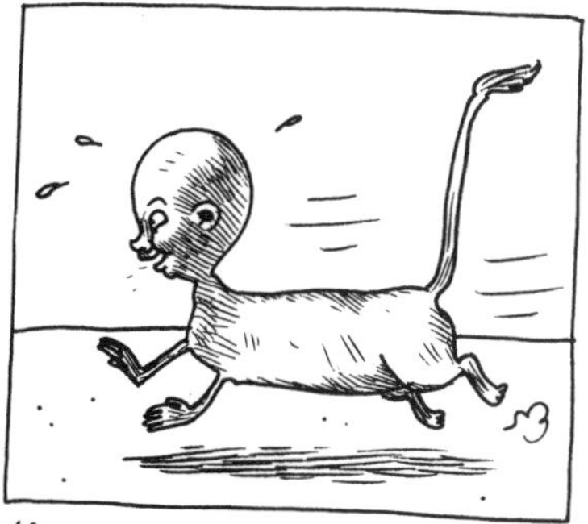

"NO ONE TAKES ME SERIOUSLY," HE BEMOANED.

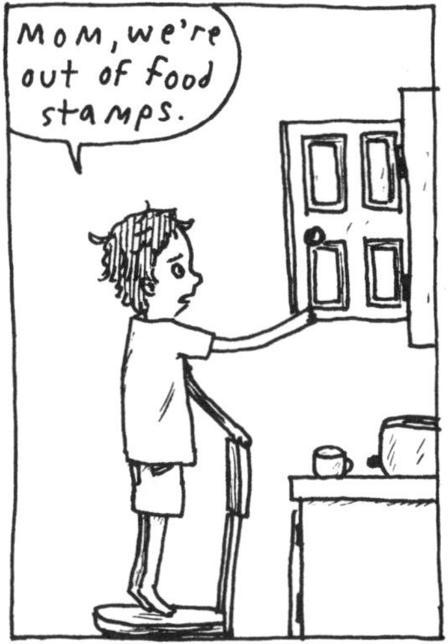
Mom, we're out of food stamps.

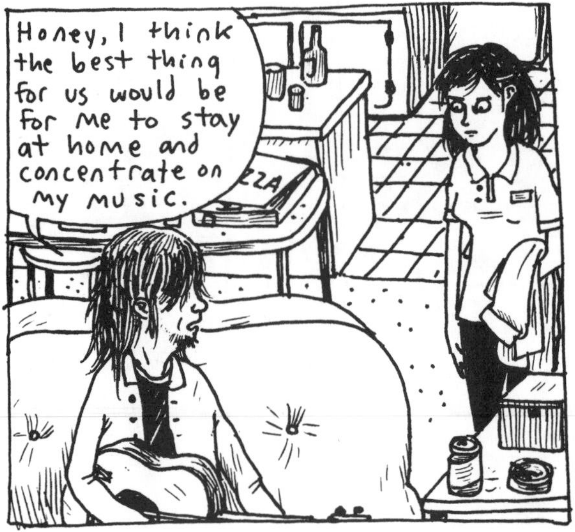
Honey, I think the best thing for us would be for me to stay at home and concentrate on my music.
ZZA

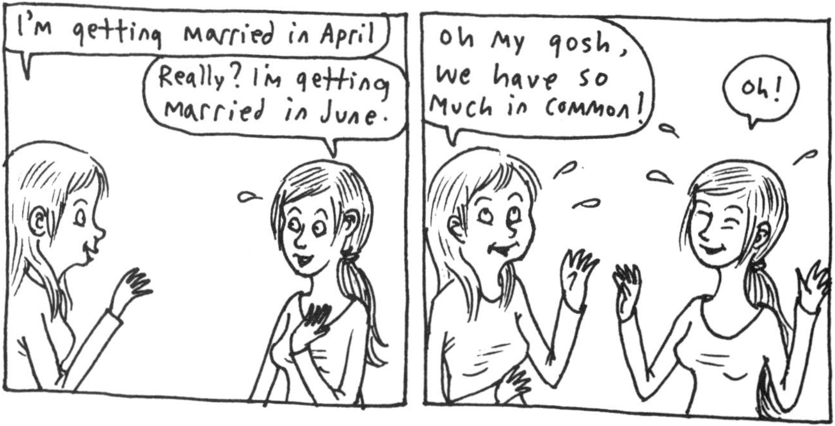
I'm getting married in April
Really? I'm getting married in June.
Oh my gosh, we have so much in common!
Oh!

YOUR CONSIDERATE POSTAL SERVICE

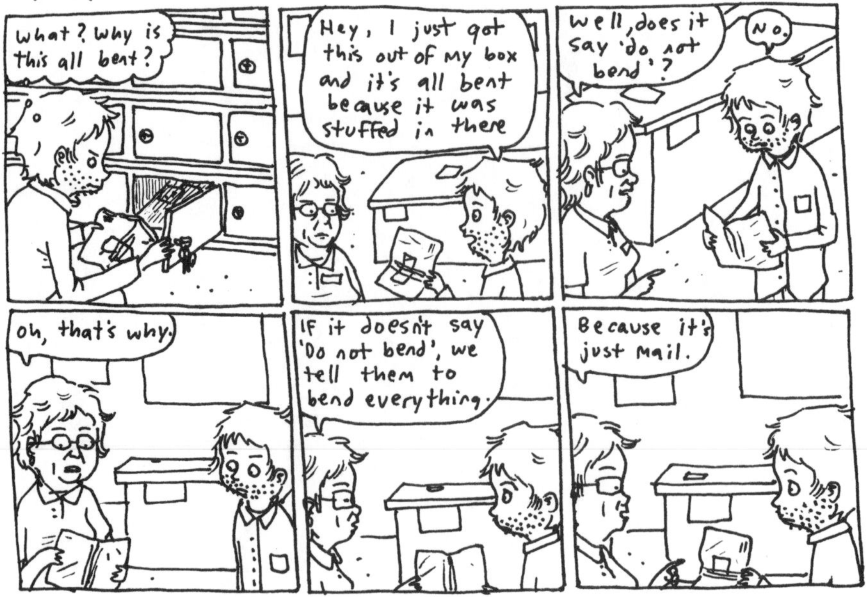
what? why is this all bent?
Hey, I just got this out of my box and it's all bent because it was stuffed in there
well, does it say 'do not bend'?
No.
oh, that's why.
If it doesn't say 'Do not bend', we tell them to bend everything.
Because it's just mail.

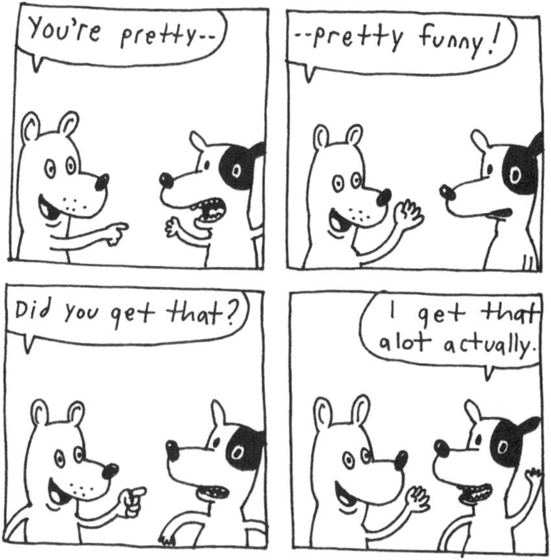
You're pretty--
--pretty funny!
Did you get that?
I get that alot actually.

DENIAL IS THE ESSENCE OF HOPE

HAHA, that house is on Fire, HA, boy, the poor sap who lives there...
That's your house.

Do you think our relationship is based on sex?
Yeah. But fortunately we have really great sex.

When are you going to apologize to me for that smear campaign you were running?

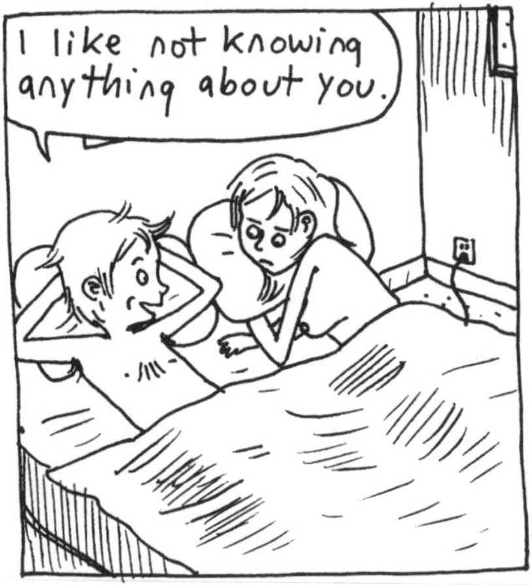
I like not knowing anything about you.

ON GREAT SEX

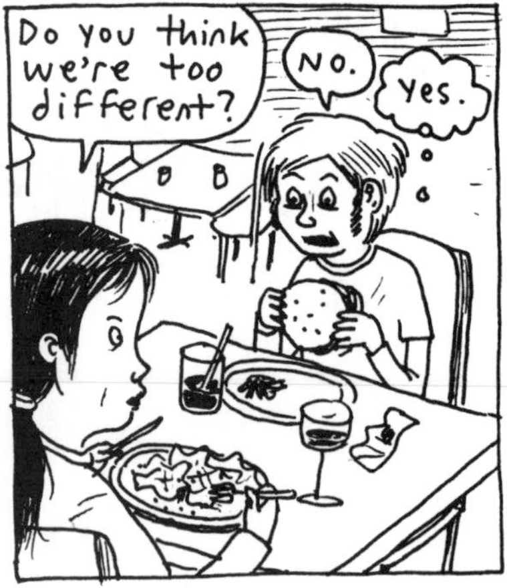
Do you think we're too different?
No.
yes.

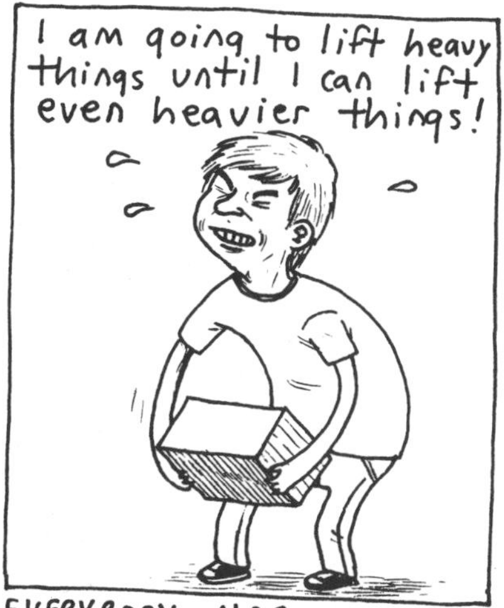
I am going to lift heavy things until I can lift even heavier things!

EVERYBODY HAS A DREAM

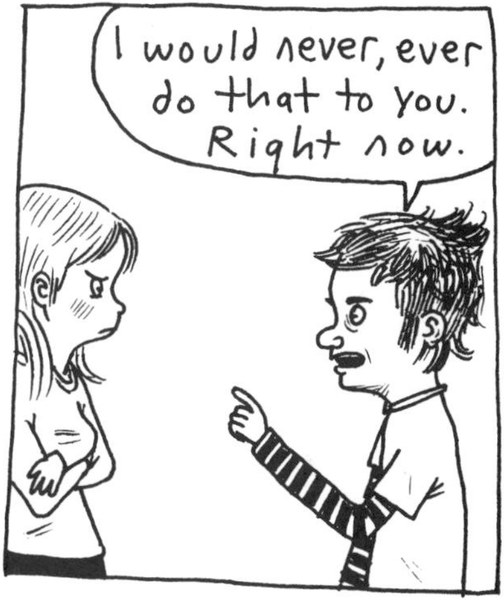
I would never, ever do that to you. Right now.

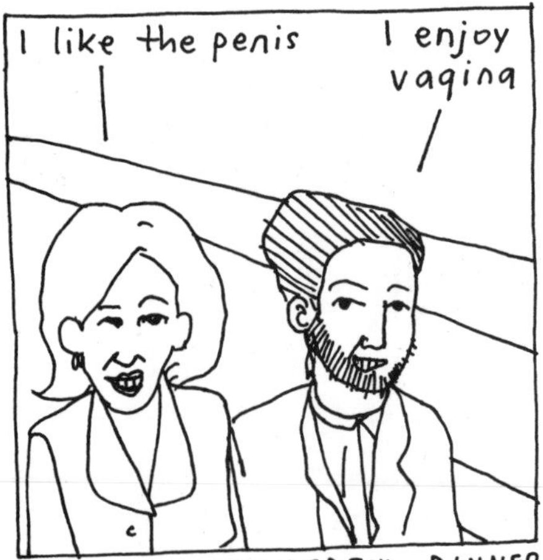
I like the penis
I enjoy vagina

IT WAS A WONDERFUL DINNER

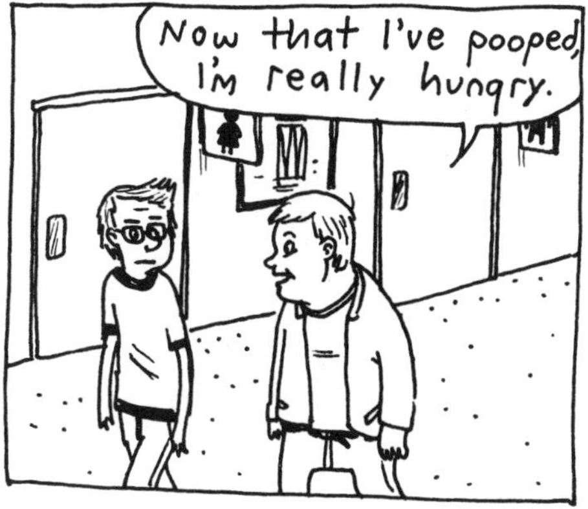
Now that I've pooped, I'm really hungry.

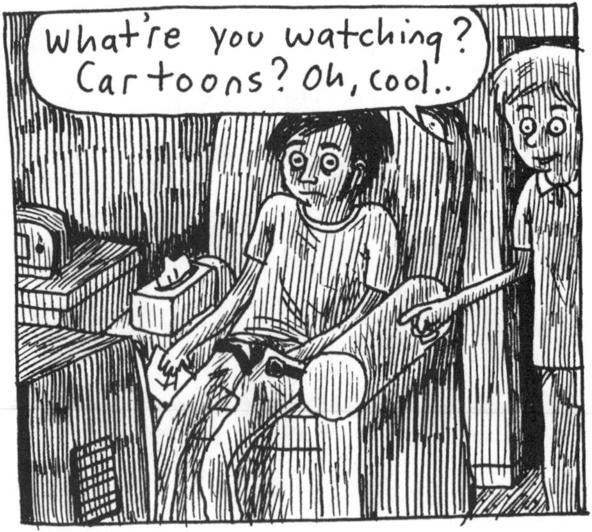
What're you watching? Cartoons? Oh, cool..

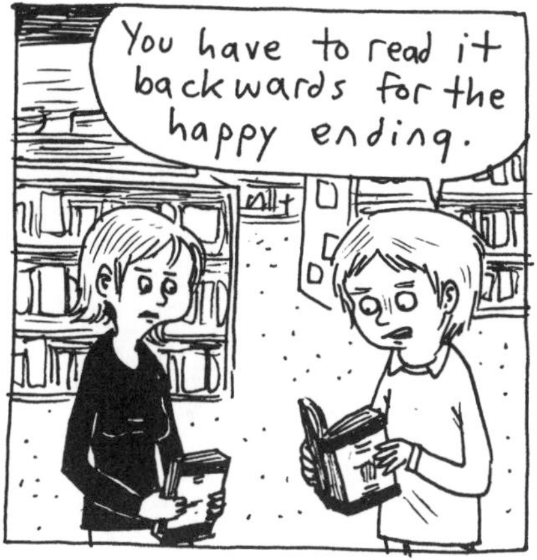
You have to read it backwards for the happy ending.

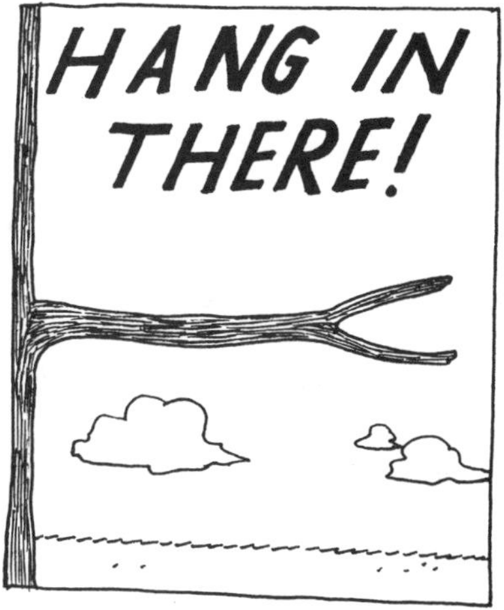
HANG IN THERE!

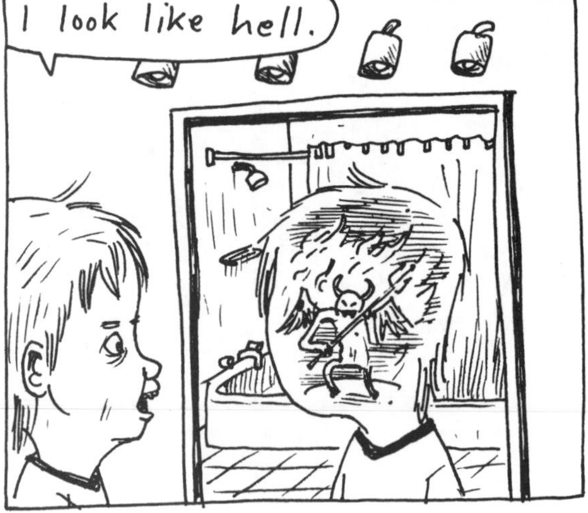
I look like hell.

WAYS TO PEE

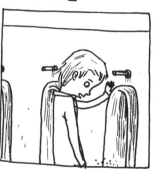

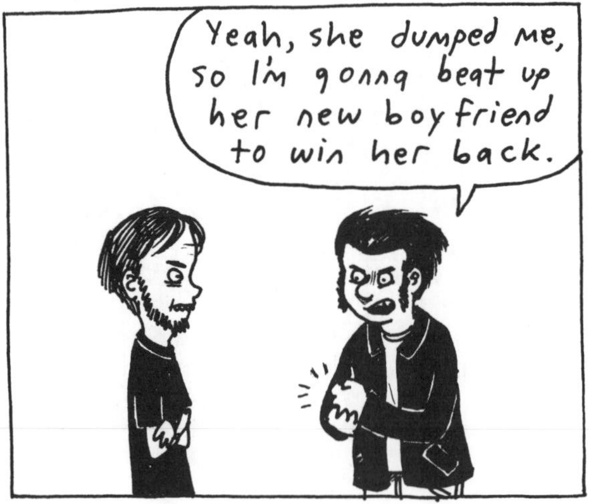
Yeah, she dumped me, so I'm gonna beat up her new boyfriend to win her back.

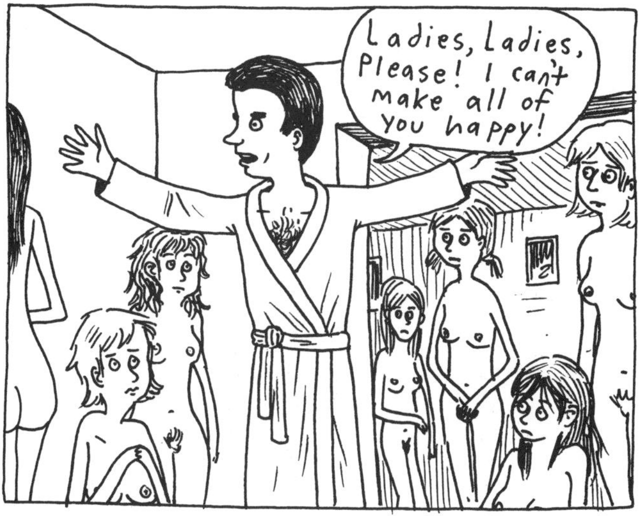
Ladies, Ladies, Please! I can't make all of you happy!

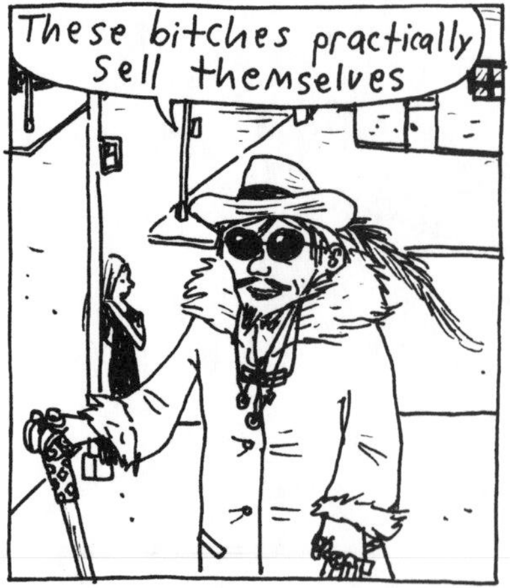
These bitches practically sell themselves

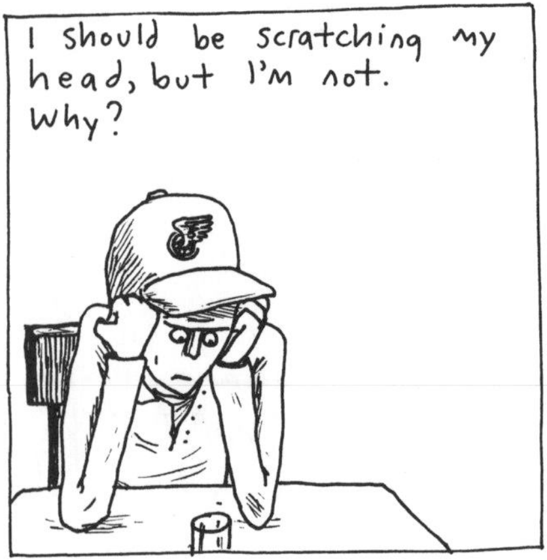
I should be scratching my head, but I'm not. Why?

THE FOUR LITTLE HORSEMEN OF THE APOCALYPSE

(TOO LITTLE TO ACTUALLY RIDE HORSES)

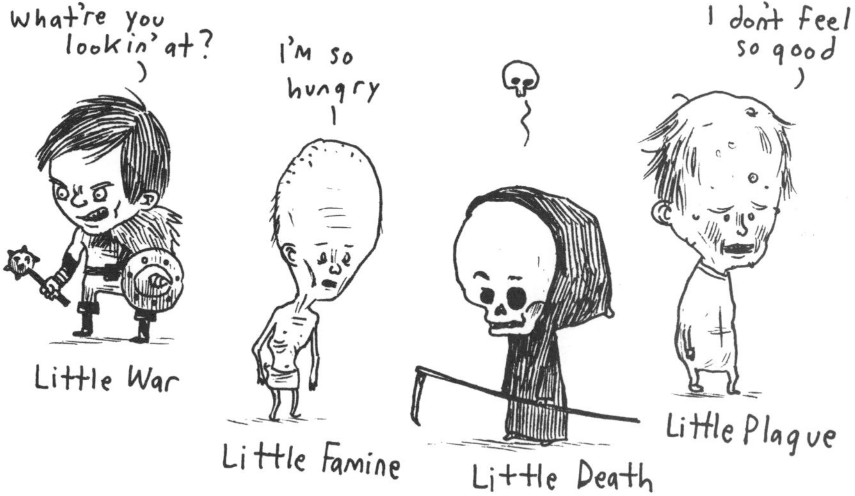
What're you lookin' at?
Little War
I'M so hungry
Little Famine
Little Death
I don't feel so good
Little Plague

~~vicious~~ cycle
~~vicious~~
~~vicious~~
vicious

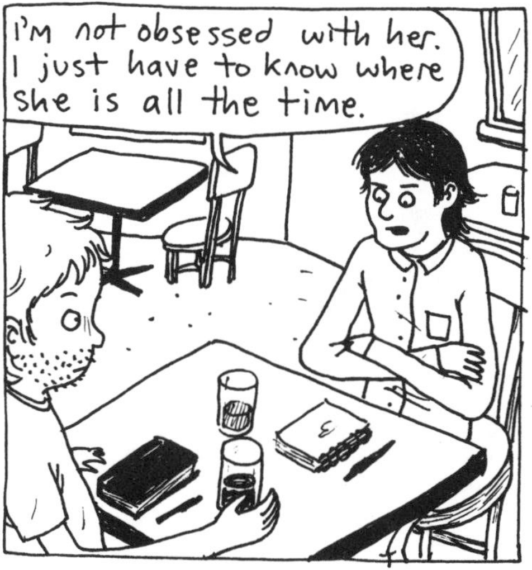
I'M not obsessed with her. I just have to know where she is all the time.

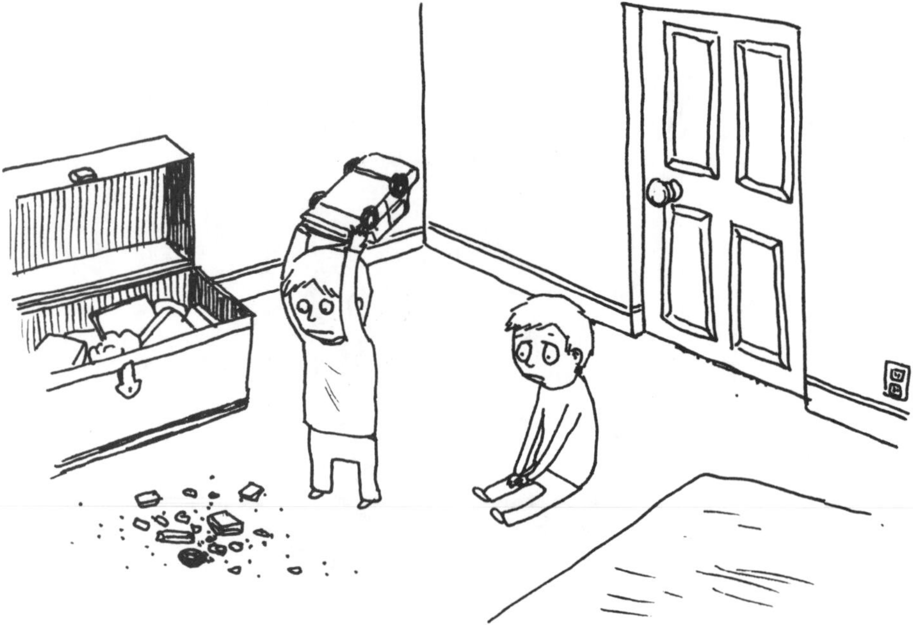

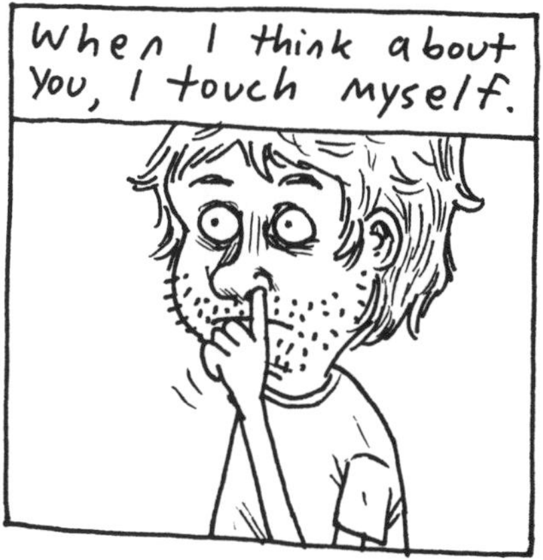
When I think about you, I touch myself.

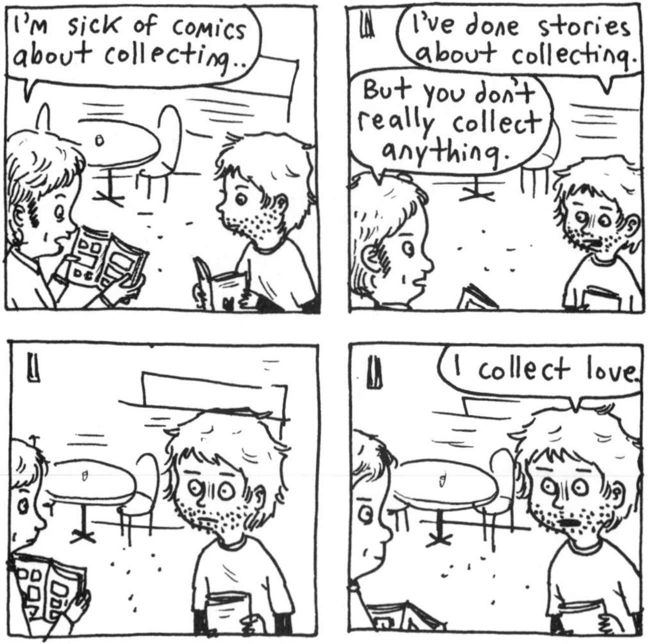
I'M SICK OF COMICS about collecting..
I've done stories about collecting.
But you don't really collect anything.
I collect love.

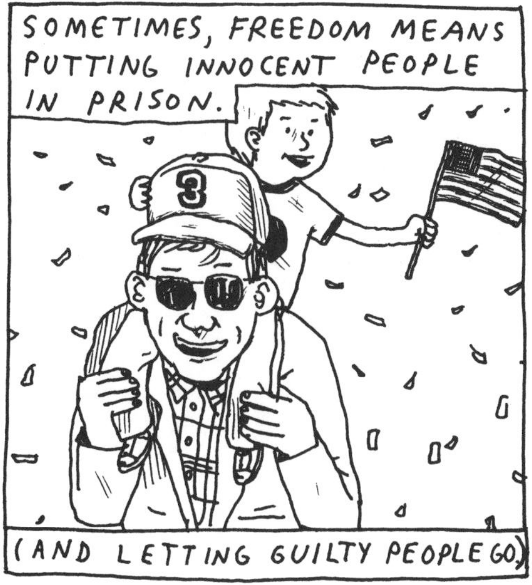
SOMETIMES, FREEDOM MEANS PUTTING INNOCENT PEOPLE IN PRISON.
3
(AND LETTING GUILTY PEOPLE GO)

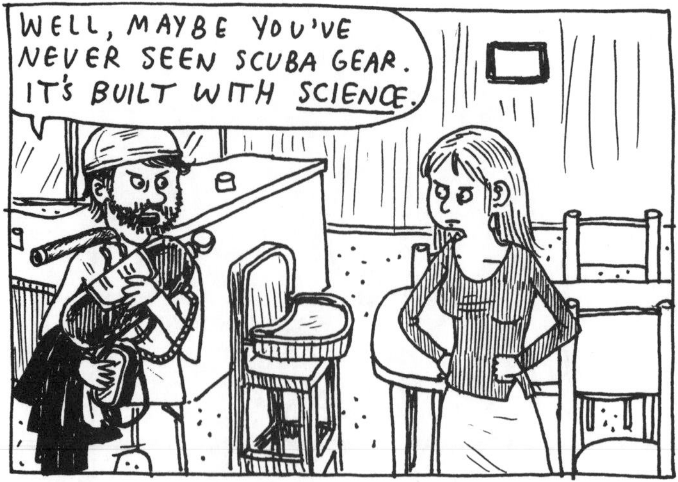
WELL, MAYBE YOU'VE NEVER SEEN SCUBA GEAR. IT'S BUILT WITH SCIENCE.

EVIDENCE OF MY MUSIC SNOBBERY

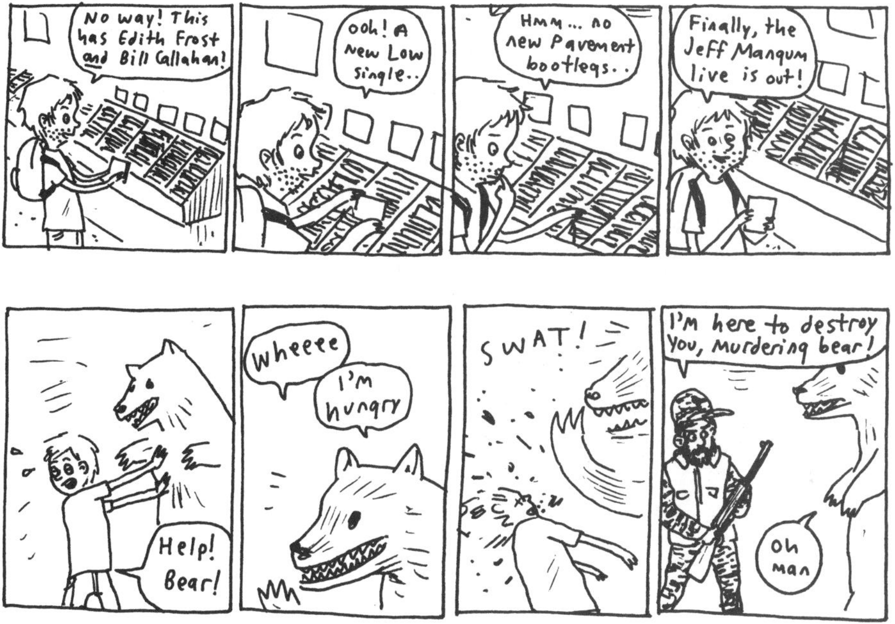
No way! This has Edith Frost and Bill Callahan!
ooh! A new Low single..
Hmm... no new Pavement bootlegs..
Finally, the Jeff Mangum live is out!
Help! Bear!
wheeee
I'm hungry
SWAT!
I'm here to destroy you, murdering bear!
Oh man

GIGANTOENCEPHALOSISYPHUS

You slept with my wife, Bighead!
As punishment, you must spend eternity pushing this boulder up this hill.
BLAM!

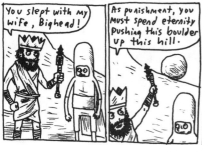

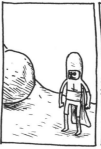

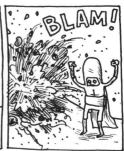

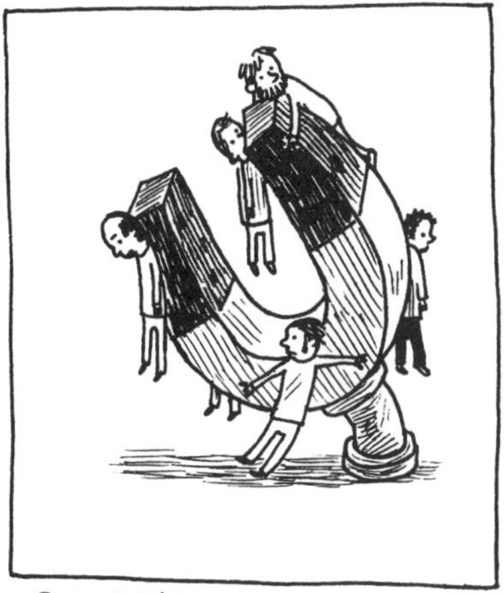

CHUCK MAGNET

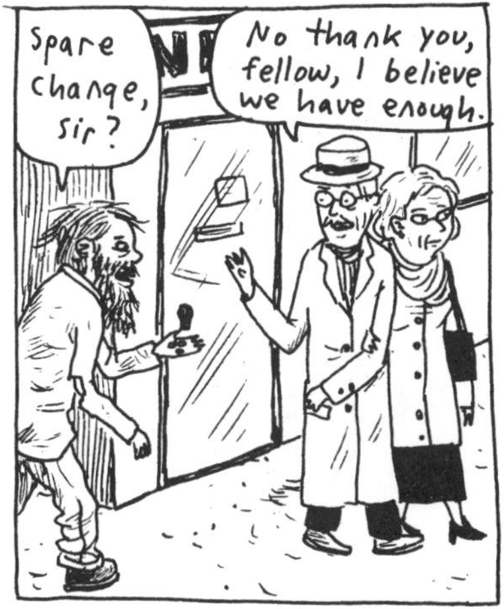

Spare change, sir?
No thank you, fellow, I believe we have enough.

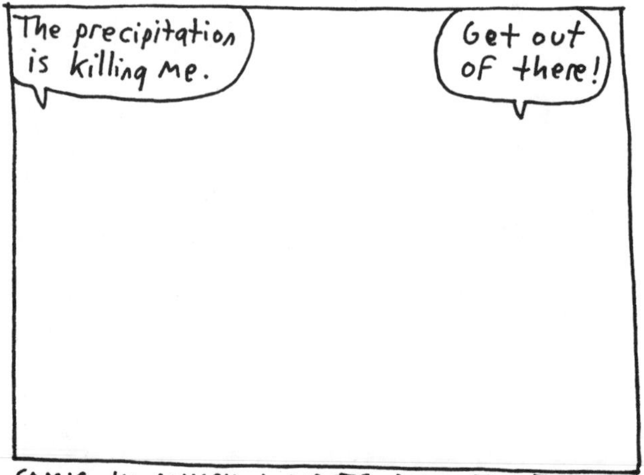
The precipitation is killing me.
Get out of there!

COMIC IN WHICH I WROTE DOWN THE TEXT AND SUBSEQUENTLY FORGOT WHAT THE IMAGE WAS SUPPOSED TO BE. SOMETHING WITH A BATHTUB, I THINK. DANG.

THE CONJOINED TWINS

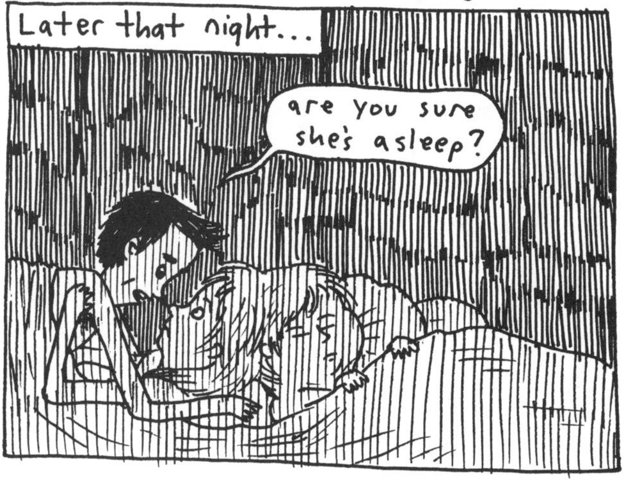
Later that night...
are you sure she's asleep?

The Tambourine Player

NO, NO, NO, you idiot! You're doing it all wrong!
You suck, Mackenzie.

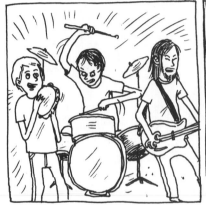

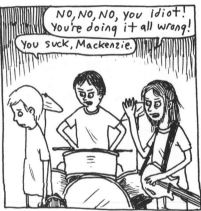

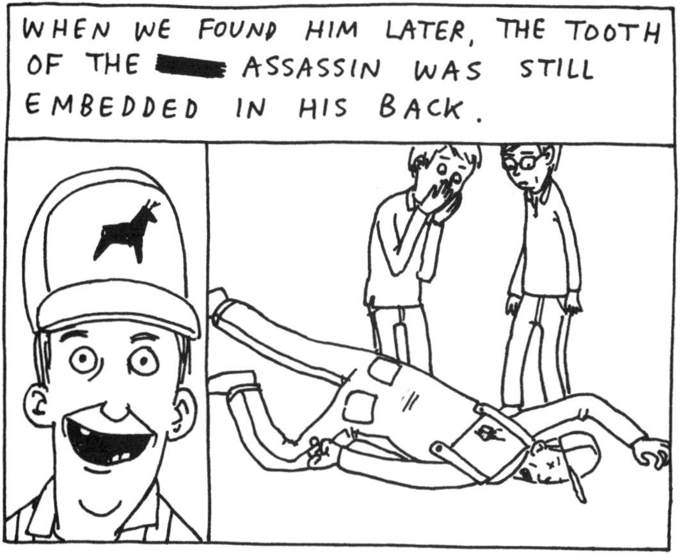
WHEN WE FOUND HIM LATER, THE TOOTH OF THE [redacted] ASSASSIN WAS STILL EMBEDDED IN HIS BACK.

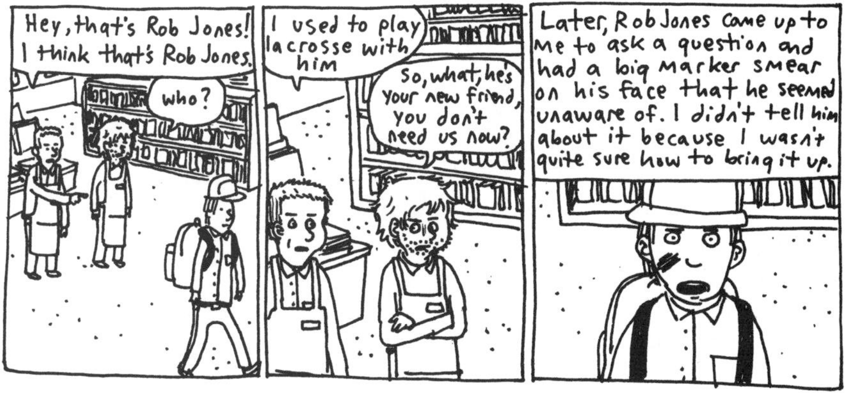
Hey, that's Rob Jones! I think that's Rob Jones.
who?
I used to play lacrosse with him
So, what, he's your new friend, you don't need us now?
Later, Rob Jones came up to me to ask a question and had a big marker smear on his face that he seemed unaware of. I didn't tell him about it because I wasn't quite sure how to bring it up.

MY LESBIAN FRIEND

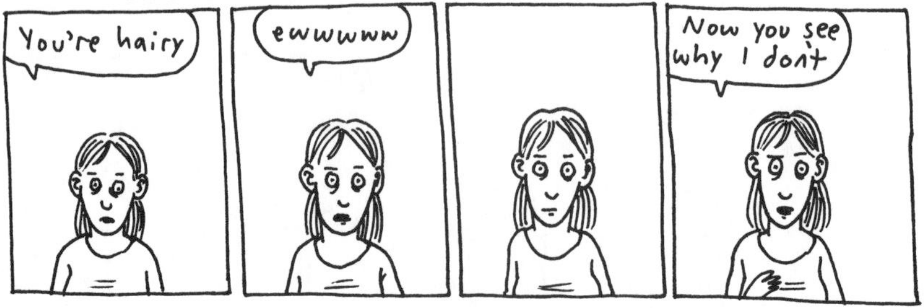
You're hairy
ewwwww
Now you see why I don't

QUIMBY'S

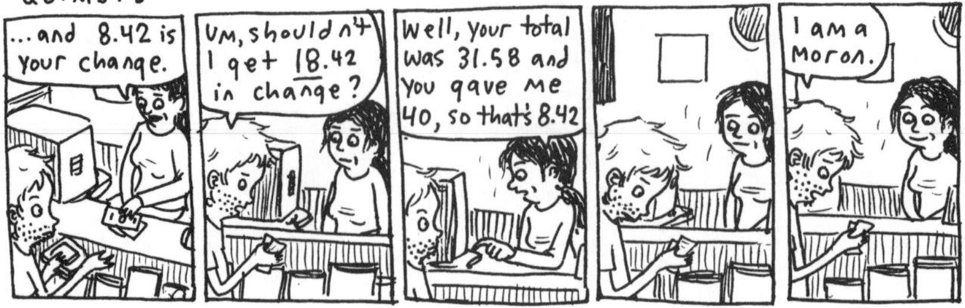
...and 8.42 is your change.
Um, shouldn't I get 18.42 in change?
Well, your total was 31.58 and you gave me 40, so that's 8.42
I am a moron.

RAT BOY

HALF-BOY, HALF-RAT

LIVES IN
PILE OF
WOOD
SHAVINGS

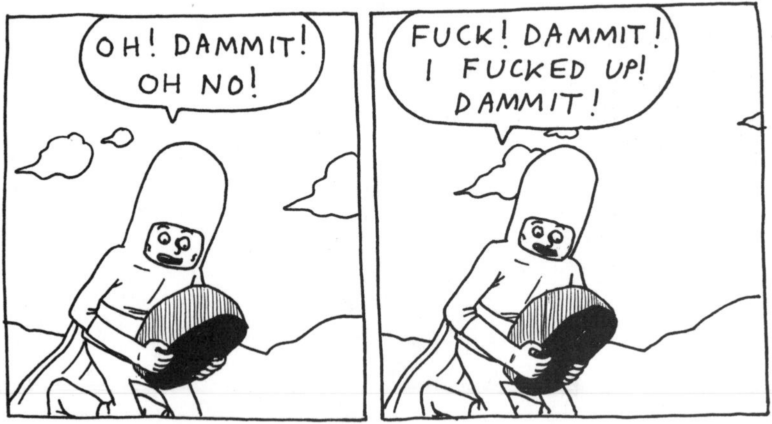
OH! DAMMIT! OH NO!
FUCK! DAMMIT! I FUCKED UP! DAMMIT!

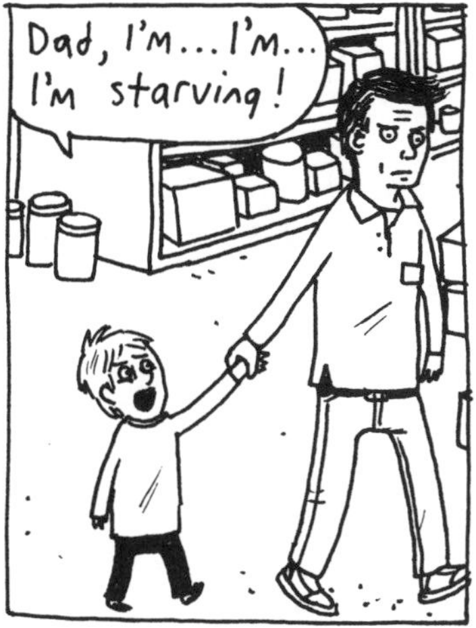
Dad, I'm... I'm...
I'm starving!

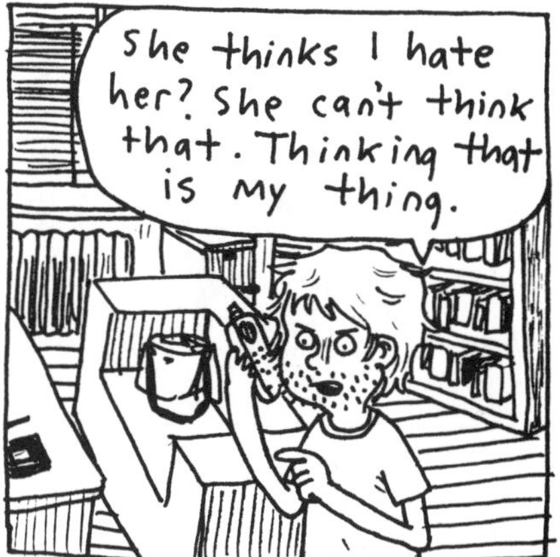
She thinks I hate her? She can't think that. Thinking that is my thing.

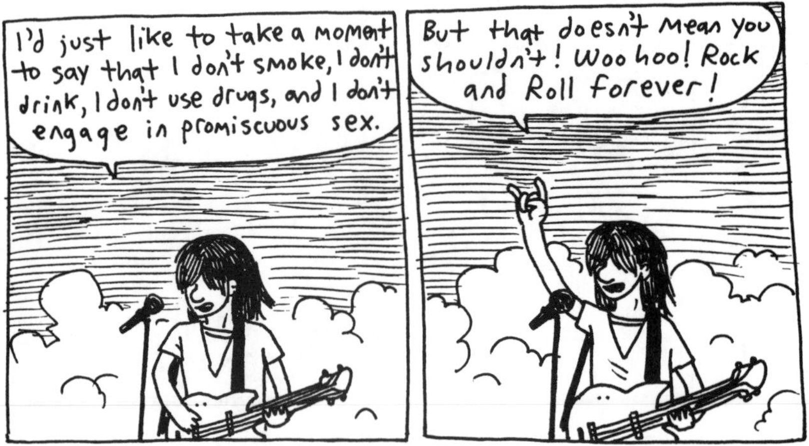
I'd just like to take a moment to say that I don't smoke, I don't drink, I don't use drugs, and I don't engage in promiscuous sex.
But that doesn't mean you shouldn't! Woo hoo! Rock and Roll forever!

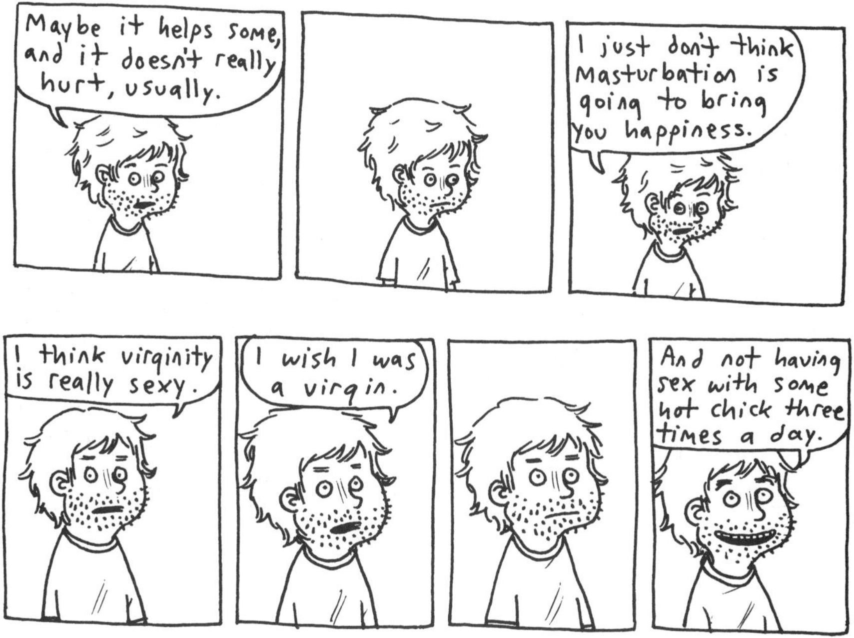
Maybe it helps some, and it doesn't really hurt, usually.
I just don't think Masturbation is going to bring you happiness.
I think virginity is really sexy.
I wish I was a virgin.
And not having sex with some hot chick three times a day.

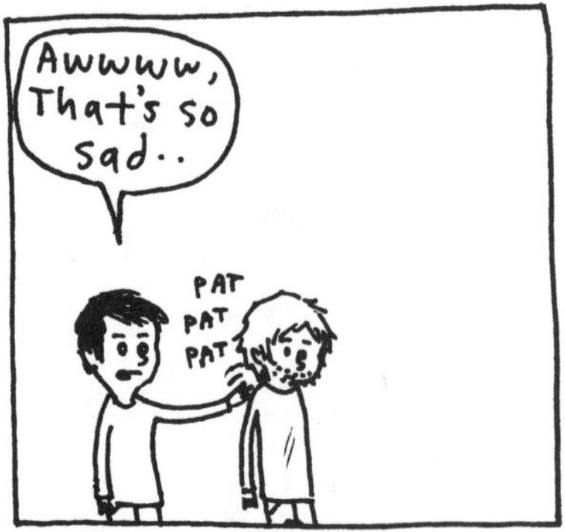
Awwww, That's so sad..
PAT PAT PAT

YOUR PITY MAKES ME FEEL EVEN MORE PATHETIC

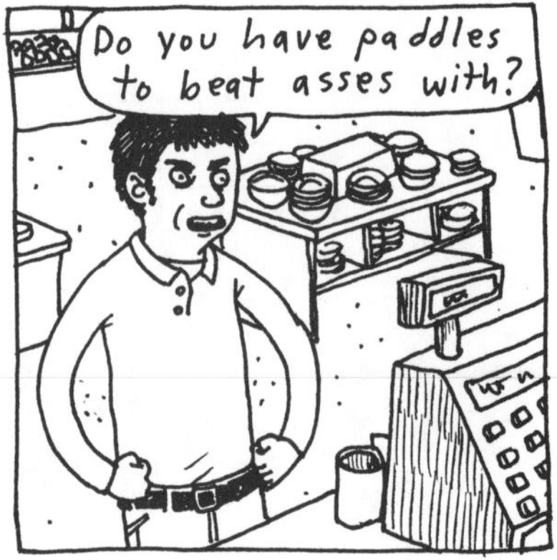
Do you have paddles to beat asses with?

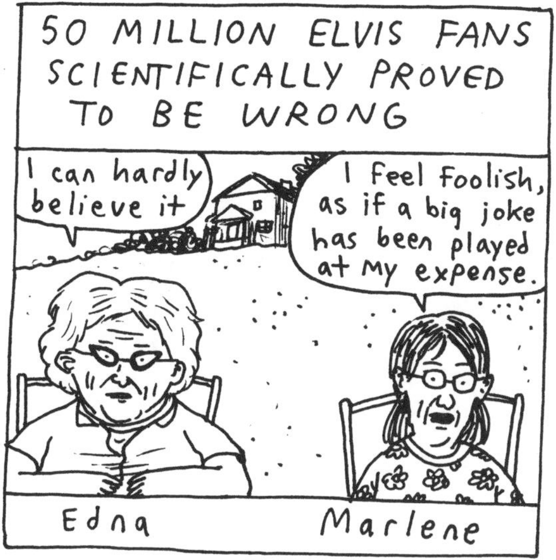
50 MILLION ELVIS FANS SCIENTIFICALLY PROVED TO BE WRONG
I can hardly believe it
I feel foolish, as if a big joke has been played at my expense.
Edna
Marlene

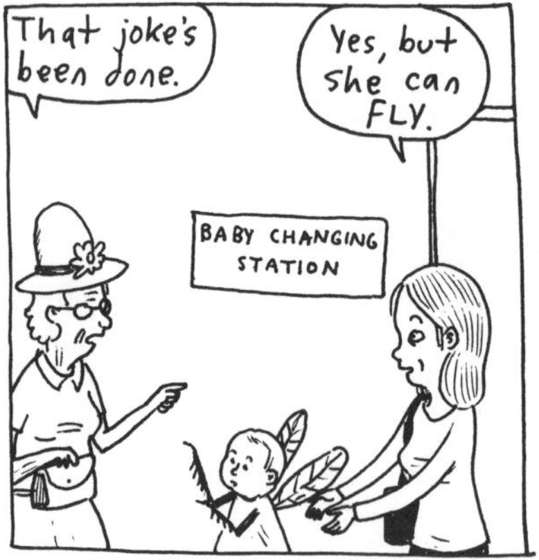
That joke's been done.
Yes, but she can FLY.
BABY CHANGING STATION

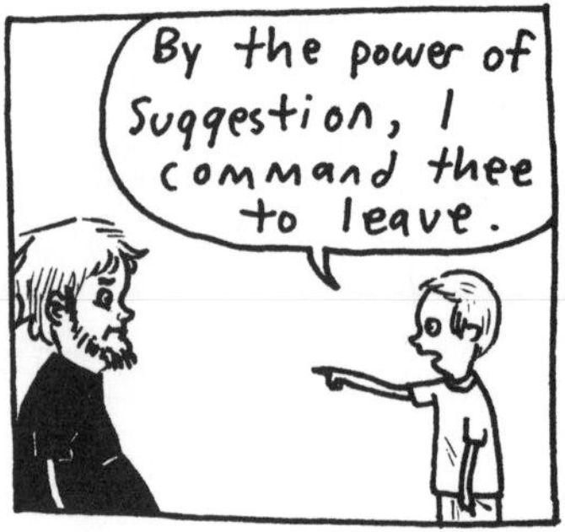
By the power of Suggestion, I command thee to leave.

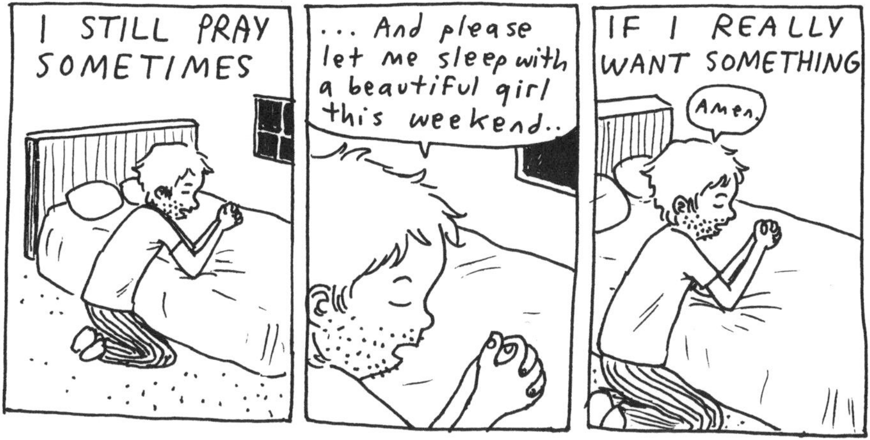
I STILL PRAY SOMETIMES
... And please let me sleep with a beautiful girl this weekend..
IF I REALLY WANT SOMETHING
Amen.

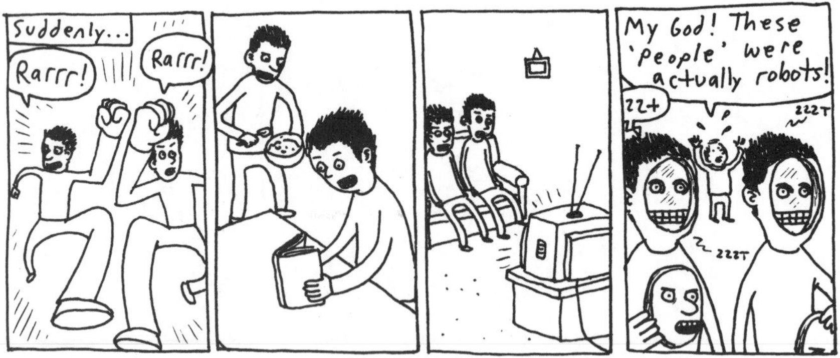
Suddenly...
Rarrr!
Rarrr!
My God! These 'people' were actually robots!
ZZT
ZZZT
ZZZT

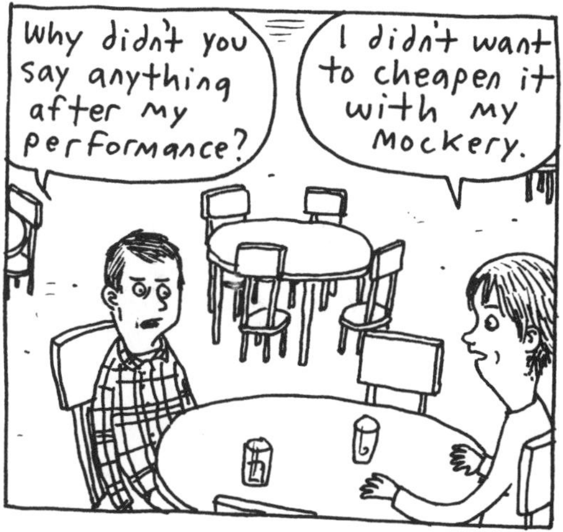
Why didn't you say anything after my performance?
I didn't want to cheapen it with my mockery.

Wouldn't <u>you</u> like to sleep with the fishes?

My poor Jeffy
Don't be so weird
Can I stick my head in your mouth?
NO.

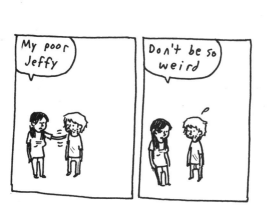

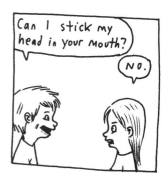

ADVERTISEMENT

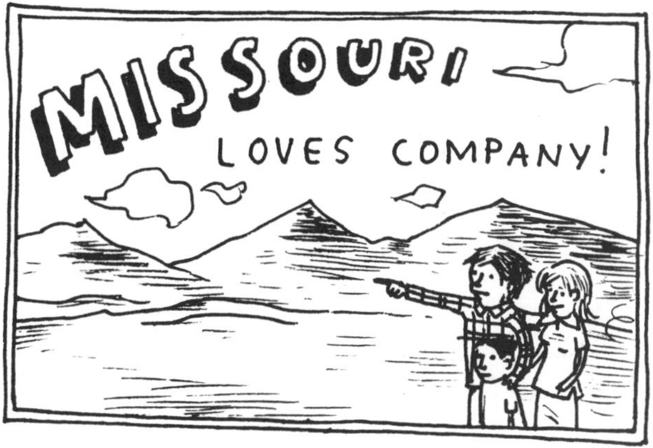
MISSOURI
LOVES COMPANY!

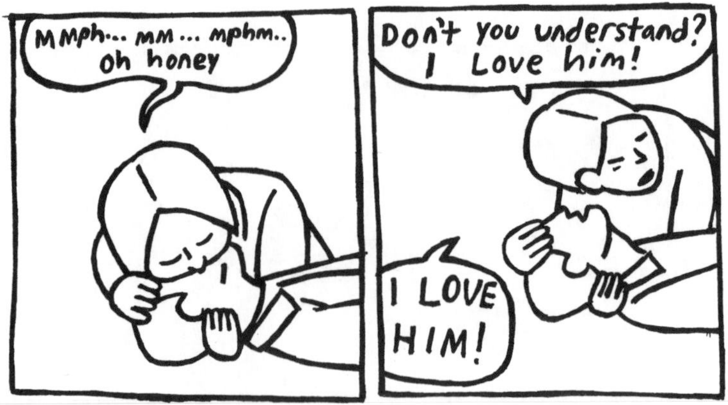
Mmph... mm... mphm.. oh honey
Don't you understand? I Love him!
I LOVE HIM!

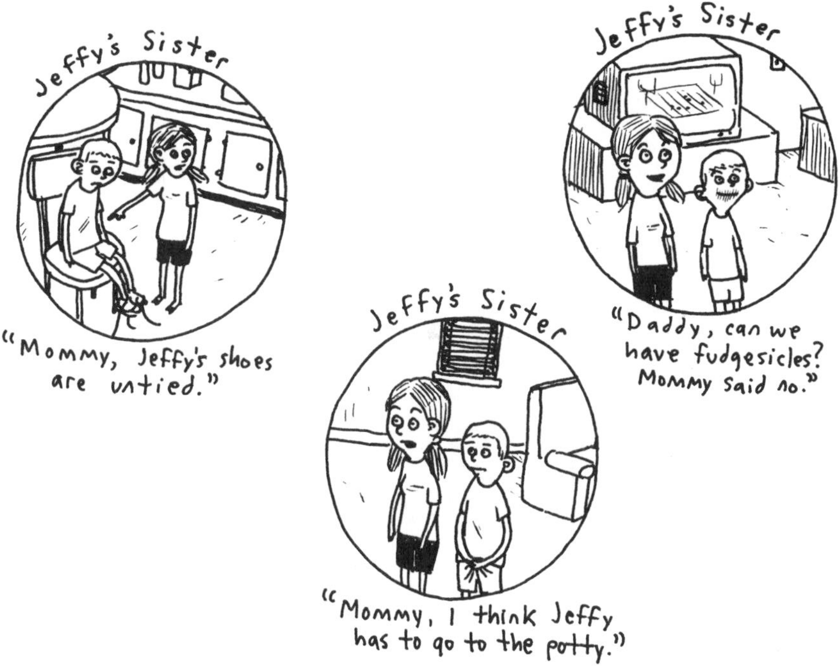
Jeffy's Sister
"Mommy, Jeffy's shoes are untied."
Jeffy's Sister
"Mommy, I think Jeffy has to go to the potty."
Jeffy's Sister
"Daddy, can we have fudgesicles? Mommy said no."

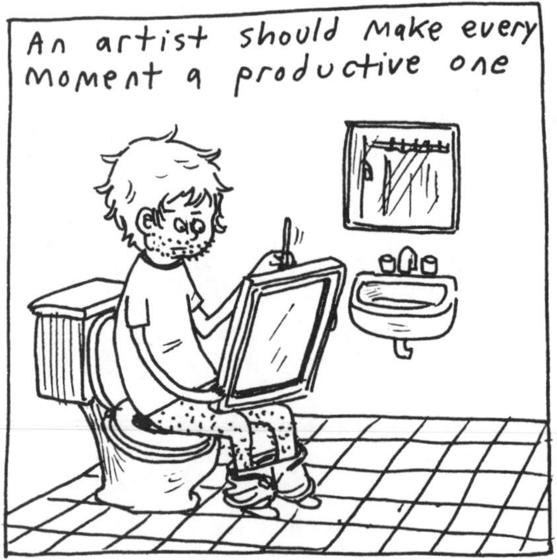
An artist should make every moment a productive one

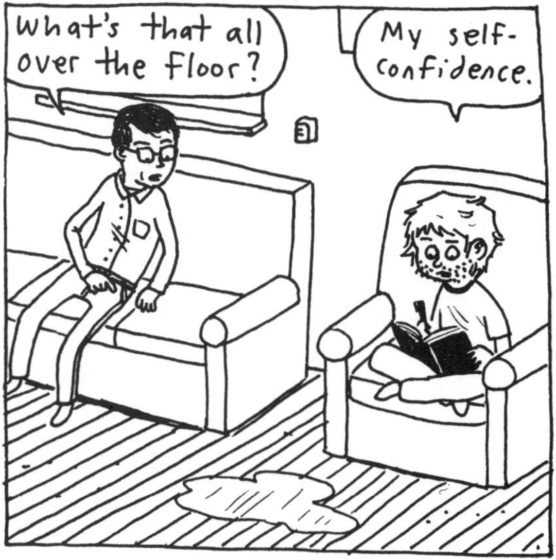
What's that all over the floor?
My self-confidence.

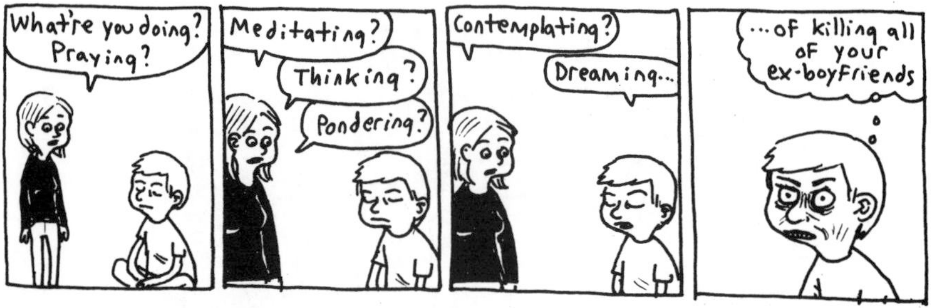
What're you doing? Praying?
Meditating?
Thinking?
Pondering?
Contemplating?
Dreaming...
...of killing all of your ex-boyfriends

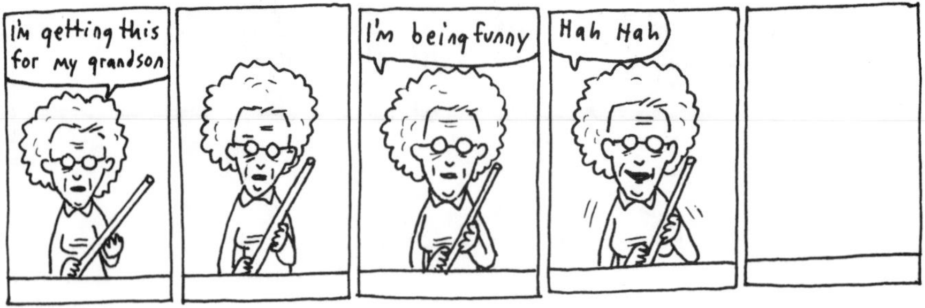
I'm getting this for my grandson
I'm being funny
Hah Hah

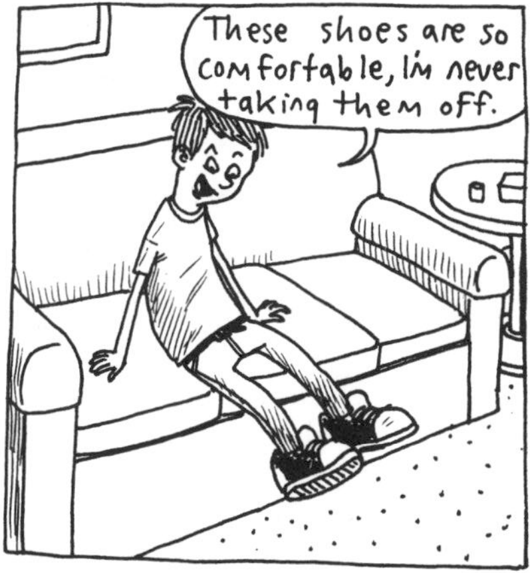
These shoes are so comfortable, I'm never taking them off.

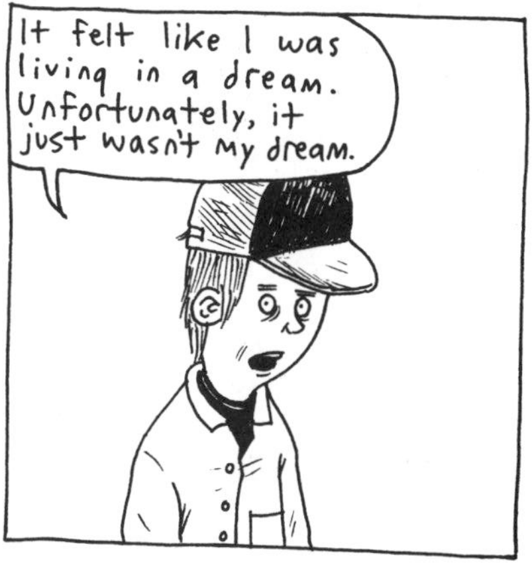
It felt like I was living in a dream. Unfortunately, it just wasn't my dream.

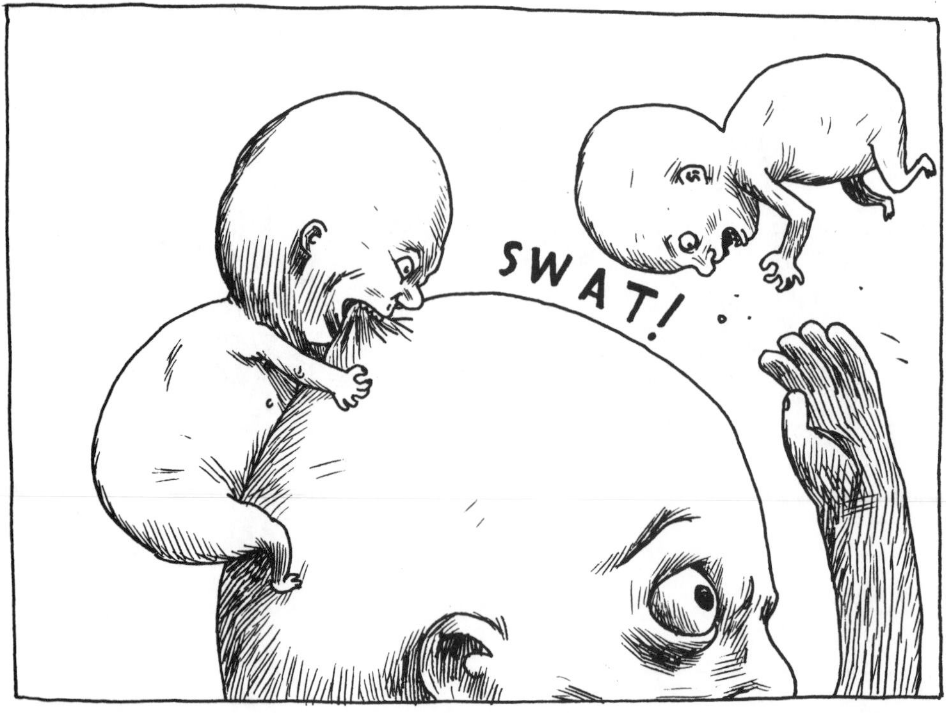
SWAT!

"Raising the Dead"

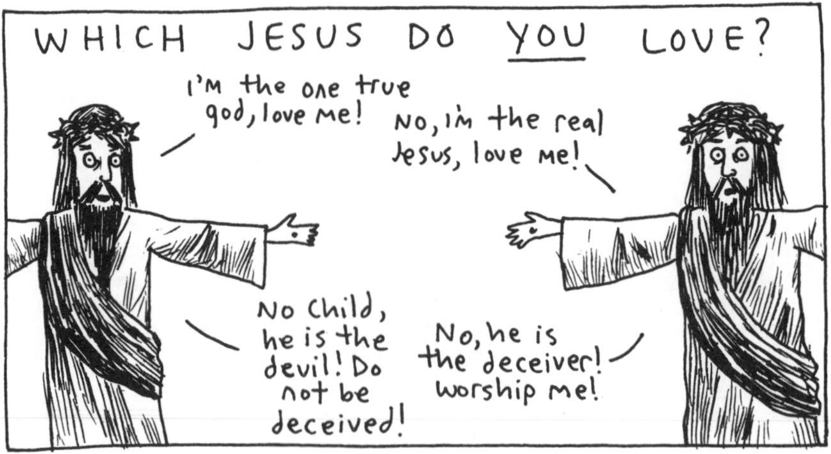
WHICH JESUS DO YOU LOVE?
I'm the one true god, love me!
No, I'm the real Jesus, love me!
No Child, he is the devil! Do not be deceived!
No, he is the deceiver! worship me!

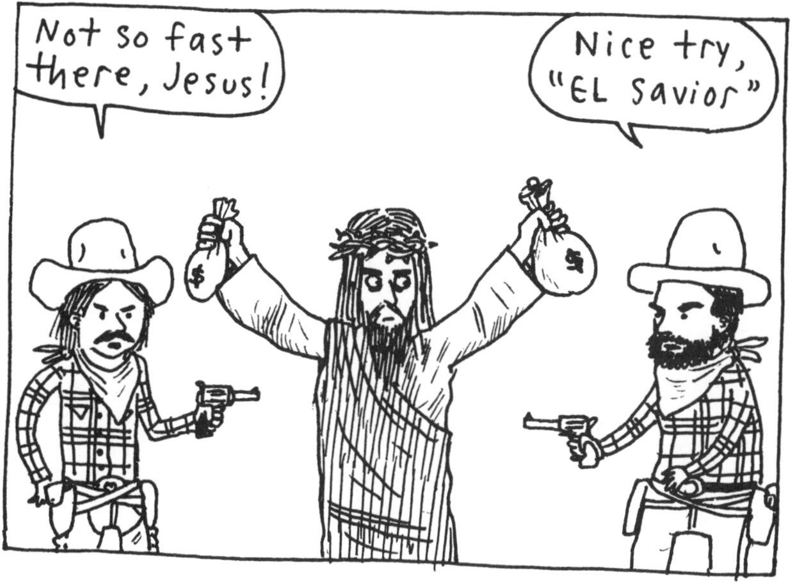
Not so fast there, Jesus!
Nice try, "EL Savior"

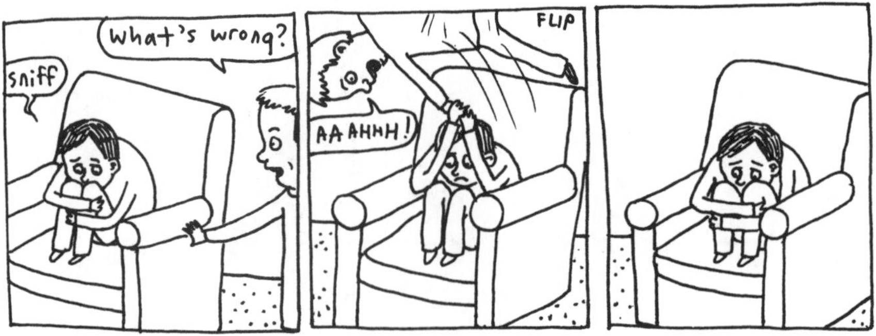
sniff
what's wrong?
AAAHHH!
FLIP

Hey, someone peed all over your filthy toilets here!
Was it you?

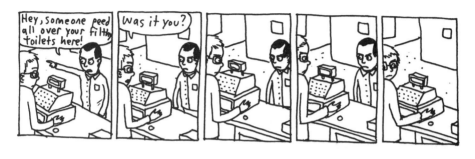

Scale of One to Ten

one
ten

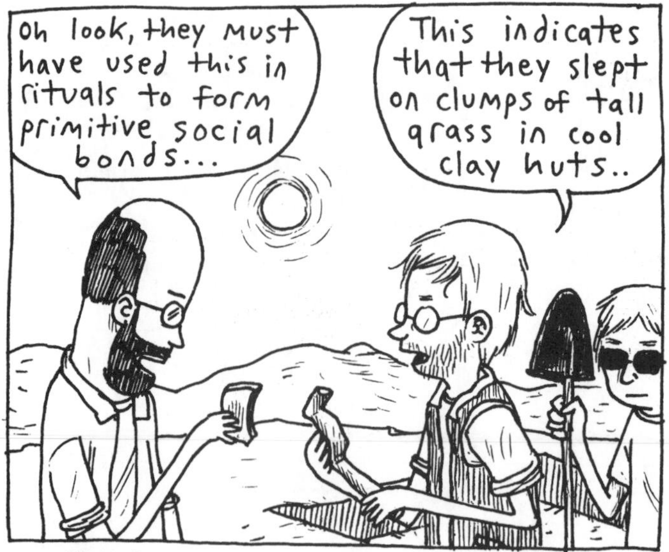
Oh look, they must have used this in rituals to form primitive social bonds...
This indicates that they slept on clumps of tall grass in cool clay huts..

THE ARCHEOLOGISTS

MONKEY DRAINS

FAITH

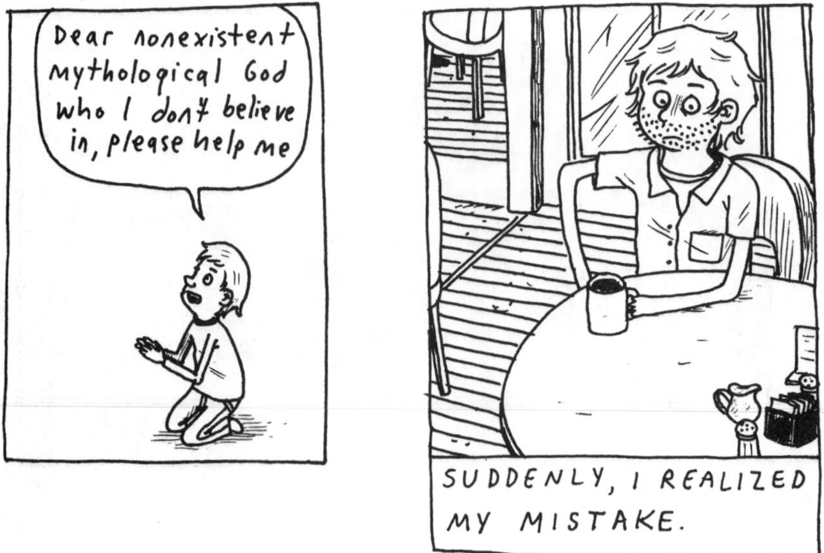
Dear nonexistent mythological God who I don't believe in, please help me
SUDDENLY, I REALIZED MY MISTAKE.

JEFFREY BROWN by Jeffrey Brown

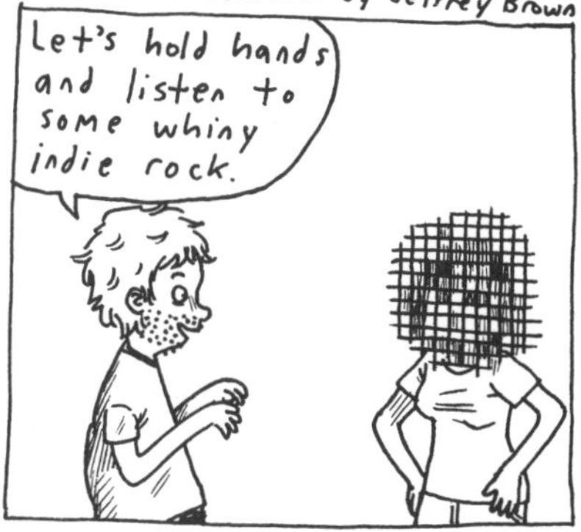
Let's hold hands and listen to some whiny indie rock.

GOOD THINGS COME TO THOSE WHO WAIT IN SMALL PACKAGES

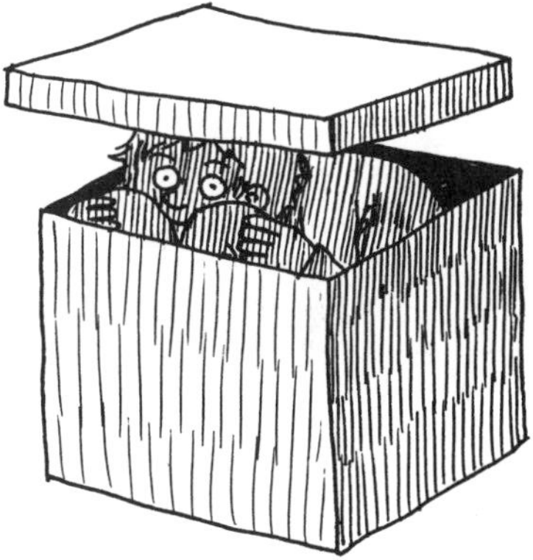

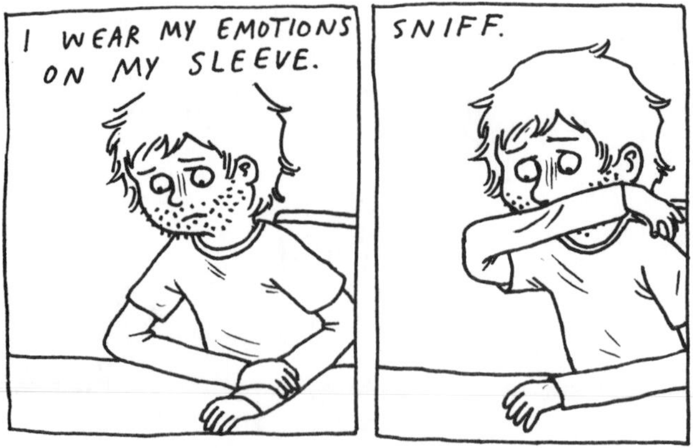
I WEAR MY EMOTIONS ON MY SLEEVE.
SNIFF.

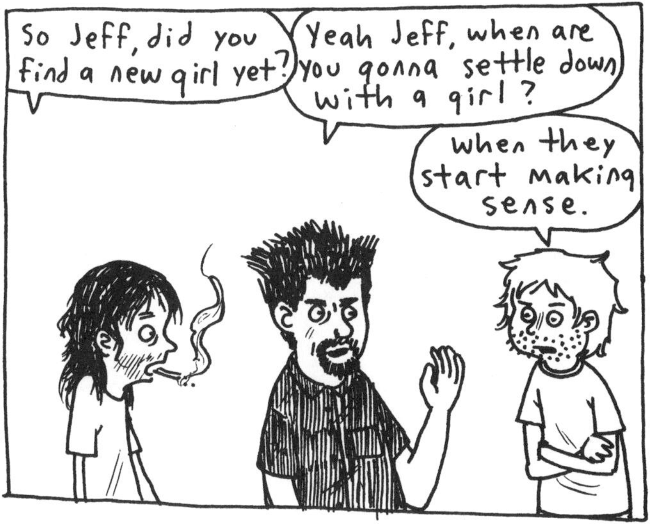
So Jeff, did you find a new girl yet?
Yeah Jeff, when are you gonna settle down with a girl?
When they start making sense.

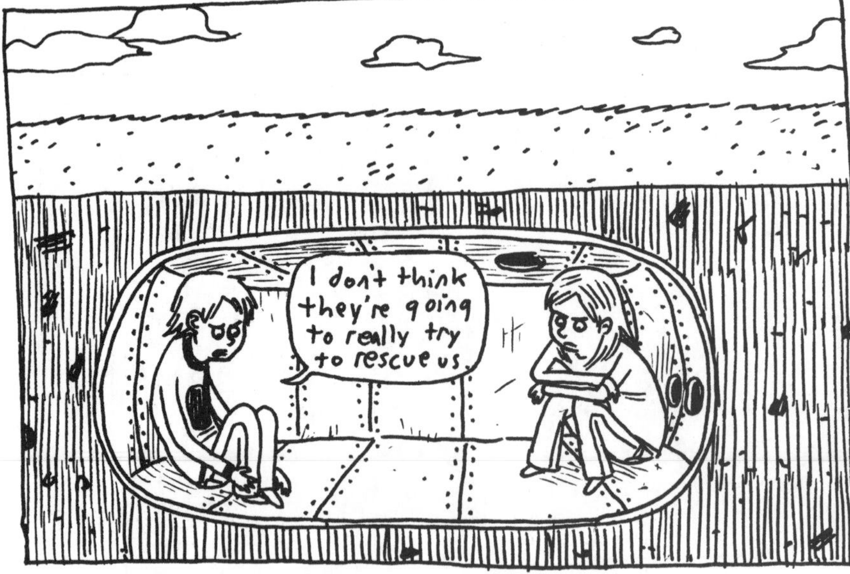
I don't think they're going to really try to rescue us

SKEPTIC TANK

IF YOU PEE ON YOUR CHUM, YOU MAKE HIM A CHUMP.

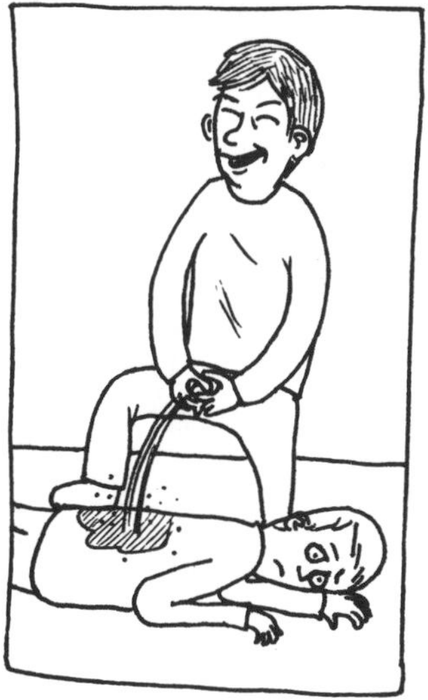

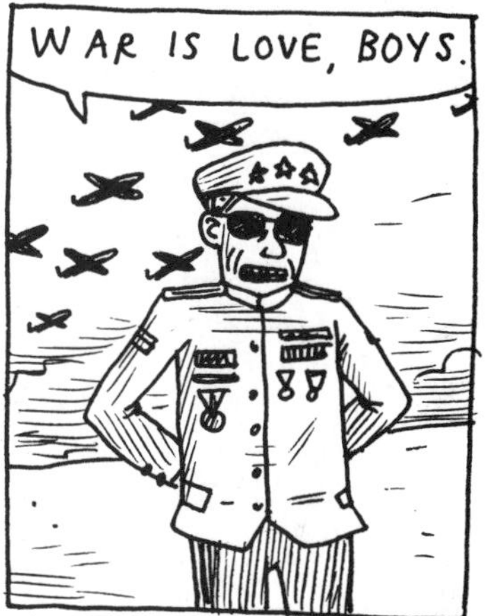
WAR IS LOVE, BOYS.

THE GENERAL CLAIMS HE IS NOT A LONELY MAN.

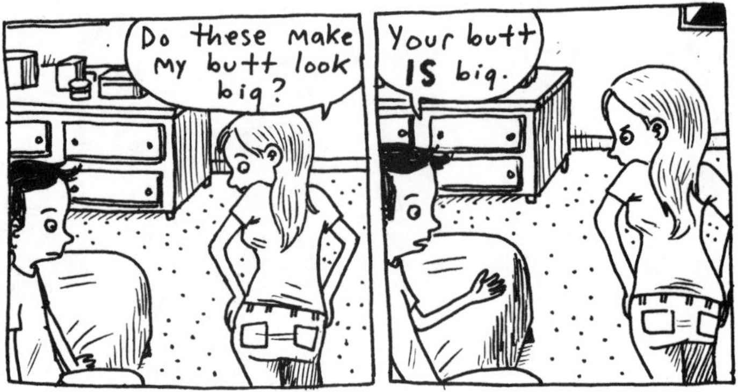
Do these make my butt look big?
Your butt IS big.

I just want to take you home and rip your pants off and screw the shit out of you.
And then cuddle.

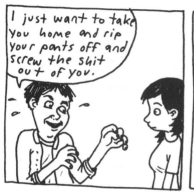

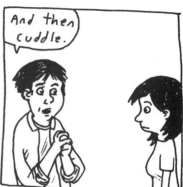

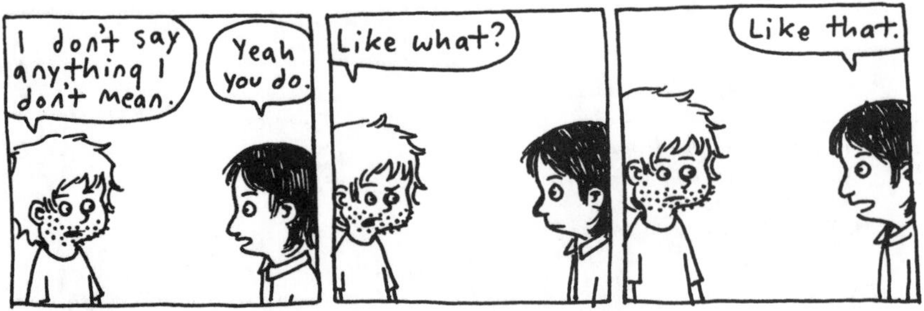
I don't say anything I don't mean.
Yeah you do.
Like what?
Like that.

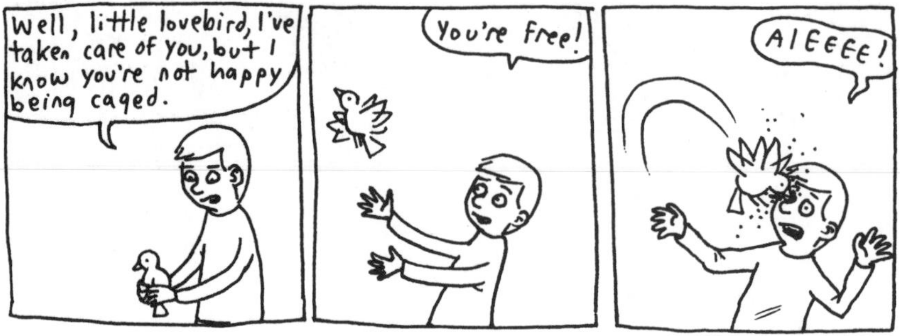
Well, little lovebird, I've taken care of you, but I know you're not happy being caged.
You're free!
AIEEEE!

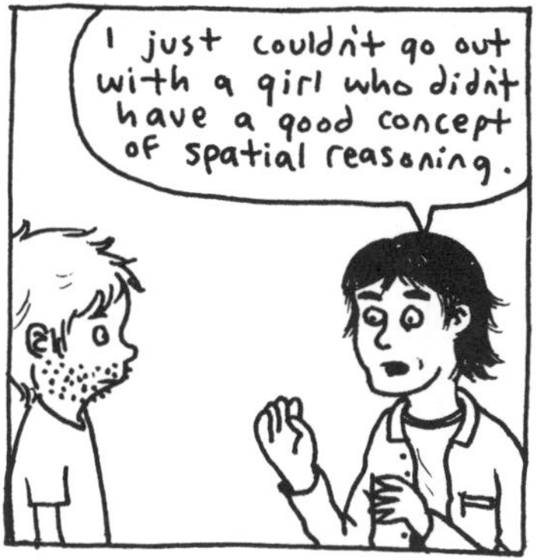
I just couldn't go out with a girl who didn't have a good concept of spatial reasoning.

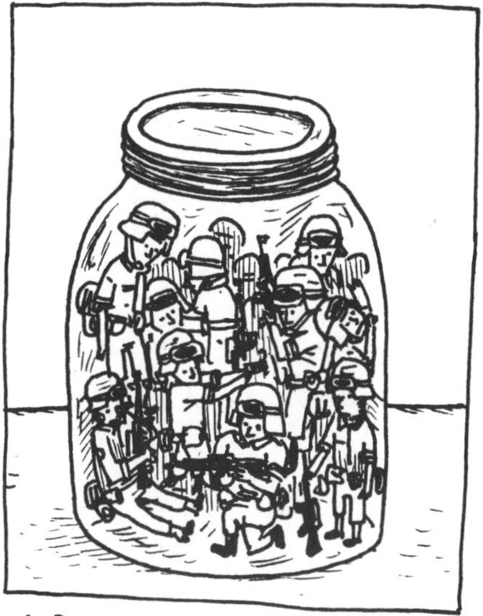

ARMY PRESERVES

I'm really pushing myself.

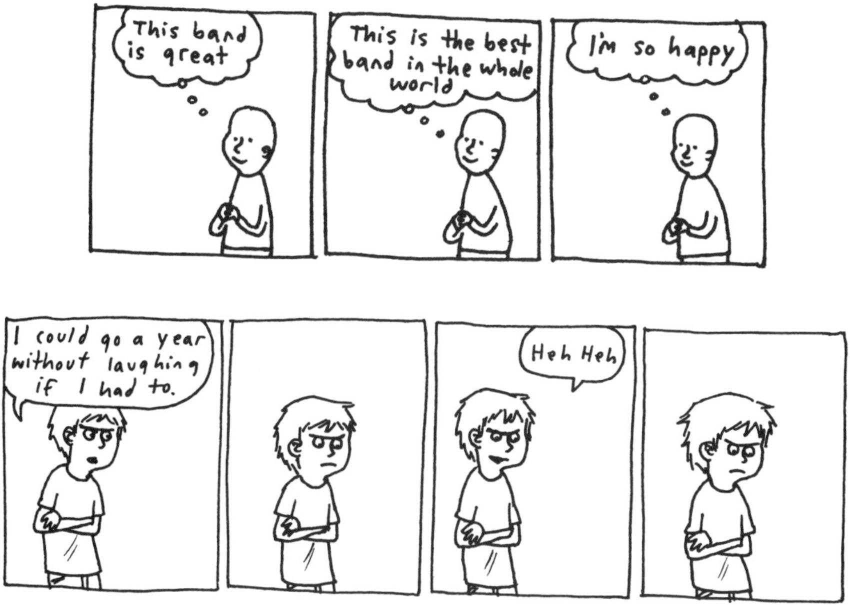
This band is great
This is the best band in the whole world
I'm so happy
I could go a year without laughing if I had to.
Heh Heh

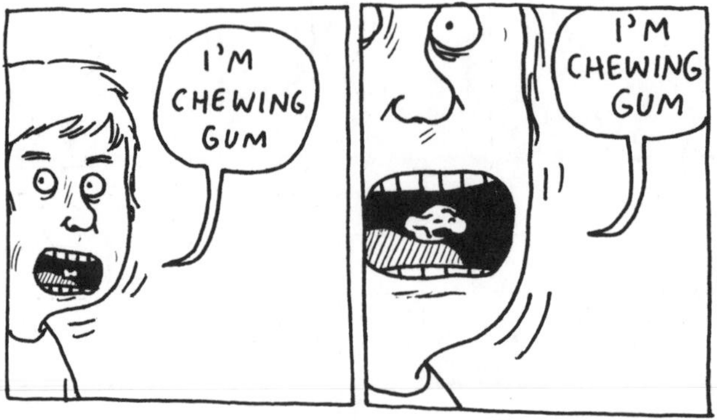
I'M CHEWING GUM
I'M CHEWING GUM

TIMMY WAS BORN
WITHOUT ARMS OR LEGS.

SO HE DOESN'T
MISS MASTURBATION.

I GUESS.

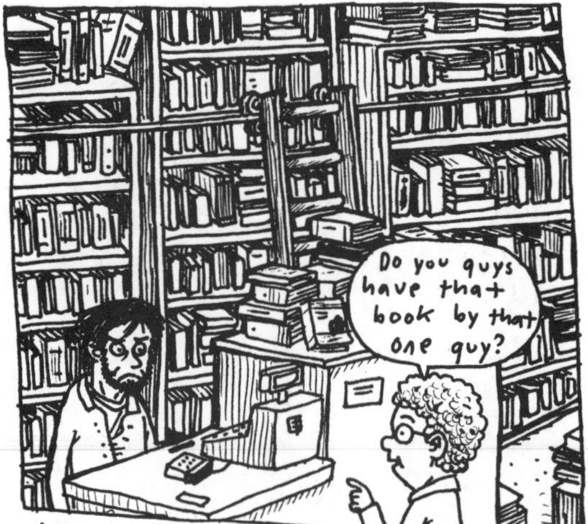
Do you guys have that book by that one guy?

AT THE LEVIATHANARIUM

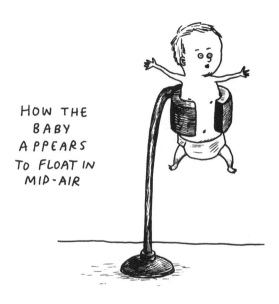

HOW THE
BABY
APPEARS
TO FLOAT IN
MID-AIR

NEW TOILETS

FLUSHHHHHH

REMOTE CONTROL
FLUSHING FUNCTION

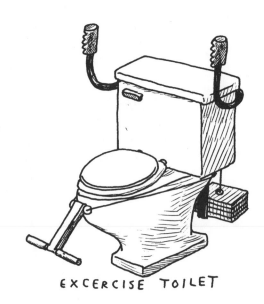

EXCERCISE TOILET

HE INVENTED A FRIENDLY ROBOT.
OF COURSE, IT WAS DESIGNED FOR
KILLING PEOPLE, BUT IT WAS STILL
VERY FRIENDLY ABOUT IT*.

*The robot pictured is a different robot that is
also friendly but is not for killing people it is
for lifting things and carrying them around.

I AM A TWO-WHEELED CART, AND I'M GOOD AT CARRYING THINGS AROUND. IF YOU NEED TO MOVE SOME HEAVY BOXES, SIMPLY STACK THEM ON ME, TILT ME BACK A LITTLE AND YOU'LL FIND PUSHING ME AROUND WILL SAVE YOU BOTH TIME AND ENERGY. YES, LIFTING HEAVY BOXES CAN BE HARD ON YOUR BACK, NEVER MIND CARRYING THEM AROUND! WITH ME ON HAND, YOUR WORK WILL BE MUCH EASIER, MY STURDY STEEL CONSTRUCTION CAN HANDLE A VERY HEAVY LOAD, AND MY TWO RUBBER TIRES REQUIRE MINIMAL CARE FOR A LONG LIFE. I AM A TWO-WHEELED CART, AND IF YOU'RE INTERESTED IN ME, CIRCLE #104.

Oh, ha ha ha, I get it, "horsing" around, he acts like a horse or something, haha!
Ha Ha, Oh, I get it, "horsing" around, because he likes horses, haha!
Haha Ha, I get it, "horsing" around, and there's a horse right over there, ha ha ha!
Haha, I get it, "horsing" around, because his Facial Features are similar to a horse
Oh, I get it, hahaha, "horsing" around, because a horse is a thing which exists, ha ha!
Quit horsing around.
Hahaha!

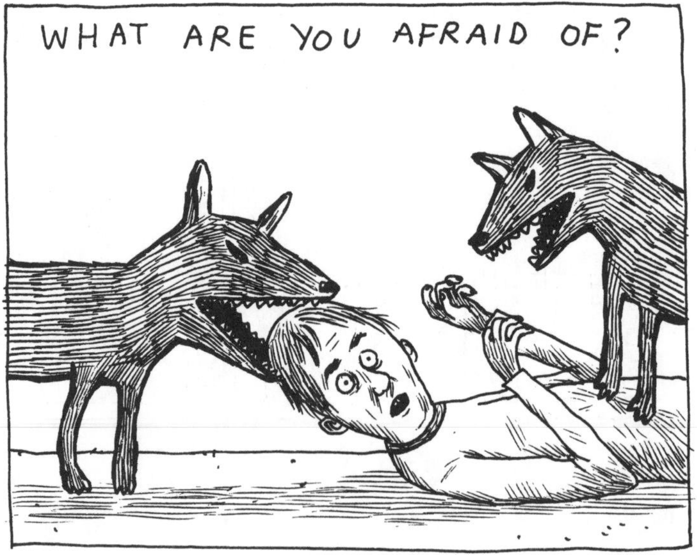
WHAT ARE YOU AFRAID OF?

So, what would you say is the one thing most preventing you from sharing our beliefs?
Common sense.

EX-GIRLFRIENDS

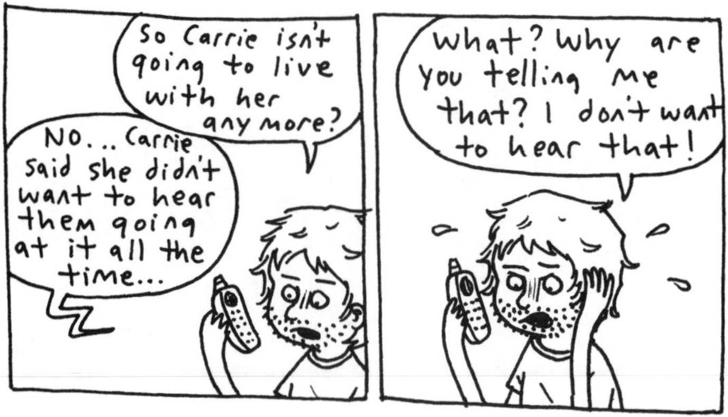
So Carrie isn't going to live with her any more?
No... Carrie said she didn't want to hear them going at it all the time...
What? Why are you telling me that? I don't want to hear that!

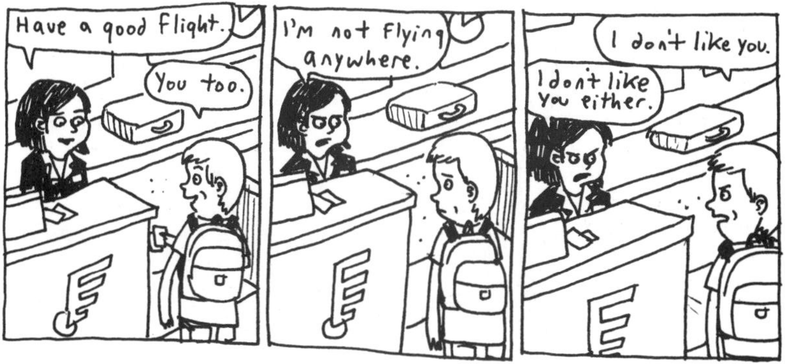
Have a good flight.
You too.
I'm not flying anywhere.
I don't like you.
I don't like you either.

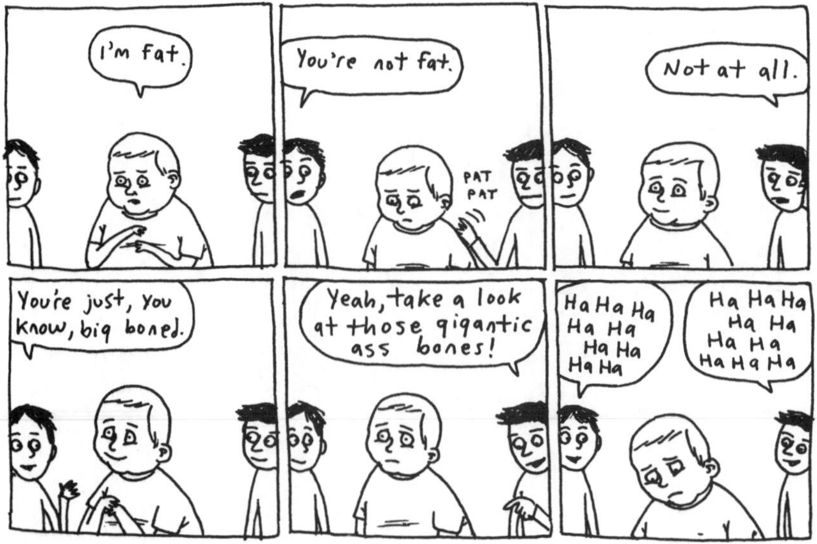
I'm fat.
You're not fat.
PAT PAT
Not at all.
You're just, you know, big boned.
Yeah, take a look at those gigantic ass bones!
Ha Ha Ha Ha Ha Ha Ha Ha Ha
Ha Ha Ha Ha Ha Ha Ha Ha Ha Ha

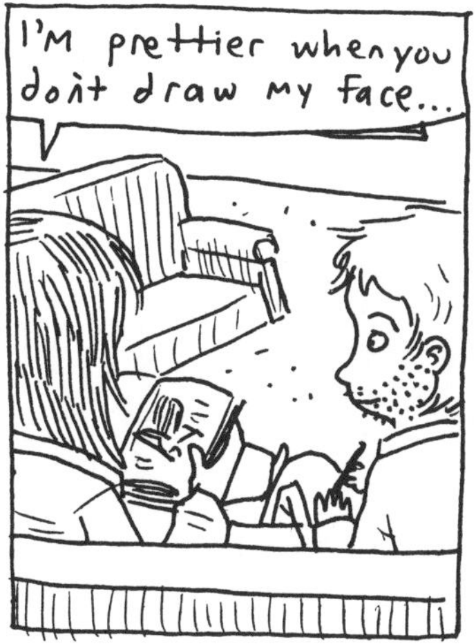
I'M prettier when you don't draw my face...

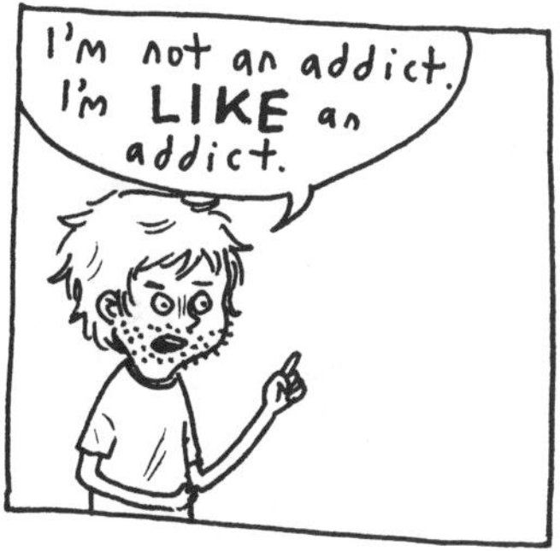
I'm not an addict. I'm LIKE an addict.

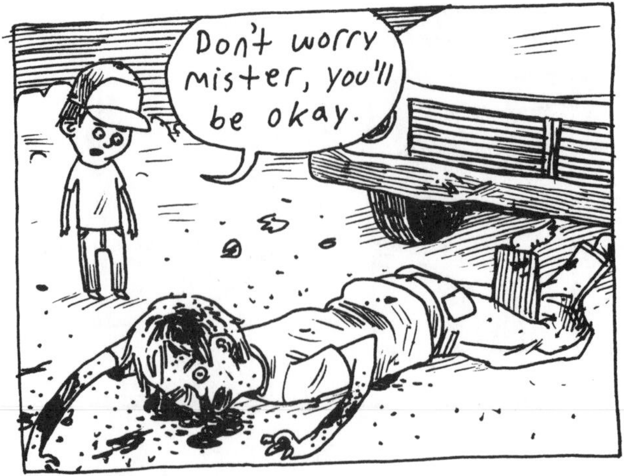
Don't worry mister, you'll be okay.

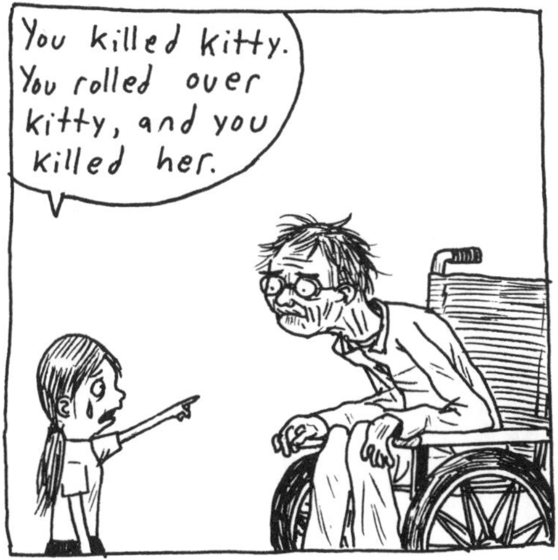
You killed kitty. You rolled over kitty, and you killed her.

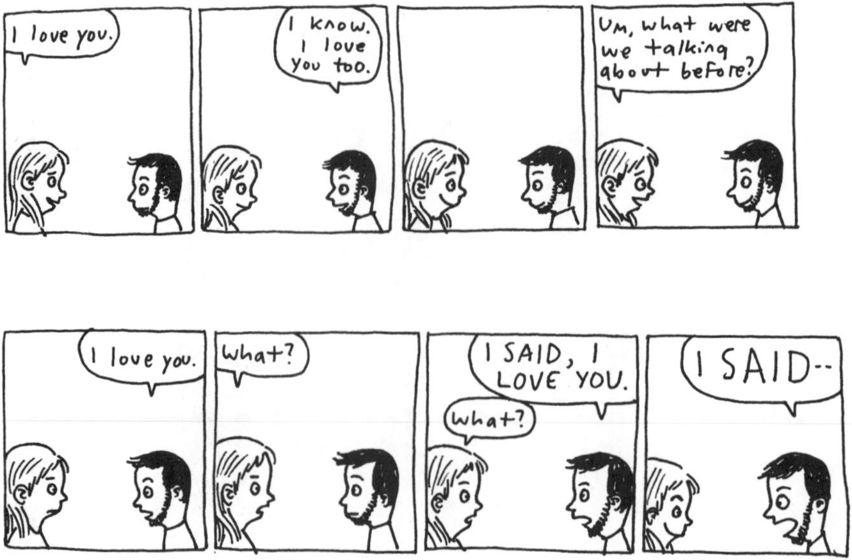
I love you.
I know. I love you too.
Um, what were we talking about before?
I love you.
What?
I SAID, I LOVE YOU.
What?
I SAID--

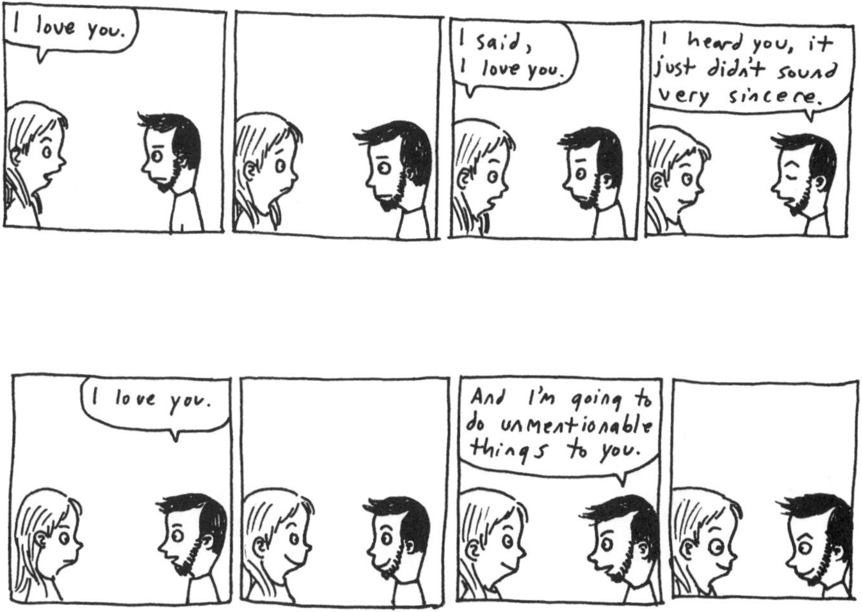
I love you.
I said, I love you.
I heard you, it just didn't sound very sincere.
I love you.
And I'm going to do unmentionable things to you.

EVERY GAME HAS A LOSER.

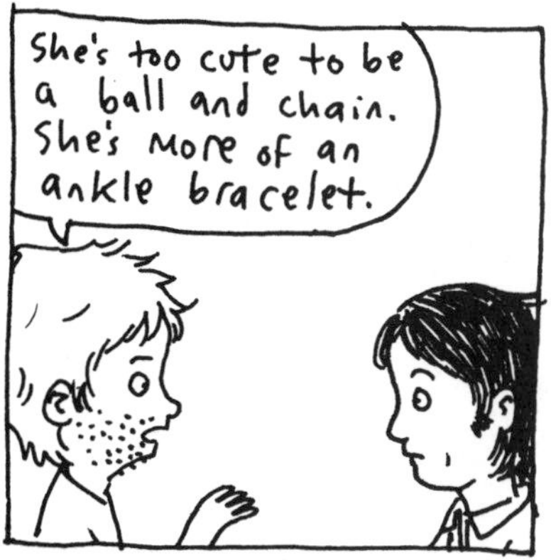
She's too cute to be a ball and chain. She's more of an ankle bracelet.

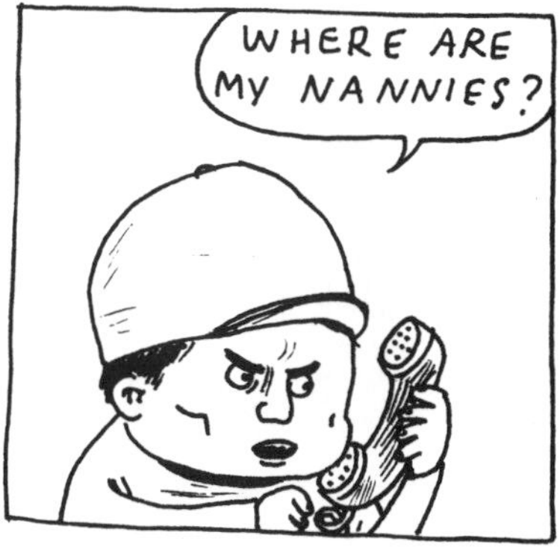
WHERE ARE MY NANNIES?

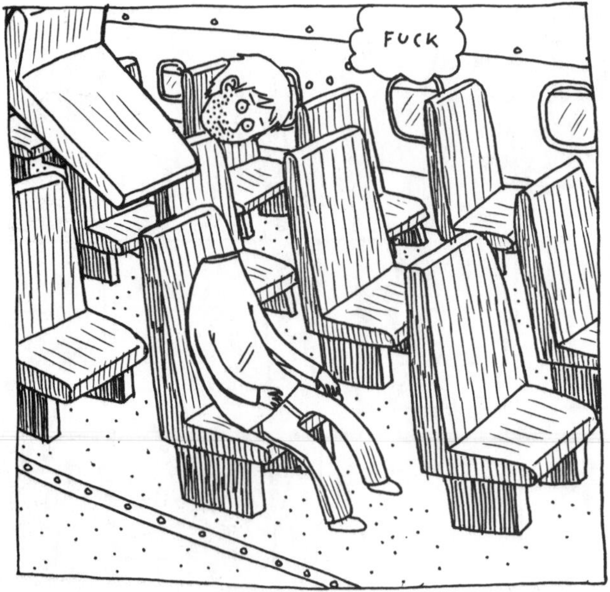
FUCK

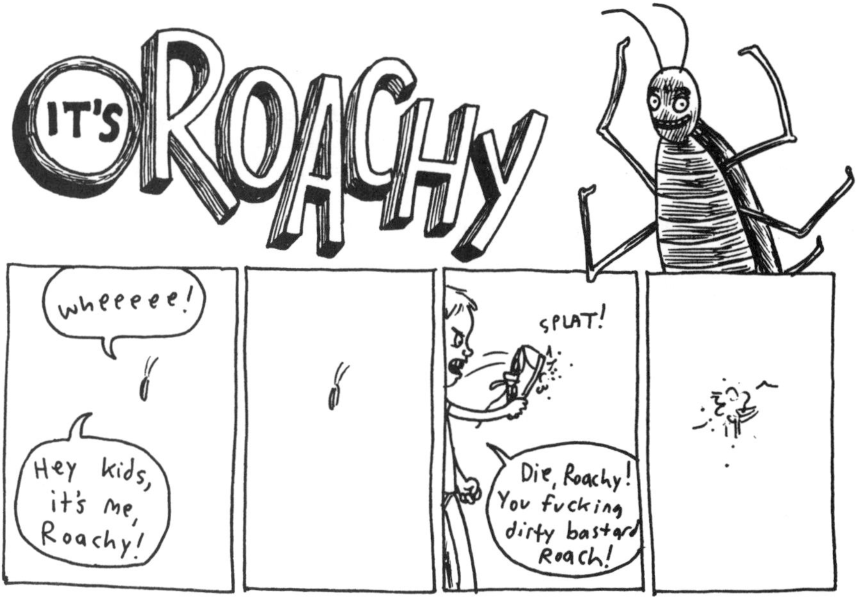

IT'S ROACHY
wheeeee!
Hey kids, it's me, Roachy!
SPLAT!
Die, Roachy! You fucking dirty bastard Roach!

Heavy Metal Fan Needs Support

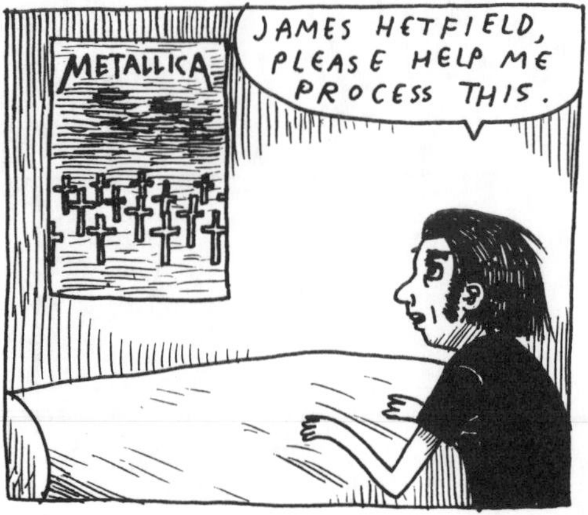
METALLICA
JAMES HETFIELD, PLEASE HELP ME PROCESS THIS.

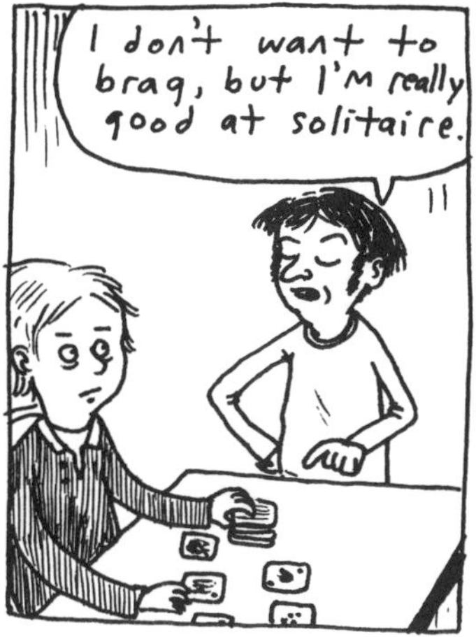
I don't want to brag, but I'm really good at solitaire.

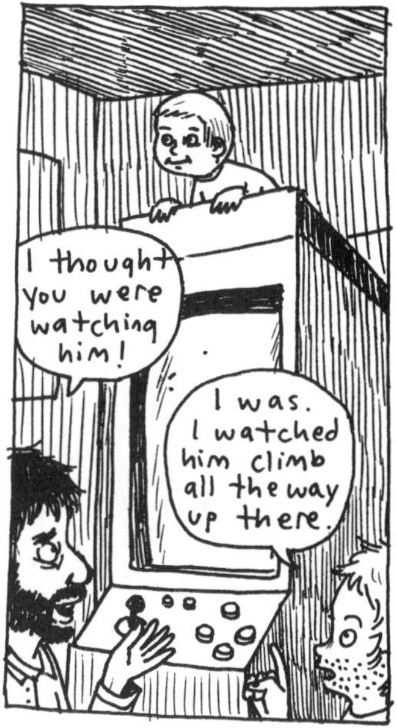
I thought you were watching him!
I was. I watched him climb all the way up there.

You washed your hands after changing the cat litter, right?
Uh, yeah, um, of course.

Honey, I'm sorry...this just isn't working. I hope this doesn't mean we can't still hang out, have sex, and say I love you.

WHO IS MORE TIREDER?

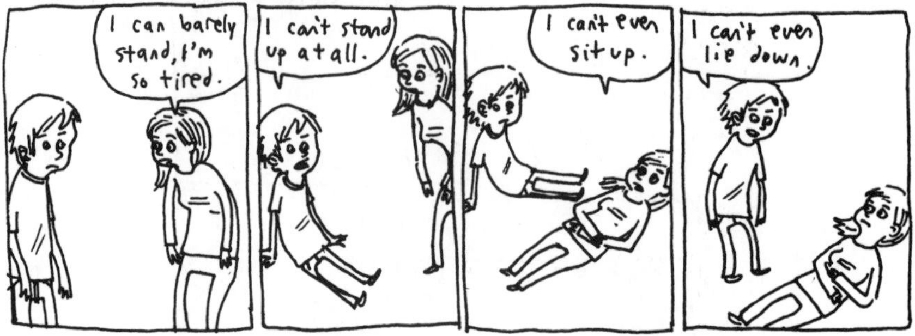
I can barely stand, I'm so tired.
I can't stand up at all.
I can't even sit up.
I can't even lie down.

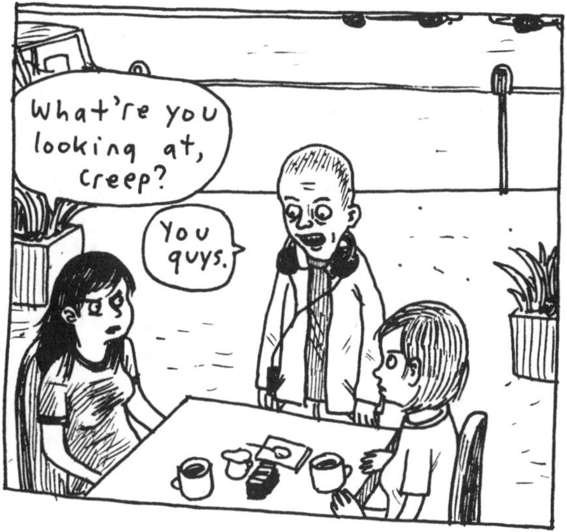
What're you looking at, creep?
You guys.

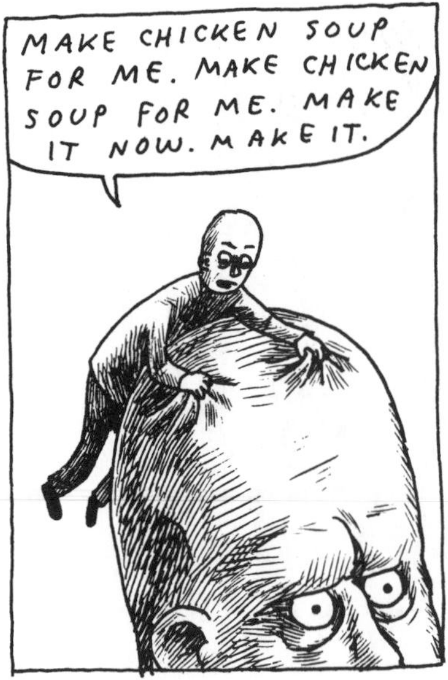
MAKE CHICKEN SOUP FOR ME. MAKE CHICKEN SOUP FOR ME. MAKE IT NOW. MAKE IT.

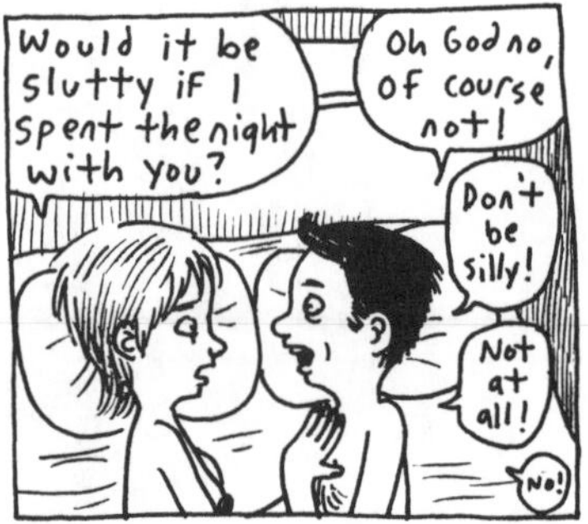
Would it be slutty if I spent the night with you?
Oh God no, of course not!
Don't be silly!
Not at all!
No!

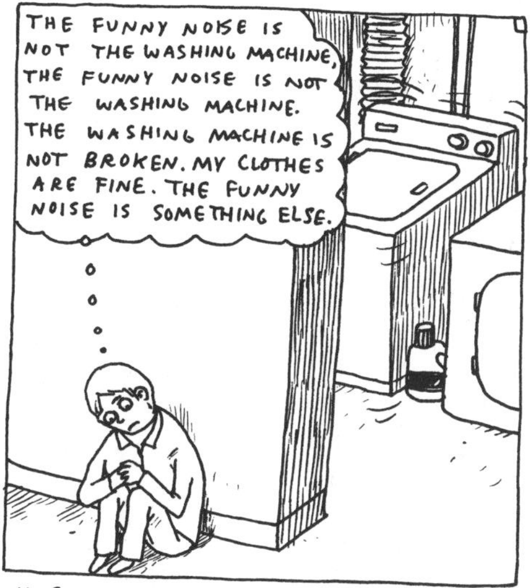
THE FUNNY NOISE IS NOT THE WASHING MACHINE, THE FUNNY NOISE IS NOT THE WASHING MACHINE. THE WASHING MACHINE IS NOT BROKEN. MY CLOTHES ARE FINE. THE FUNNY NOISE IS SOMETHING ELSE.

HIS CLOTHES WILL BE CLEAN SOON

...and I said to him, if you need to rely on semantics to win an argument, professor, maybe you need to go do more research. He still gave me a 'B' on my paper, but I've earned his grudging respect.

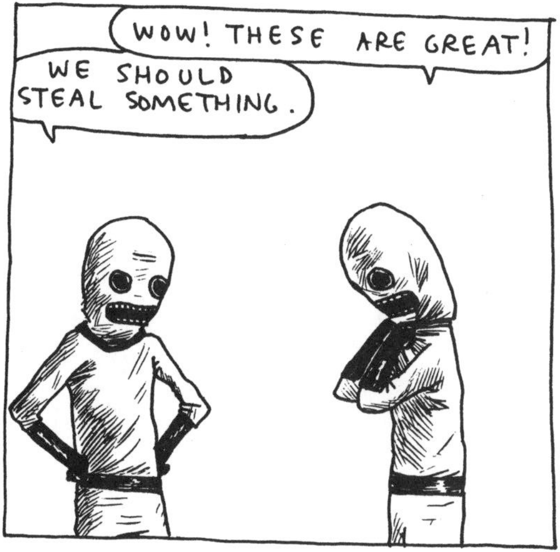
WE SHOULD STEAL SOMETHING.
WOW! THESE ARE GREAT!

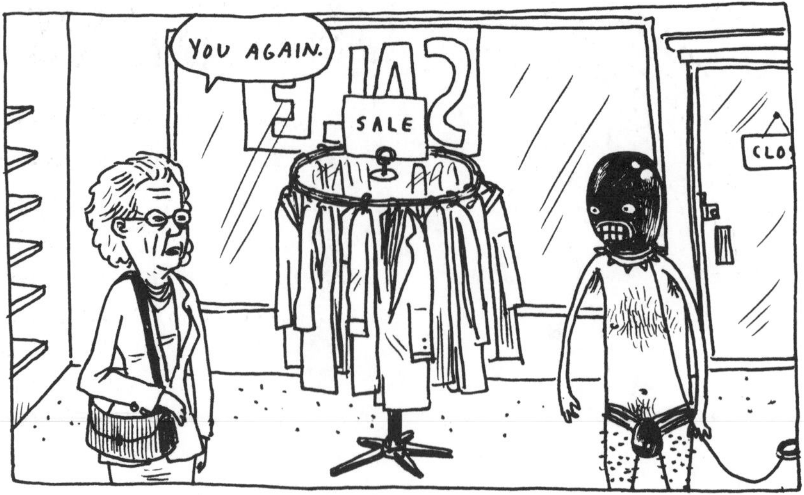

YOU AGAIN.
SALE
CLO

UNICORNS

Unicorns have teeth. These devious beasts have come up with ~~diseng~~ really good plans for the systematic elimination of certain persons who stand in the way of the Unicorn Master directives. One time a unicorn stood on it's hind legs and flailed its front ones at me. What did I ever do to you, you stupid unicorn?

WHAT IF MEN COULD HAVE BABIES TOO?

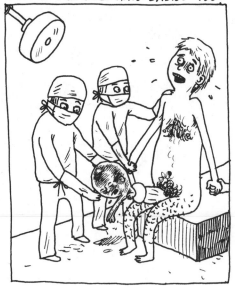

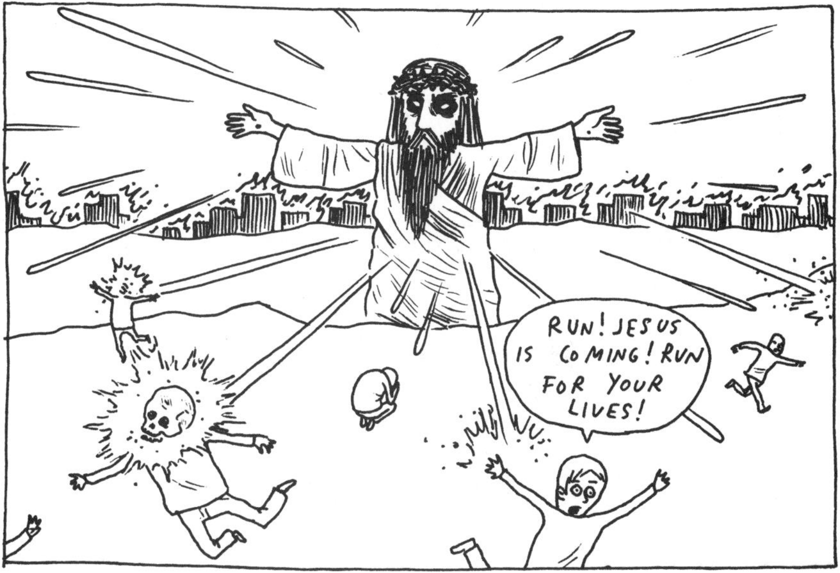
RUN! JESUS IS COMING! RUN FOR YOUR LIVES!

I'm kind of scared of the penis.
You shouldn't be scared. The penis is nothing to be afraid of.
Oh, no, I'm not scared of yours. It's kind of small.

HOPELESS ROMANTICS

...and his girlfriend died in the crash with him.
That's sad.
Not really. They died together.

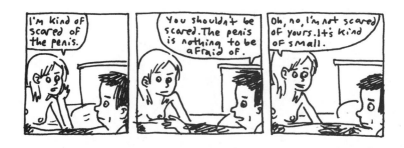

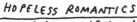

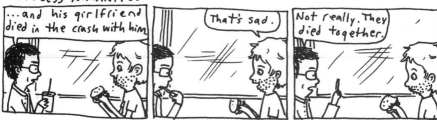

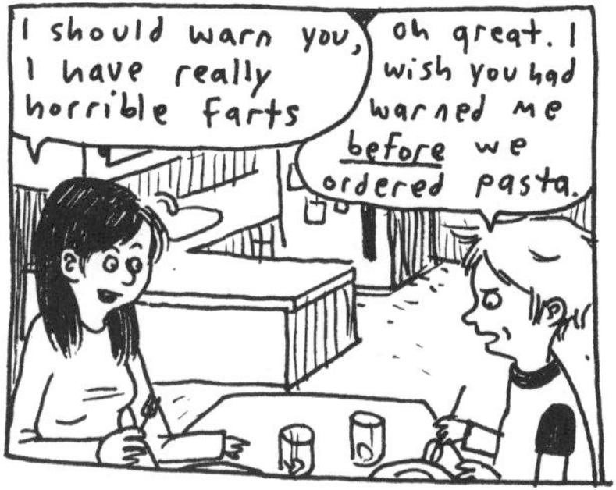
I should warn you, I have really horrible farts
oh great. I wish you had warned me before we ordered pasta.

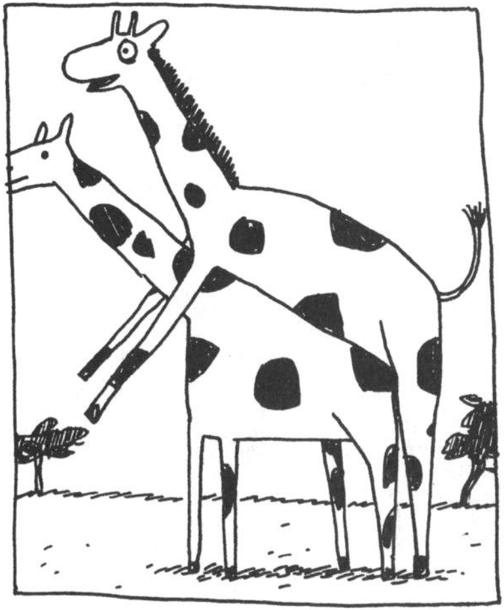

NATURE SHOW

MOMENT I KNEW IT WOULDN'T WORK

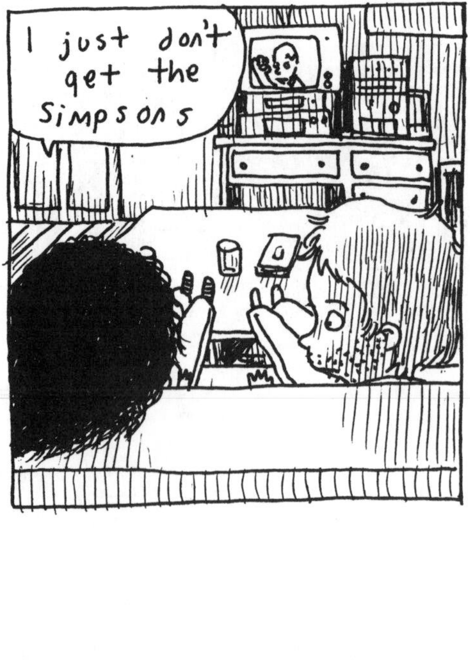
I just don't get the Simpsons

Romance

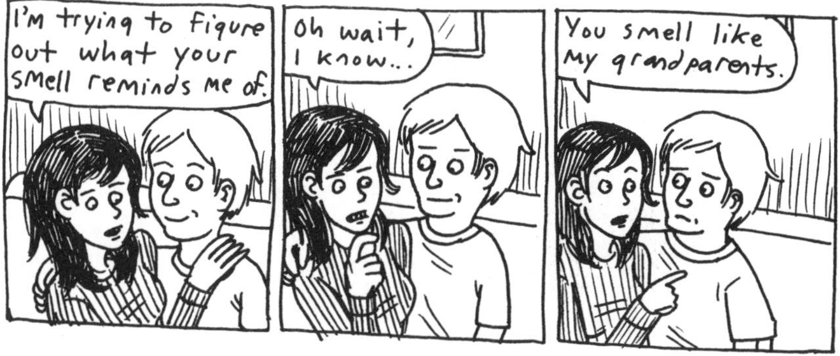
I'm trying to figure out what your smell reminds me of.
Oh wait, I know...
You smell like my grandparents.

The Physicists Fall Out Of Love

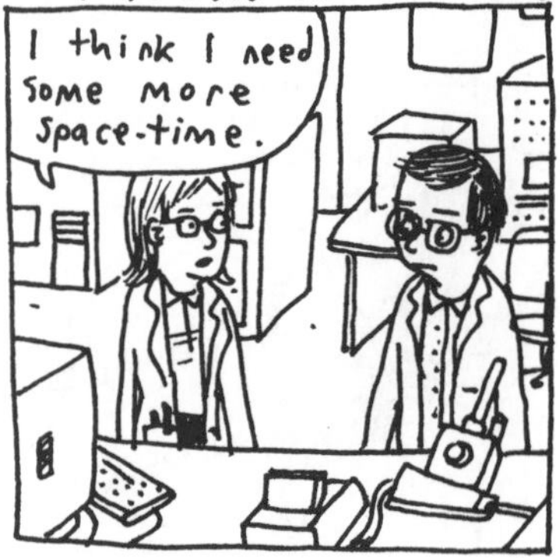
I think I need some more space-time.

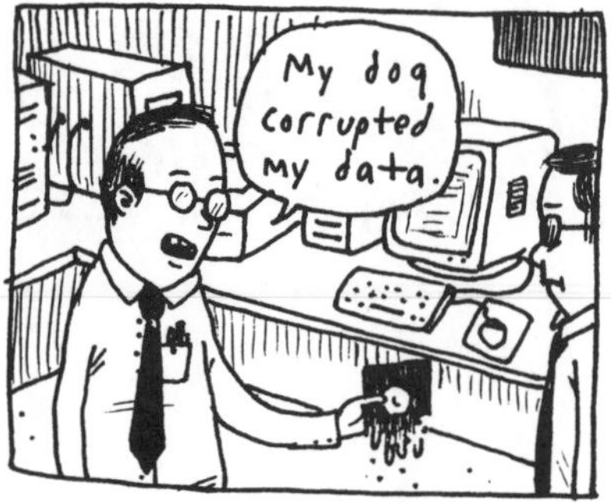
My dog corrupted my data.

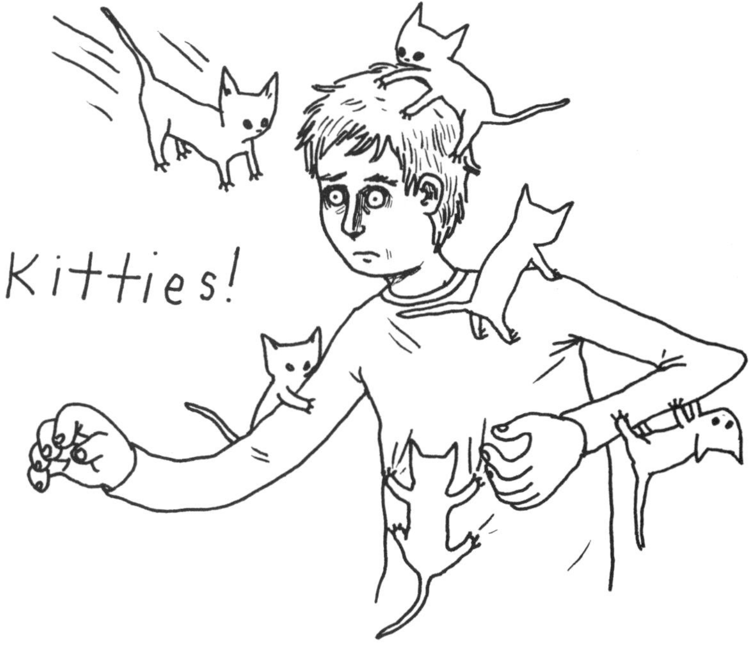
Kitties!

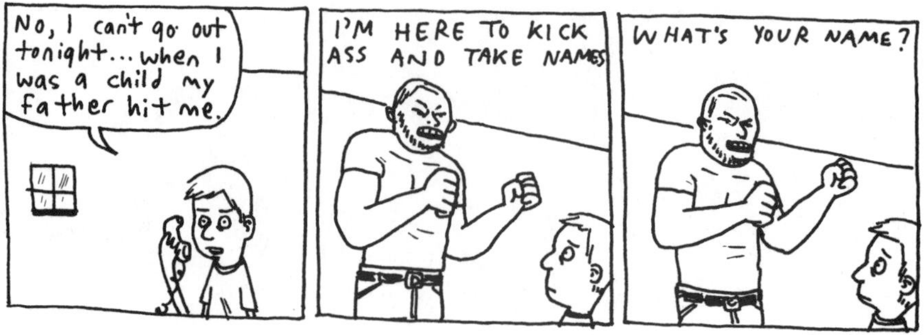
No, I can't go out tonight... when I was a child my father hit me.
I'M HERE TO KICK ASS AND TAKE NAMES
WHAT'S YOUR NAME?

DRAMA

AAAHHHHHH!
WHA--?!
WHA--?!
SQUEEEEEEEL!

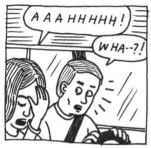

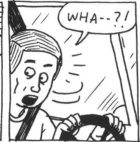

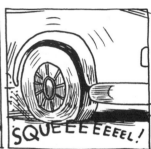

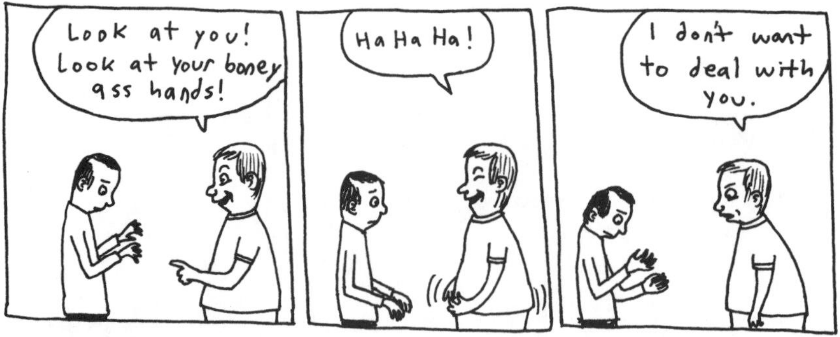
Look at you!
Look at your boney ass hands!
Ha Ha Ha!
I don't want to deal with you.

IS IT GROSS?

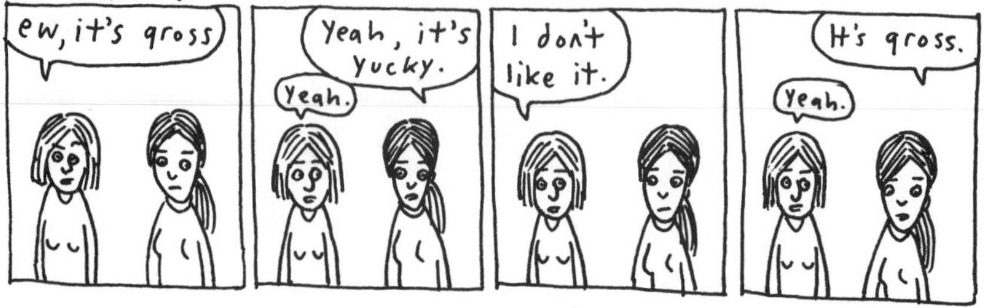
ew, it's gross
Yeah, it's yucky.
Yeah.
I don't like it.
It's gross.
Yeah.

OOF!
WHUMP
Asshole!

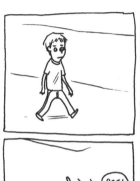

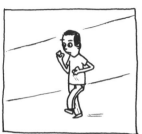

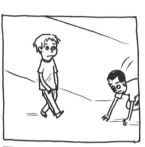

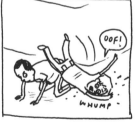

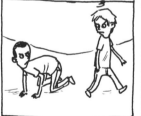

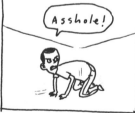

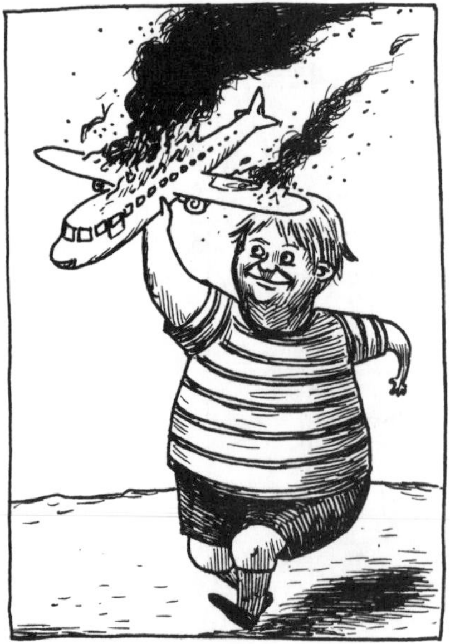

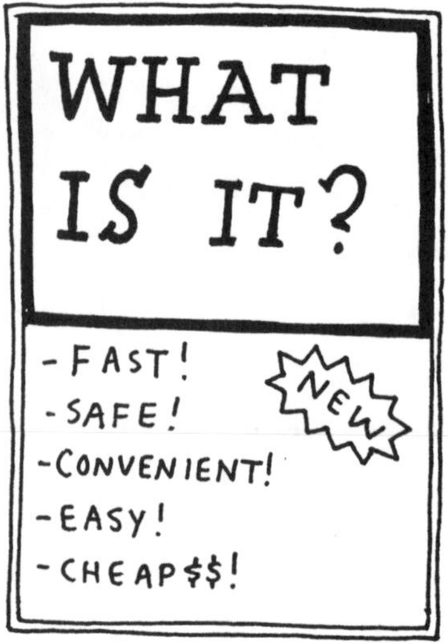

WHAT IS IT?
-FAST!
-SAFE!
-CONVENIENT!
-EASY!
-CHEAP$$!
NEW

Your cheerleader existence isn't satisfying anymore.

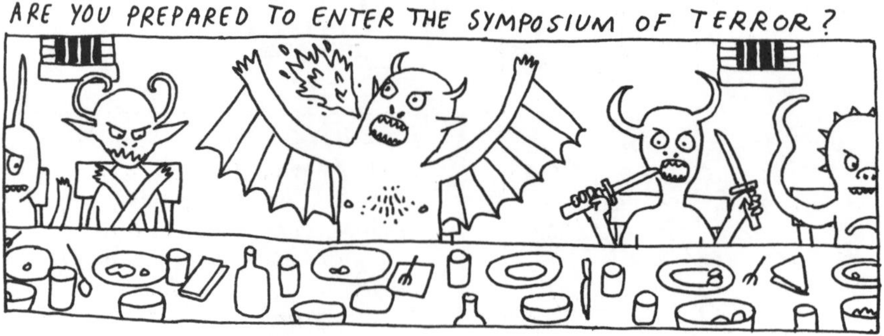
ARE YOU PREPARED TO ENTER THE SYMPOSIUM OF TERROR?

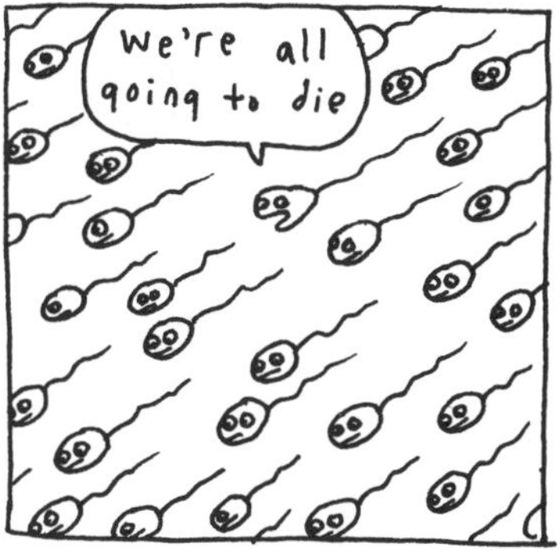
We're all going to die

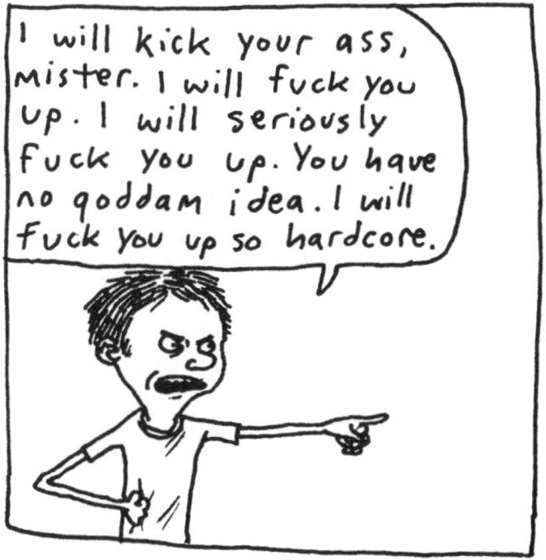
I will kick your ass, mister. I will fuck you up. I will seriously fuck you up. You have no goddam idea. I will fuck you up so hardcore.

NINJA PARADISE

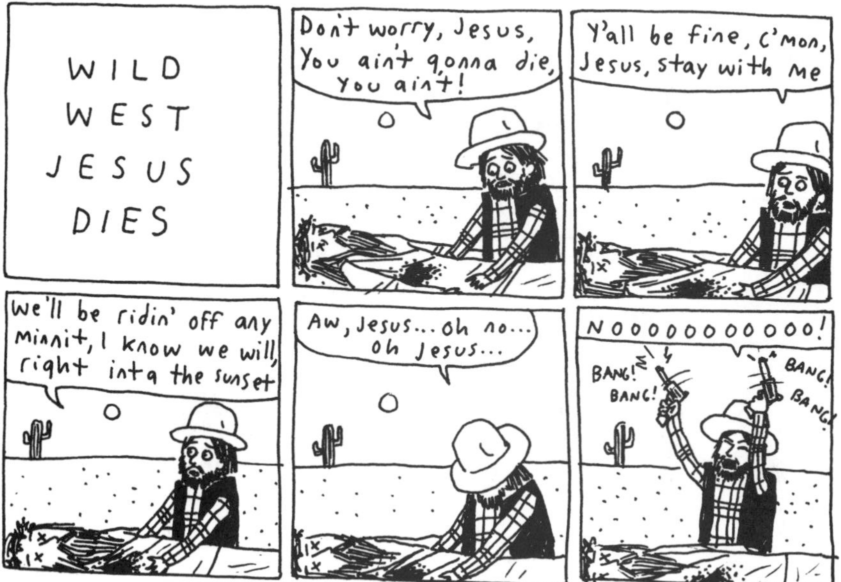
WILD WEST JESUS DIES
Don't worry, Jesus, You ain't gonna die, You ain't!
Y'all be fine, C'mon, Jesus, stay with me
We'll be ridin' off any minnit, I know we will, right inta the sunset
Aw, Jesus... oh no... oh Jesus...
NOOOOOOOOOOOO!
BANG! BANG!
BANG! BANG!

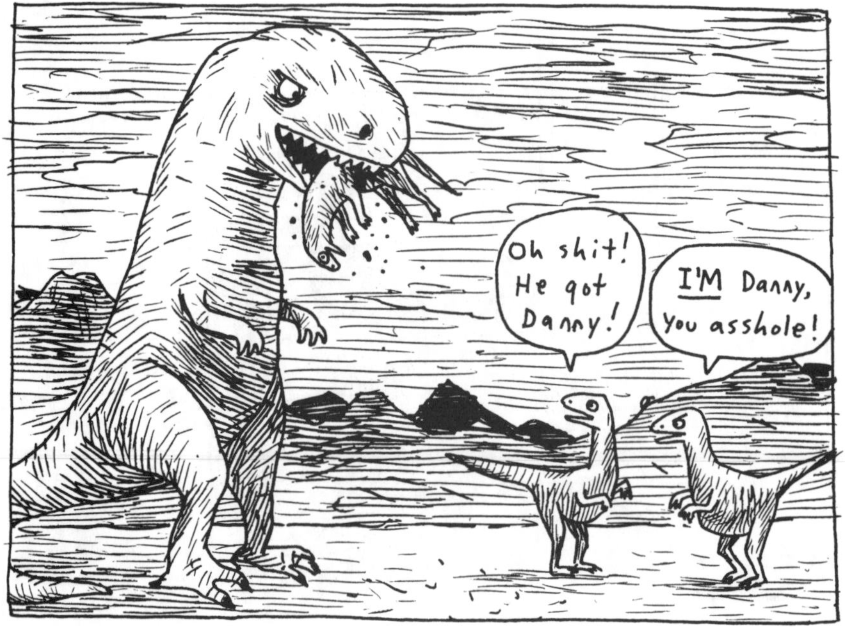
Oh shit! He got Danny!
I'M Danny, you asshole!

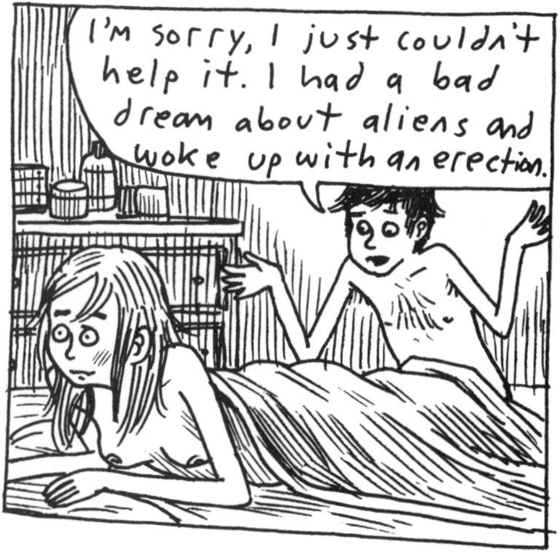
I'm sorry, I just couldn't help it. I had a bad dream about aliens and woke up with an erection.

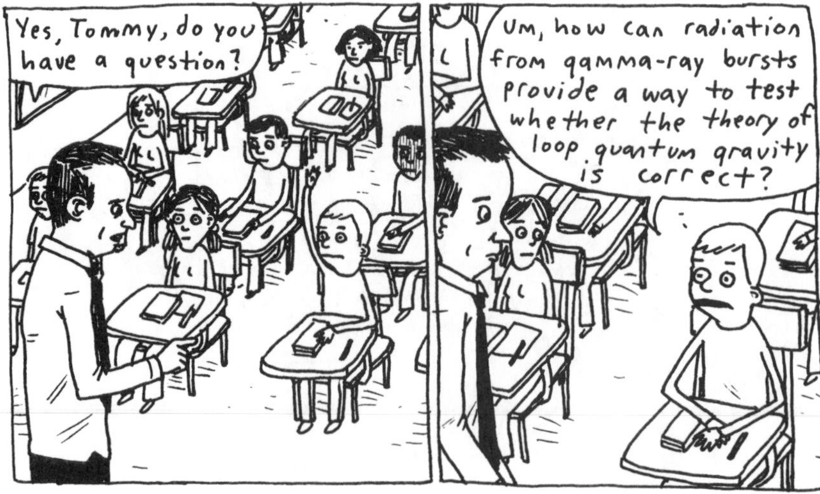
Yes, Tommy, do you have a question?
Um, how can radiation from gamma-ray bursts provide a way to test whether the theory of loop quantum gravity is correct?

FILM DESIGN | SOLDIER'S COSTUMES

Helmet

Helmet back

Braids

Robe design

Soldiers Marching off to penetrate enemy lines

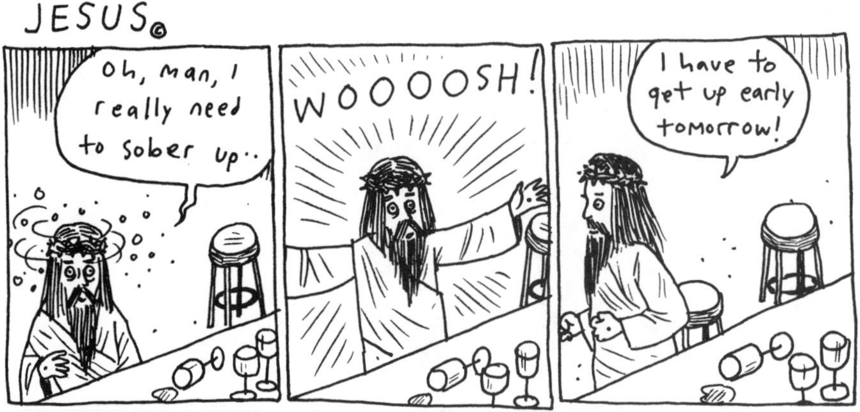
JESUS©
Oh, man, I really need to sober up..
WOOOOOSH!
I have to get up early tomorrow!

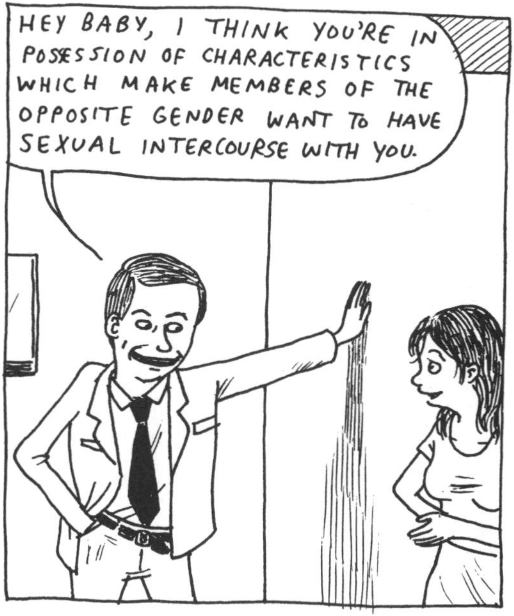
HEY BABY, I THINK YOU'RE IN POSSESSION OF CHARACTERISTICS WHICH MAKE MEMBERS OF THE OPPOSITE GENDER WANT TO HAVE SEXUAL INTERCOURSE WITH YOU.

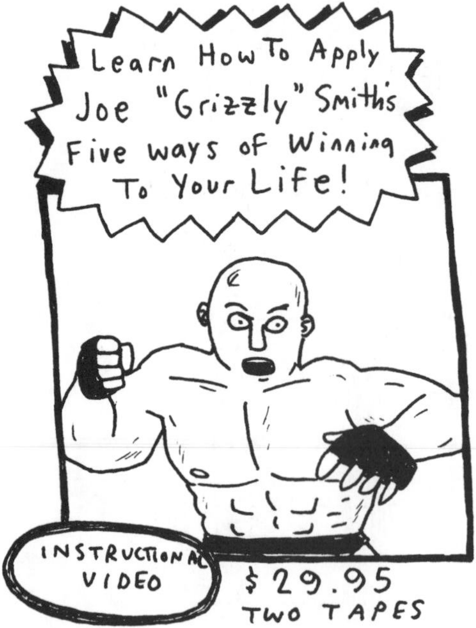
Learn How To Apply Joe "Grizzly" Smith's Five ways of Winning To Your Life!
INSTRUCTIONAL VIDEO
$29.95
TWO TAPES

1. Knockout!
2. Submission!
3. Referee stops fight!
4. Doctor stops fight!
5. Corner throws in towel!

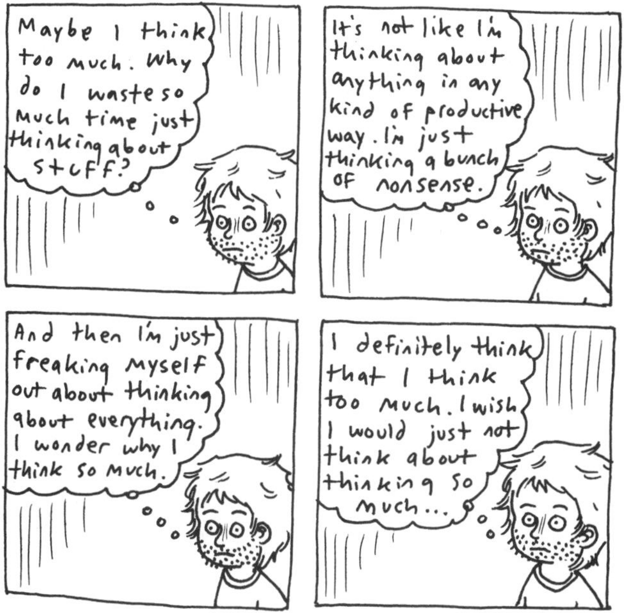
Maybe I think too much. Why do I waste so much time just thinking about stuff?
It's not like I'm thinking about anything in any kind of productive way. I'm just thinking a bunch of nonsense.
And then I'm just freaking myself out about thinking about everything. I wonder why I think so much.
I definitely think that I think too much. I wish I would just not think about thinking so much...

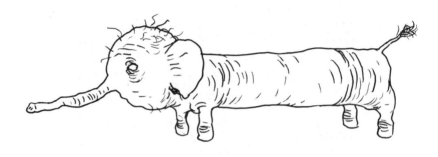

Elephallus

NEW YEAR'S RESOLUTION

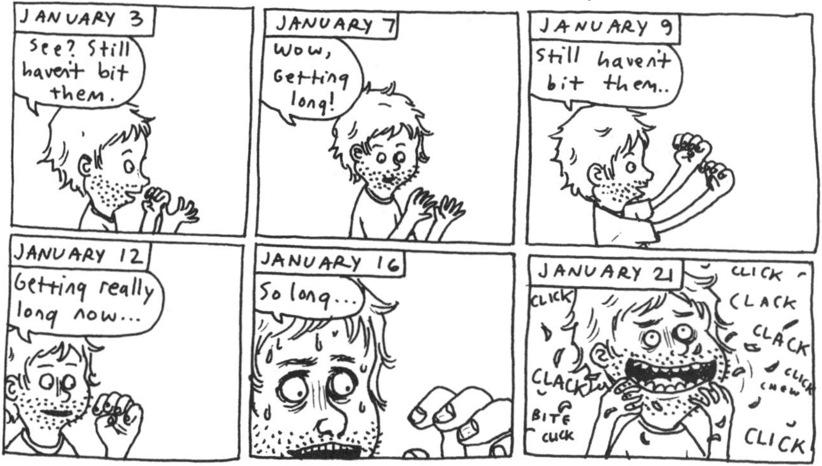
JANUARY 3
See? Still haven't bit them.
JANUARY 7
Wow, Getting long!
JANUARY 9
Still haven't bit them..
JANUARY 12
Getting really long now...
JANUARY 16
So long...
JANUARY 21
CLICK
CLICK
CLACK
CLACK
CLACK
CLICK
CHEW
BITE
CLICK
CLICK

THE FATHER OF YOUR CHILD:

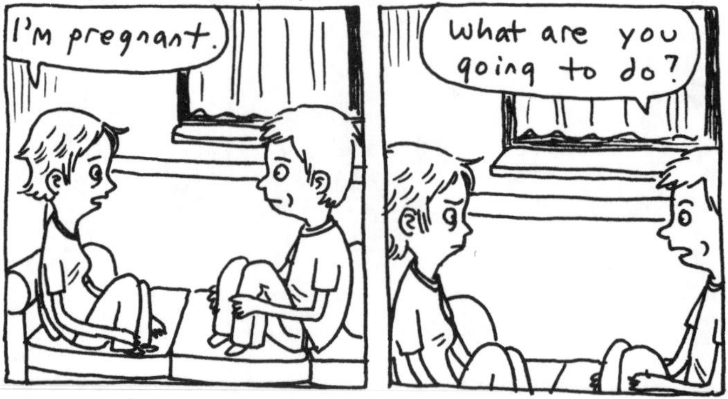

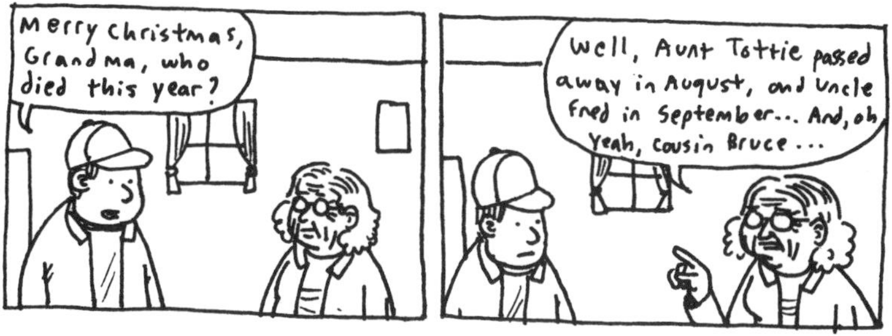
Merry Christmas, Grandma, who died this year?
Well, Aunt Tottie passed away in August, and Uncle Fred in September... And, oh yeah, cousin Bruce...

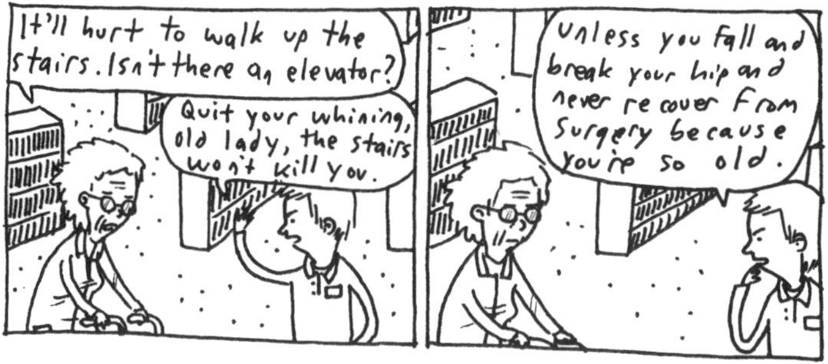
It'll hurt to walk up the stairs. Isn't there an elevator?
Quit your whining, old lady, the stairs won't kill you.
Unless you fall and break your hip and never recover from surgery because you're so old.

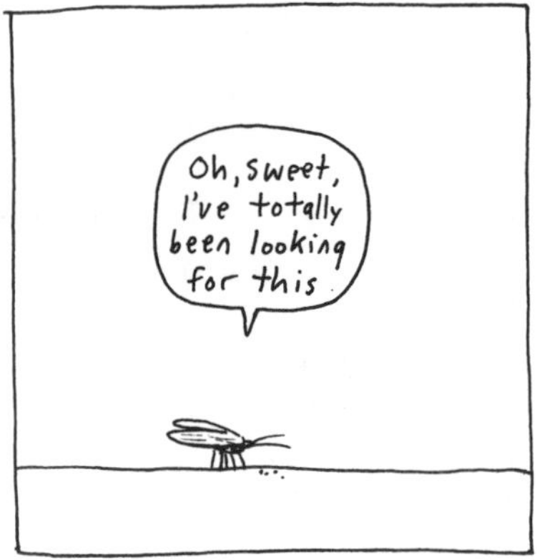
Oh, sweet, I've totally been looking for this.

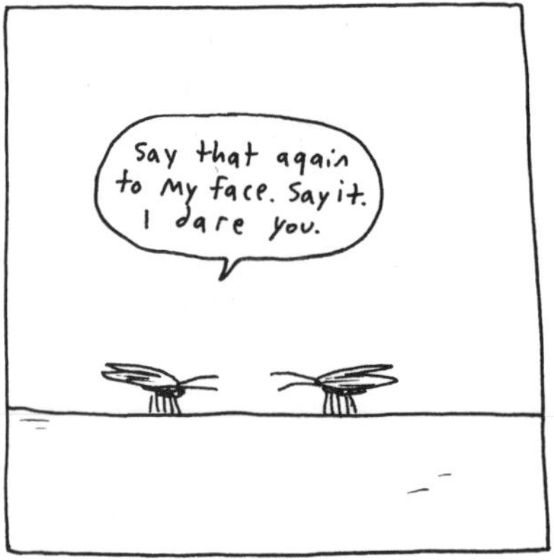
Say that again to my face. Say it. I dare you.

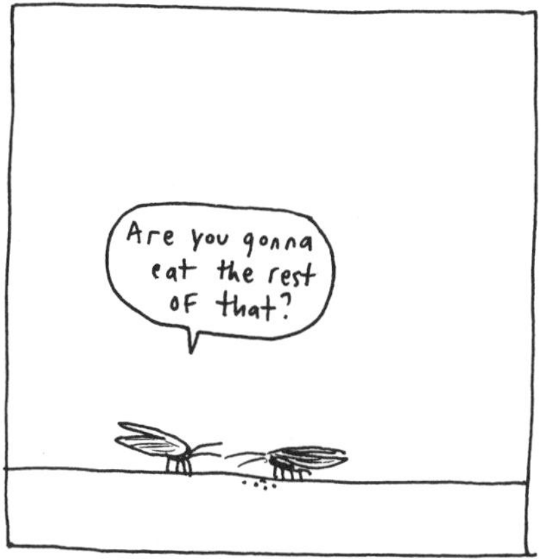
Are you gonna eat the rest of that?

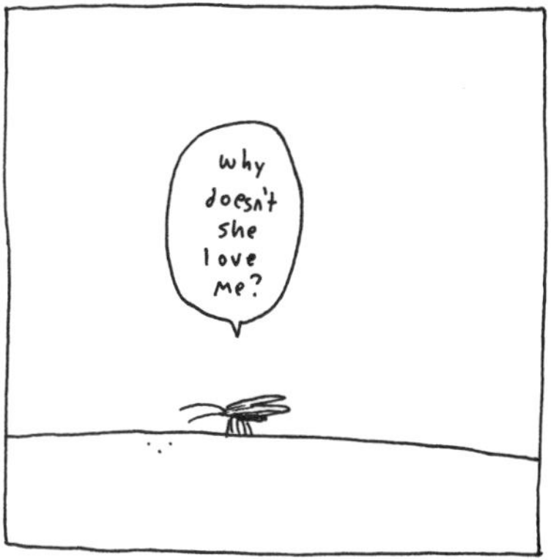
why doesn't she love me?

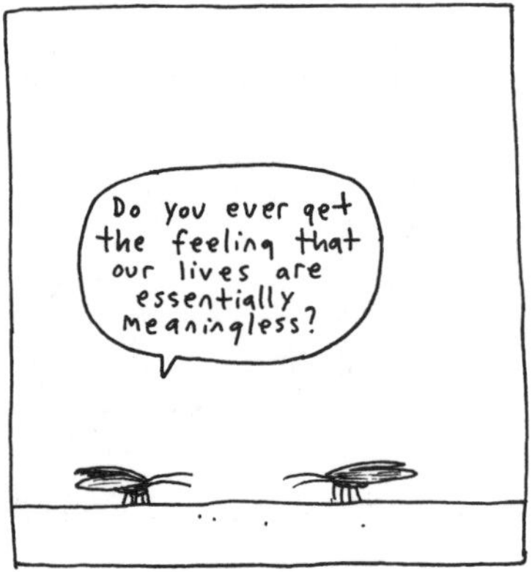
Do you ever get the feeling that our lives are essentially meaningless?

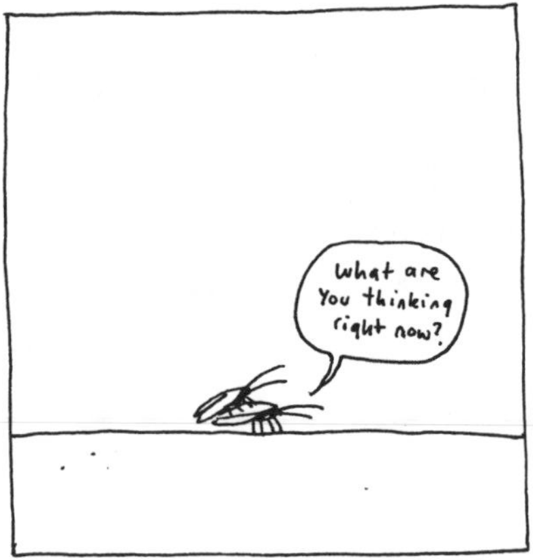
What are you thinking right now?

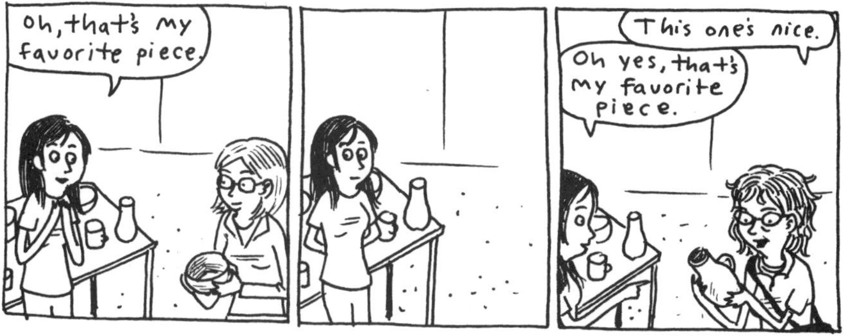
Oh, that's my favorite piece.
This one's nice.
Oh yes, that's my favorite piece.

MY SURGERY COMIC

ohhhhh
cough
No, No, Mr. Loving. It's not just about the hard things.
It's about the joys.
It's about the joys.

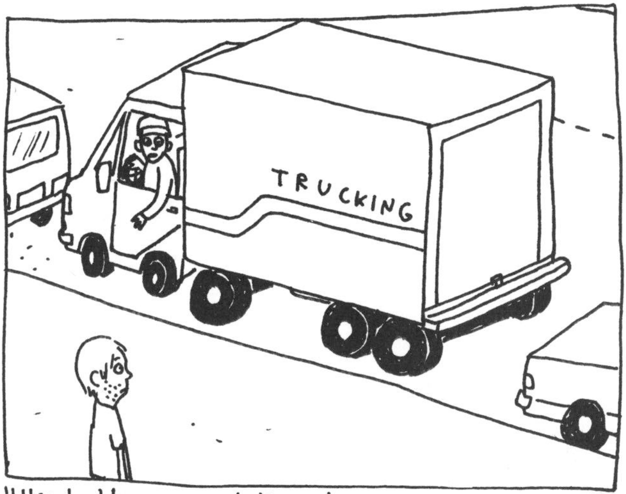
TRUCKING

"Hey buddy, can you tell me how much room I have?"

Jammin' with the CD

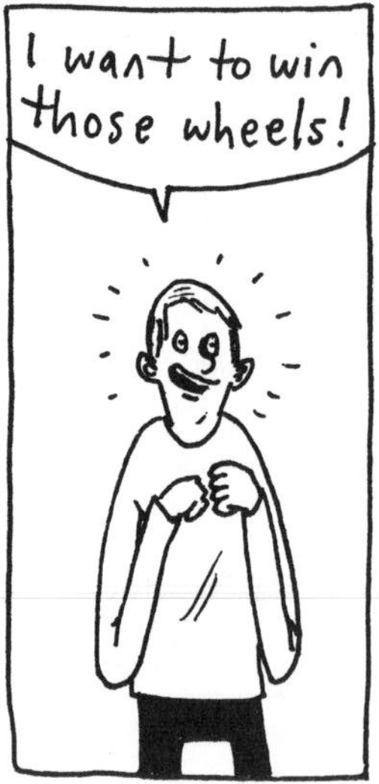
I want to win those wheels!

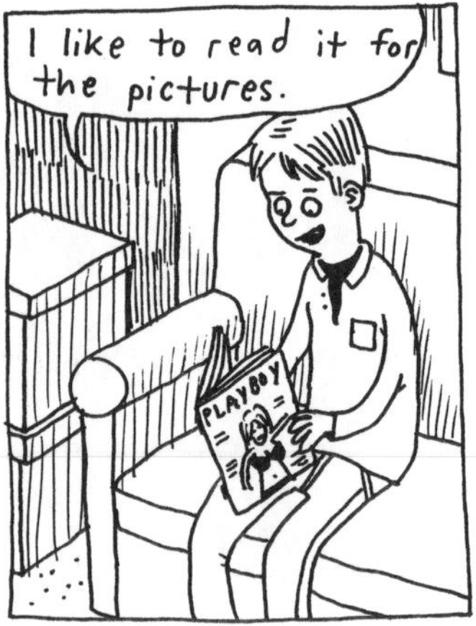
I like to read it for the pictures.
PLAYBOY

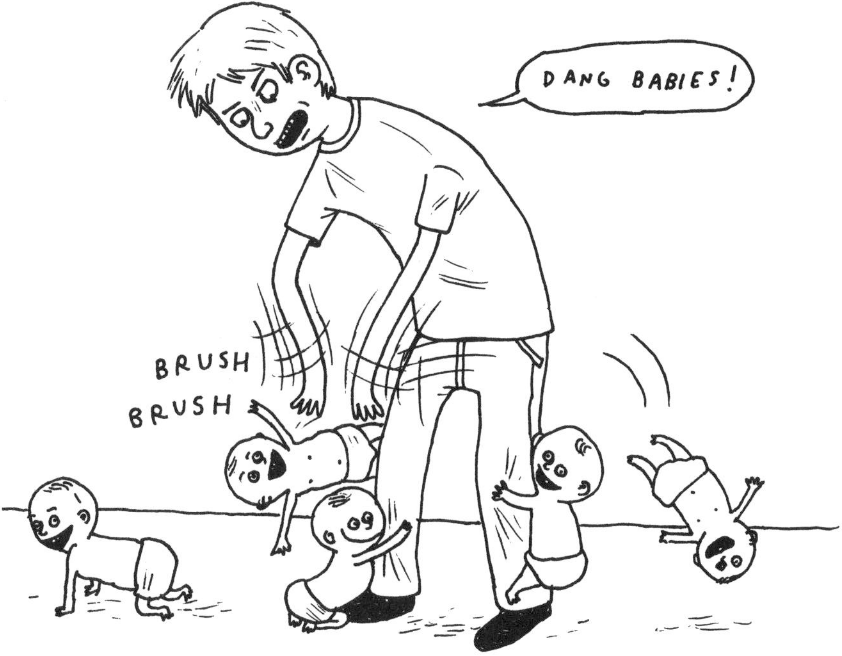
DANG BABIES!
BRUSH
BRUSH

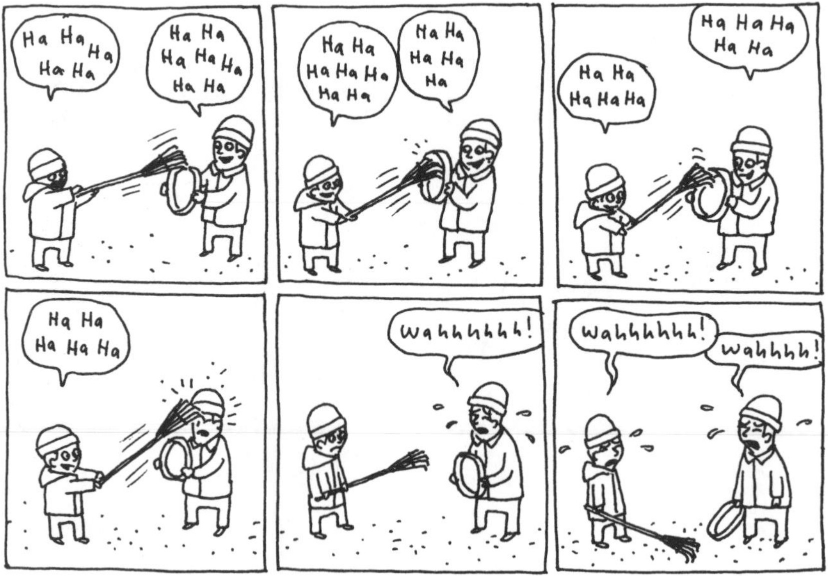

Ha Ha Ha Ha Ha
Ha Ha Ha Ha Ha Ha Ha
Ha Ha Ha Ha Ha Ha Ha
Ha Ha Ha Ha Ha
Ha Ha Ha Ha Ha
Ha Ha Ha Ha Ha
Ha Ha Ha Ha Ha
wahhhhhh!
wahhhhhhh!
wahhhh!

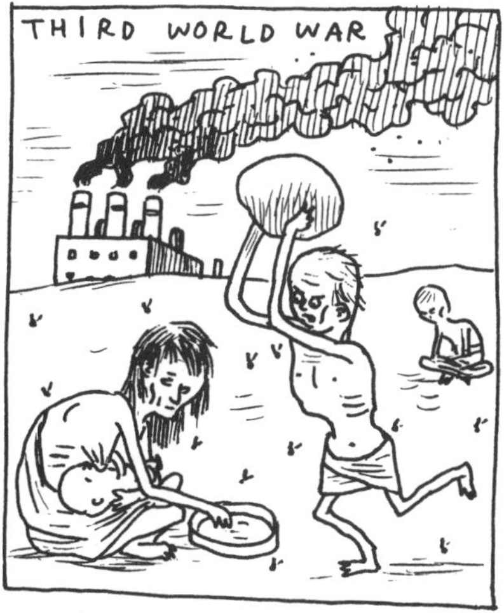
THIRD WORLD WAR

KIDS LOVE PORN

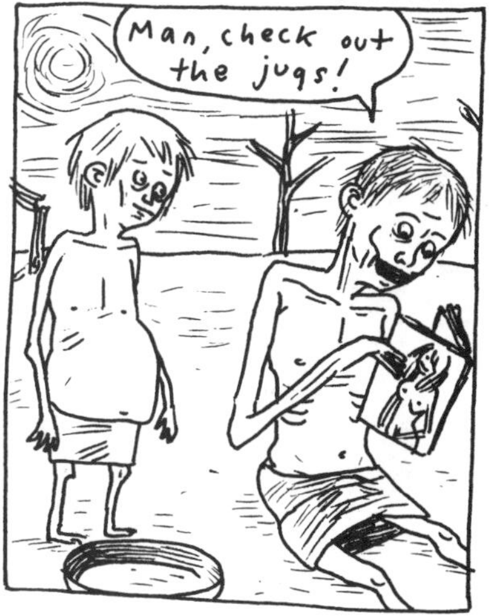
Man, check out the jugs!

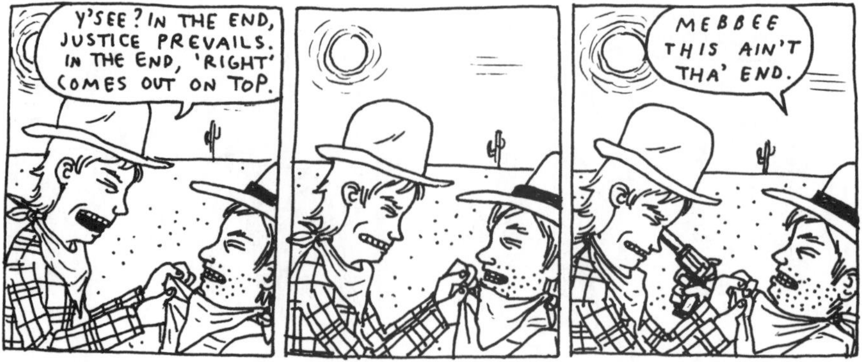
Y'SEE? IN THE END, JUSTICE PREVAILS. IN THE END, 'RIGHT' COMES OUT ON TOP.
MEBBEE THIS AIN'T THA' END.

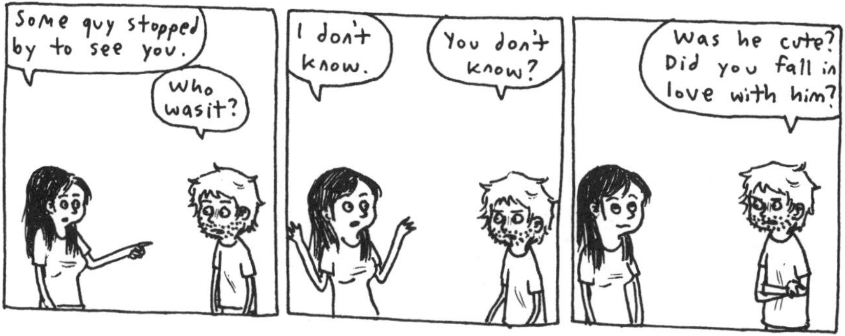
Some guy stopped by to see you.
Who wasit?
I don't know.
You don't know?
Was he cute? Did you fall in love with him?

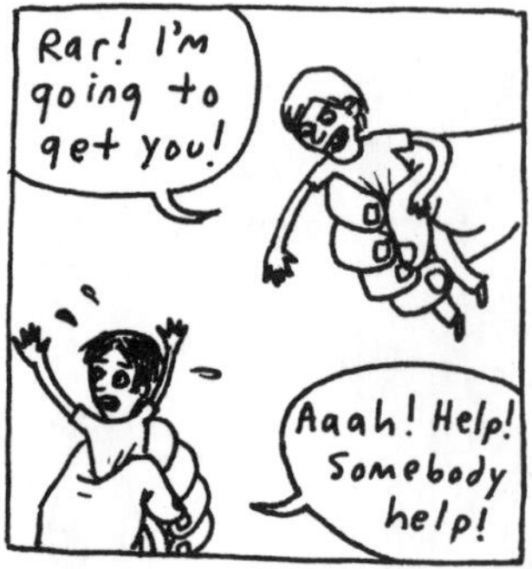
Rar! I'm going to get you!
Aaah! Help! Somebody help!

Theirs was a forbidden love.

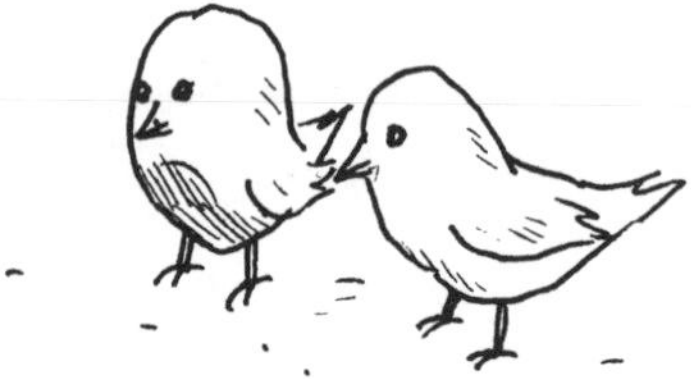

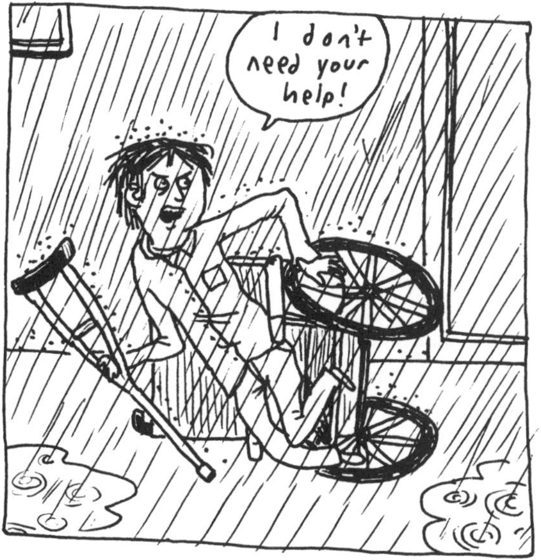
I don't need your help!

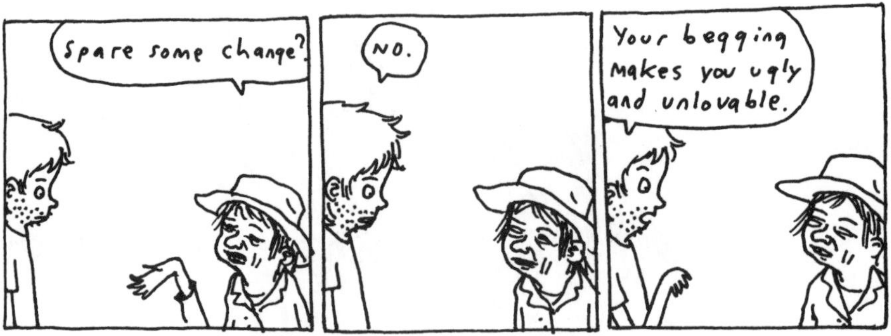
Spare some change?
NO.
Your begging makes you ugly and unlovable.

IT IS HARD TO THROW THINGS AWAY

Ah! Dammit! Goddam Garbage cans!
Ah, Fuck it.

YOU WANT TO KEEP THEM FOREVER

Man, you know who else was huge in college?
Huge Man.
Man, he was huge.
Oh, yeah. Huge Man. Totally.

Did you miss me?
Huh? When?
While you were asleep, silly!

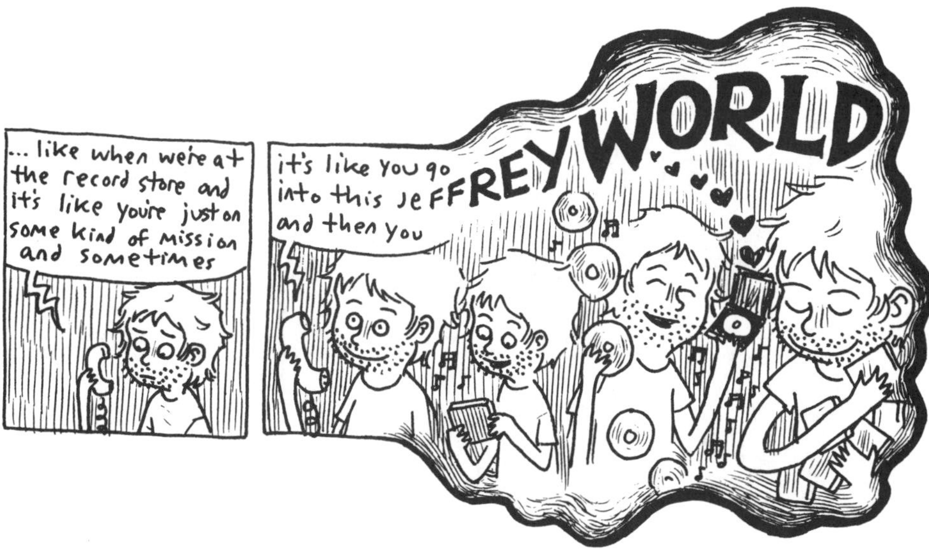

... like when we're at the record store and it's like you're just on some kind of mission and sometimes
it's like you go into this JEFFREY WORLD and then you

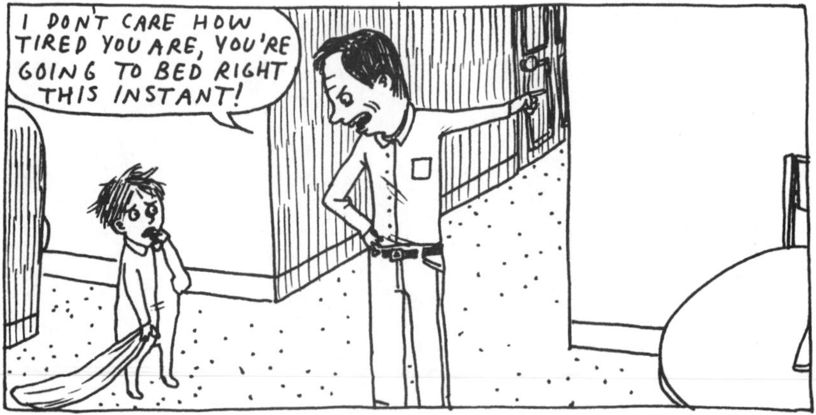
I DON'T CARE HOW TIRED YOU ARE, YOU'RE GOING TO BED RIGHT THIS INSTANT!

Romance.

I'LL GIVE YOU SOMETHING TO CRY ABOUT, YOU BITCH!
Will you marry me?

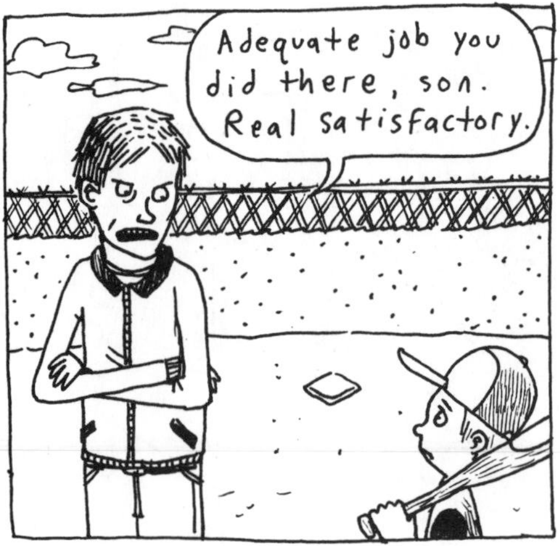
Adequate job you did there, son. Real satisfactory.

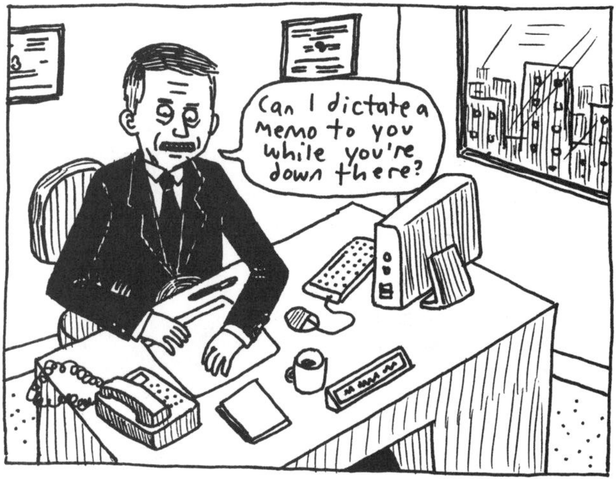
Can I dictate a memo to you while you're down there?

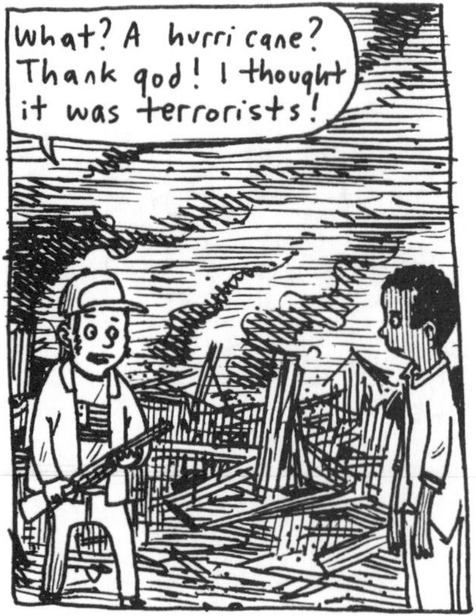
What? A hurricane? Thank god! I thought it was terrorists!

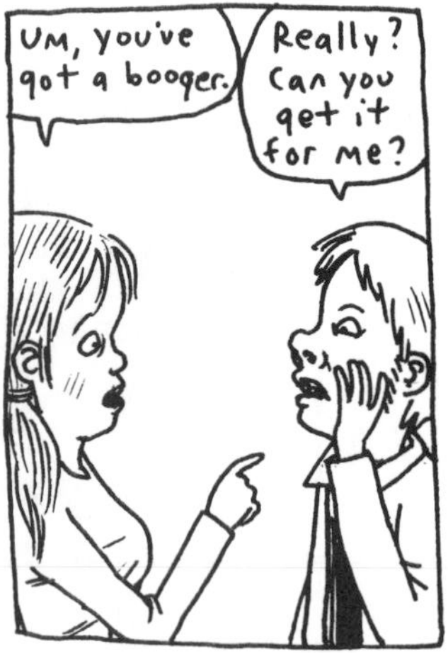
Um, you've got a booger.
Really? Can you get it for me?

Hey man, can you spare $250,000?
Oh, I-
Don't talk to him, honey, he's a CEO

The good news is we've completely repaired your intestines. The bad news is there's a few parts we forgot to put back in afterward.

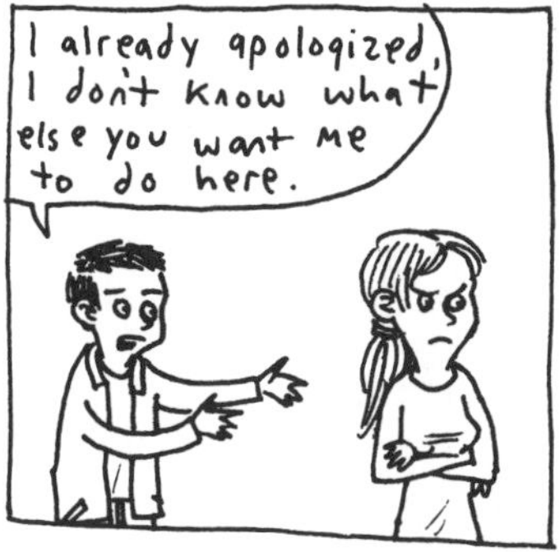
I already apologized, I don't know what else you want me to do here.

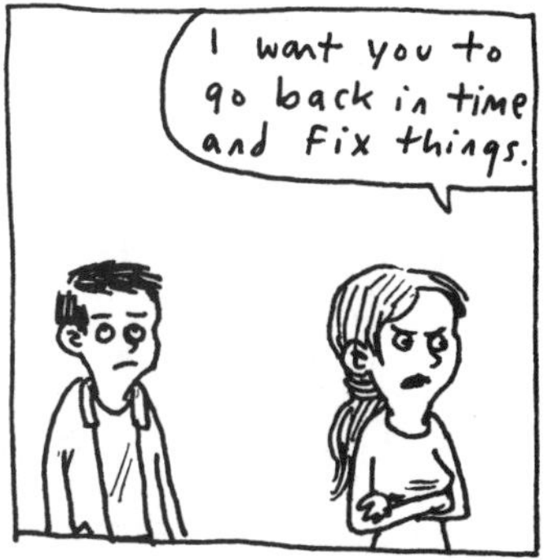
I want you to go back in time and fix things.

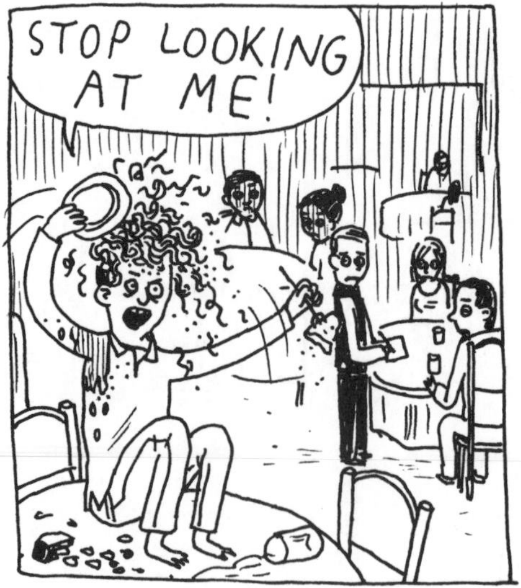
STOP LOOKING AT ME!

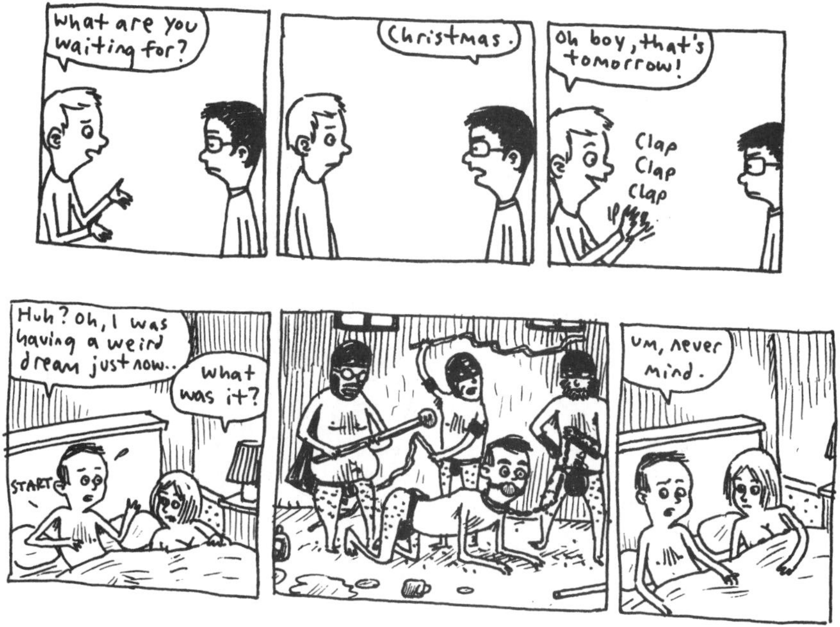
What are you waiting for?
Christmas.
Oh boy, that's tomorrow!
Clap Clap Clap
Huh? Oh, I was having a weird dream just now..
START
What was it?
Um, never mind.

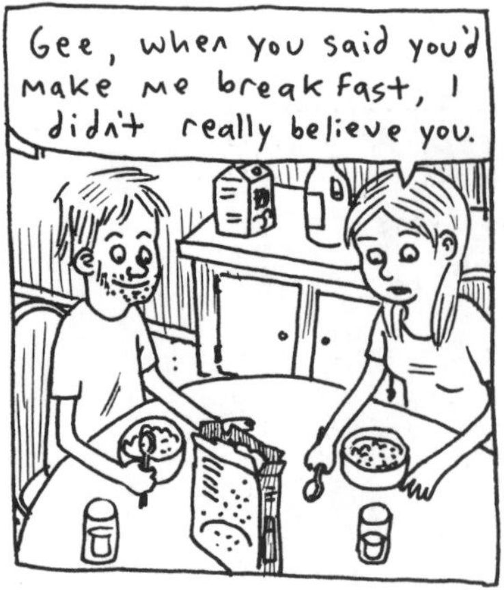
Gee, when you said you'd make me breakfast, I didn't really believe you.

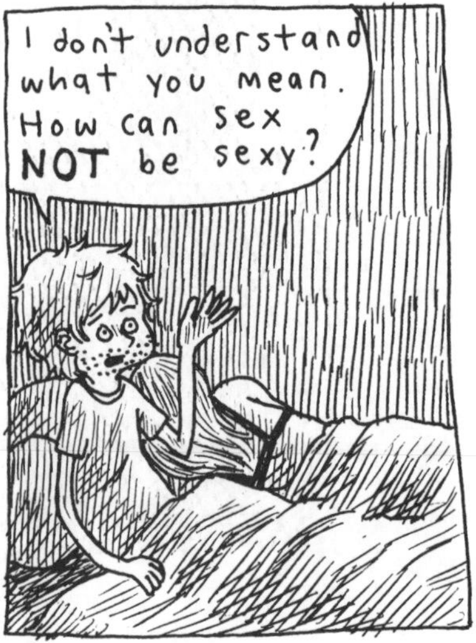
I don't understand what you mean. How can sex NOT be sexy?

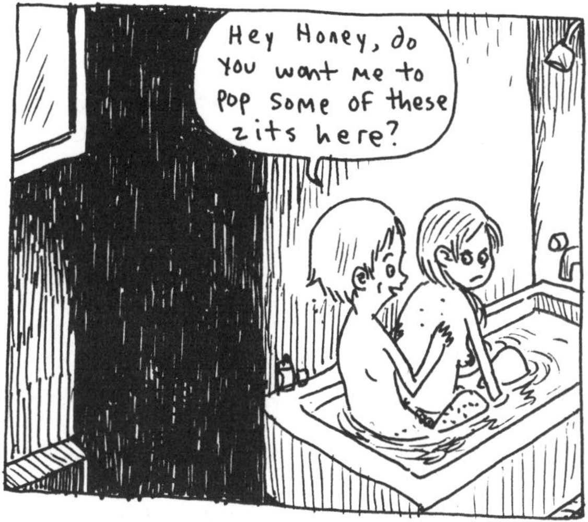
Hey Honey, do you want me to pop some of these zits here?

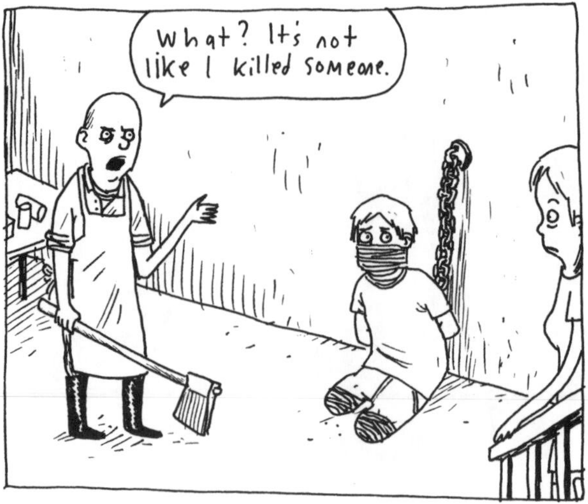
What? It's not like I killed someone.

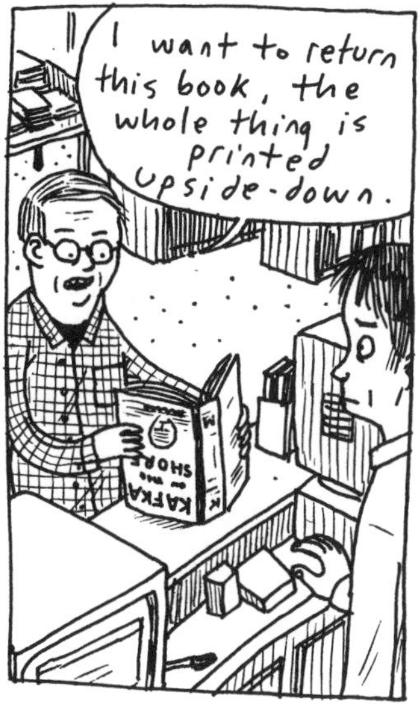
I want to return this book, the whole thing is printed upside-down.
KAFKA
SHORE

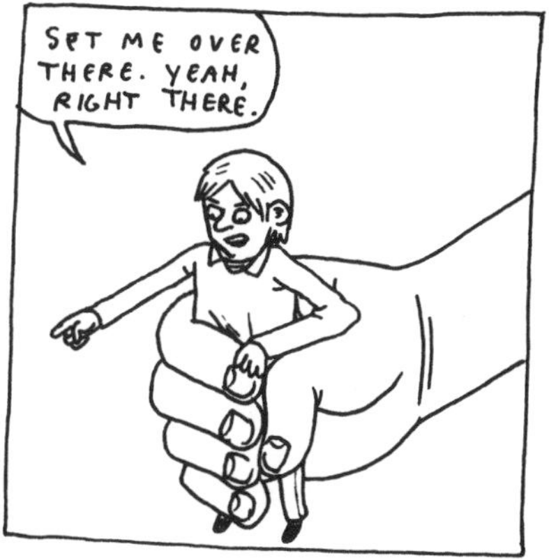
SET ME OVER THERE. YEAH, RIGHT THERE.

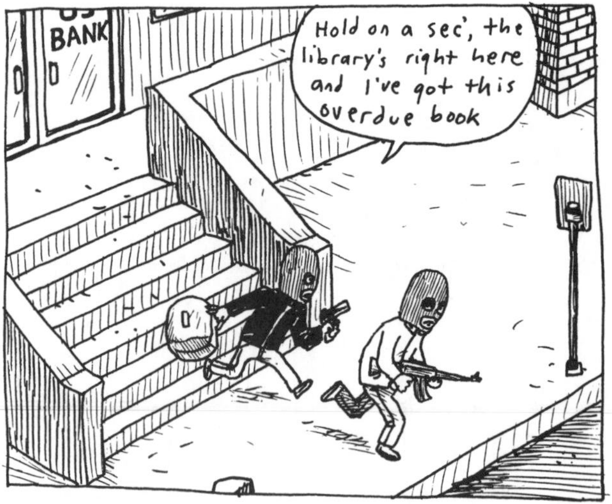
BANK
Hold on a sec', the library's right here and I've got this overdue book

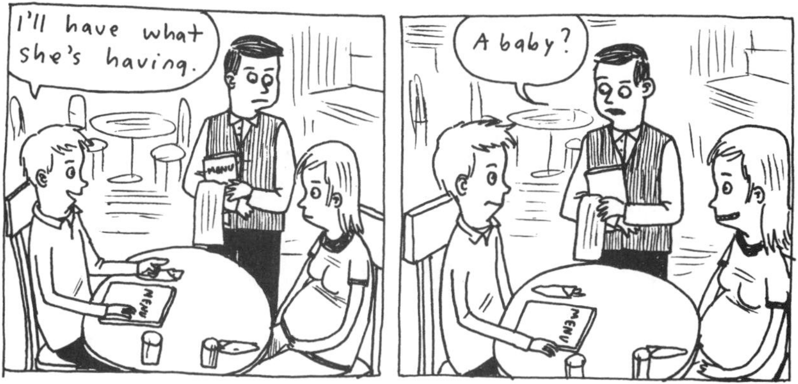
I'll have what she's having.
MENU
MENU
A baby?
MENU

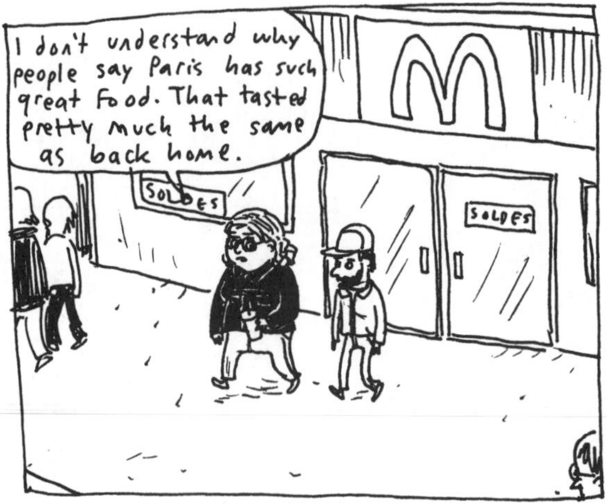
I don't understand why people say Paris has such great food. That tasted pretty much the same as back home.
SOLDES
SOLDES

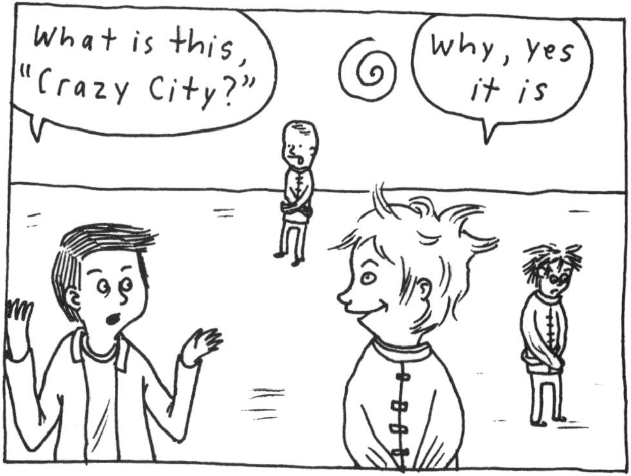
What is this, "Crazy City?"
Why, yes it is

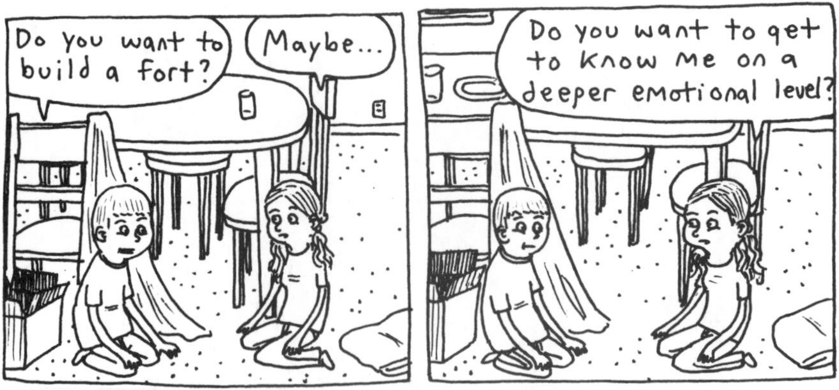
Do you want to build a fort?
Maybe...
Do you want to get to know me on a deeper emotional level?

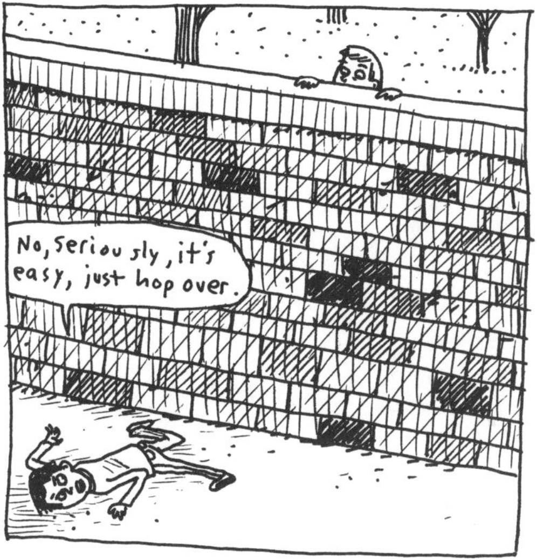
No, seriously, it's easy, just hop over.

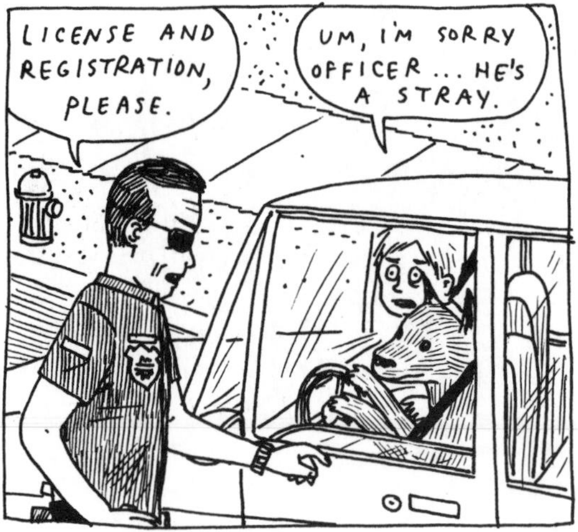
LICENSE AND REGISTRATION, PLEASE.
UM, I'M SORRY OFFICER... HE'S A STRAY.

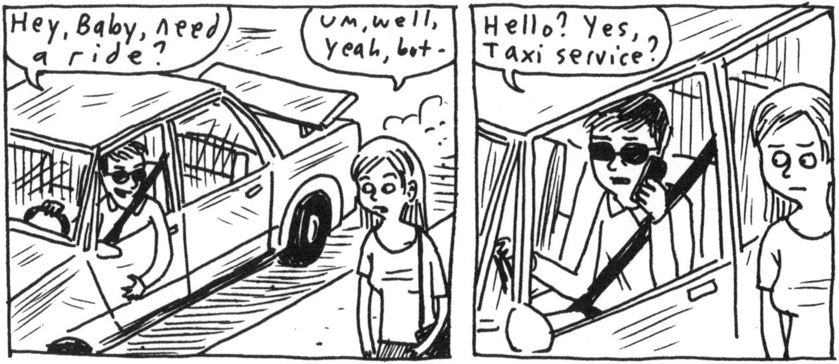
Hey, Baby, need a ride?
um, well, yeah, but-
Hello? Yes, Taxi service?

HOW TO MAKE SOMETHING CUTER

INCREASE HEAD SIZE
INCREASE EYE SIZE

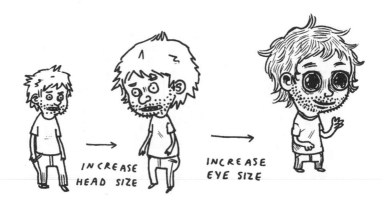

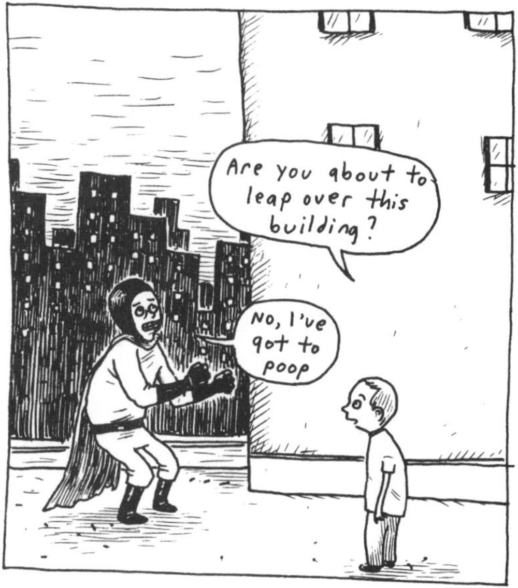
Are you about to leap over this building?
No, I've got to poop

I thought I'd scare her away by sticking my feet in her face, but it turns out she has a foot fetish.
Oh, yeah, I had the same thing happen with this girl I peed on.

MY BROTHER AND I AT THE MOVIES

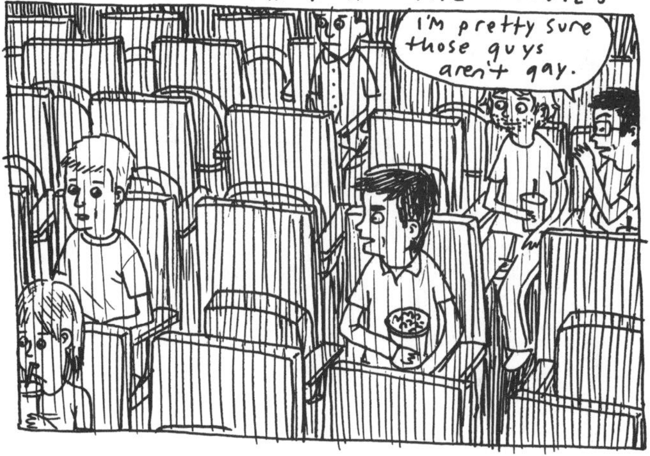

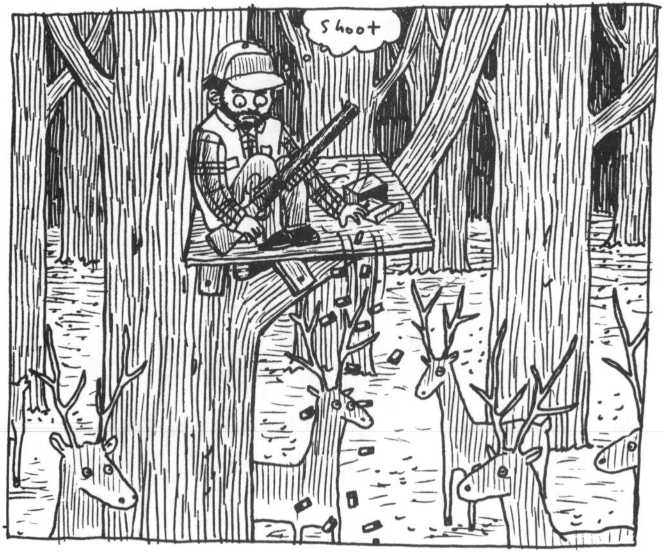
Shoot

HEY KIDS!

GAMES!

Can you find at least nine differences between the two pictures?

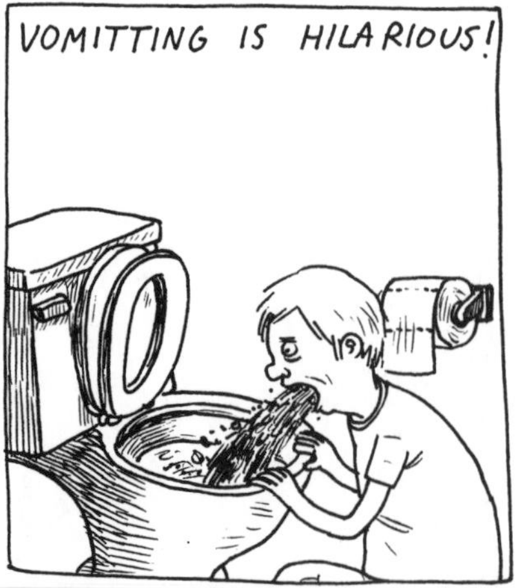
VOMITTING IS HILARIOUS!

REASONS PEOPLE WOULD WANT TO BEAT ME UP

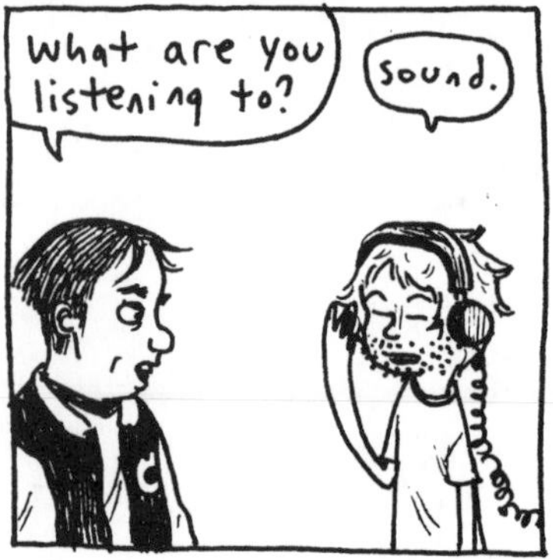
What are you listening to?
Sound.

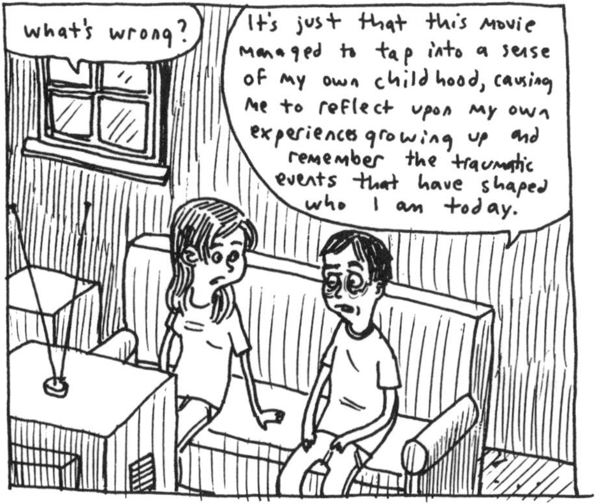
what's wrong?
It's just that this movie managed to tap into a sense of my own childhood, causing me to reflect upon my own experiences growing up and remember the traumatic events that have shaped who I am today.

WHY ARE YOU CRYING?

My house was destroyed by a tornado. I lost everything.

My husband just died in a tragic and unexpected accident.

Thousands of people were killed in a terrorist bombing today.

My favorite sports team lost a game.

Hm, let's see... There's hellfire, demons that attack you, pits of despair, and lakes of molten lava... but you can drive SUV's and there's lots of Walmarts.
Hm.

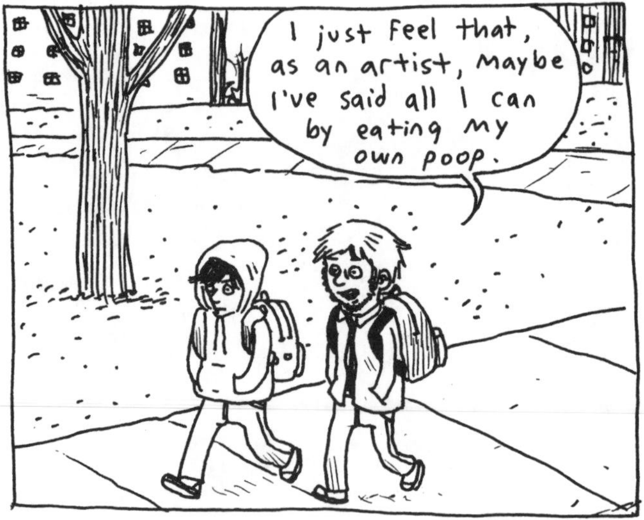
I just feel that, as an artist, maybe I've said all I can by eating my own poop.

APPEARANCES

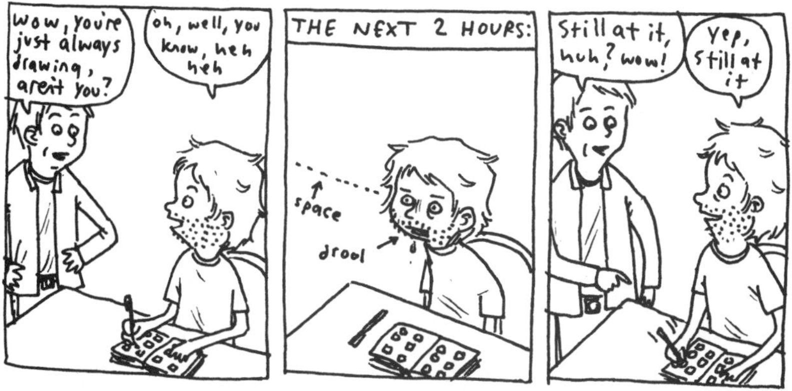

wow, you're just always drawing, aren't you?
oh, well, you know, heh heh
THE NEXT 2 HOURS:
space
drool
Still at it, huh? wow!
yep, still at it

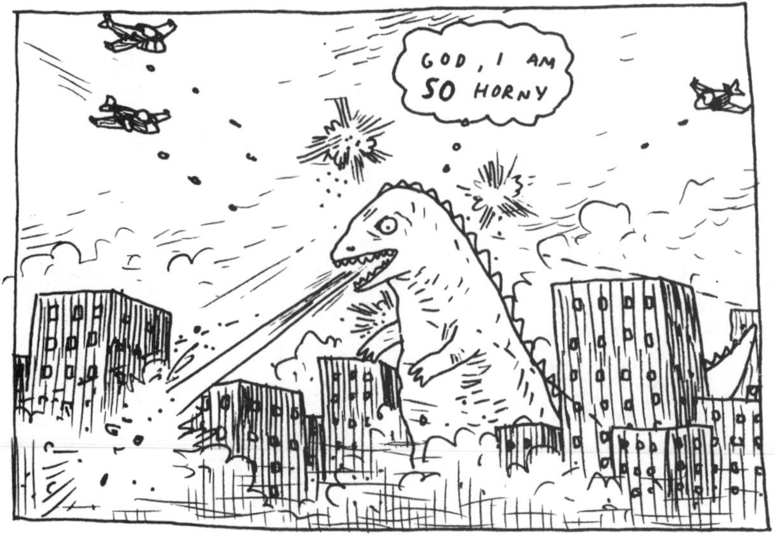
GOD, I AM SO HORNY

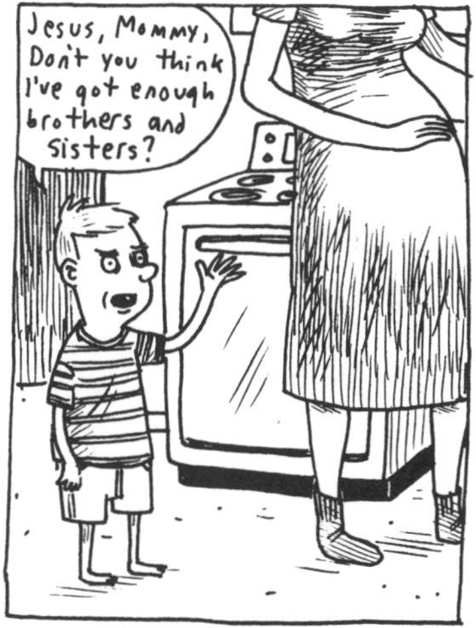
Jesus, Mommy, Don't you think I've got enough brothers and sisters?

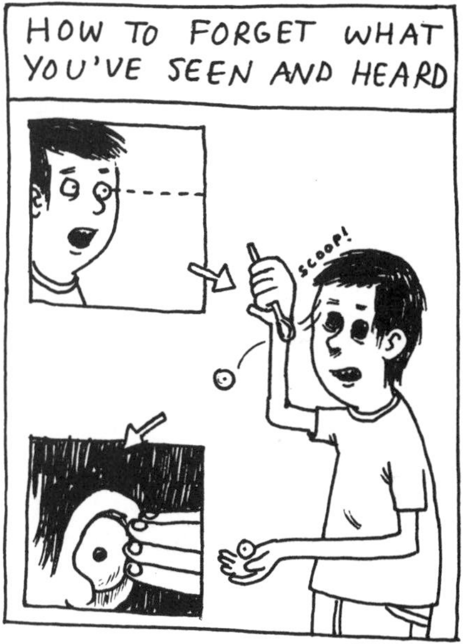
HOW TO FORGET WHAT YOU'VE SEEN AND HEARD
SCOOP!

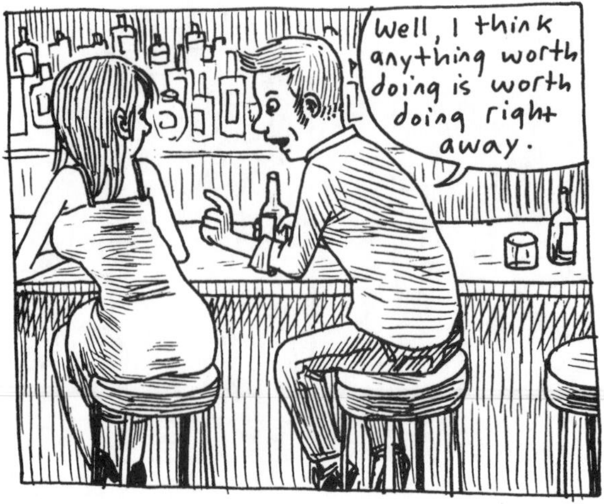
Well, I think anything worth doing is worth doing right away.

THE AGING ROCK STARS
This song sounds familiar...
well, it's one of yours.
Oh yeah.

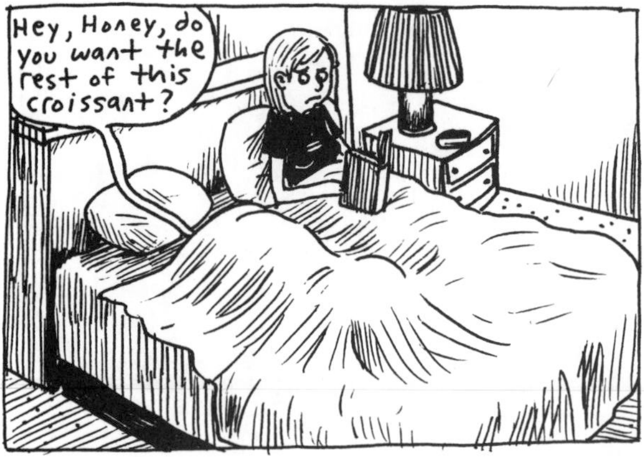
Hey, Honey, do you want the rest of this croissant?

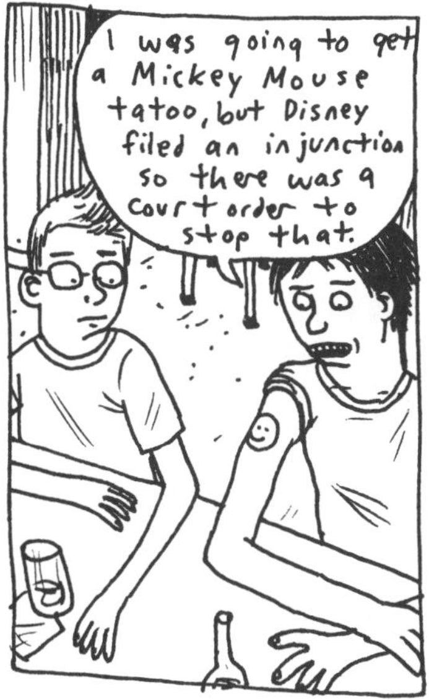
I was going to get a Mickey Mouse tatoo, but Disney filed an injunction so there was a court order to stop that.

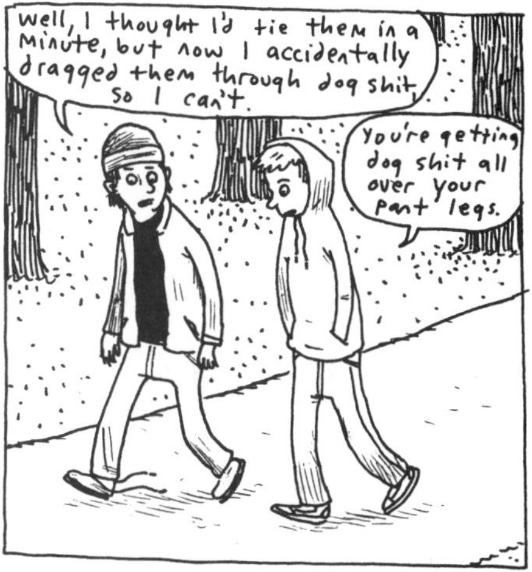
Well, I thought I'd tie them in a minute, but now I accidentally dragged them through dog shit, so I can't.
You're getting dog shit all over your pant legs.

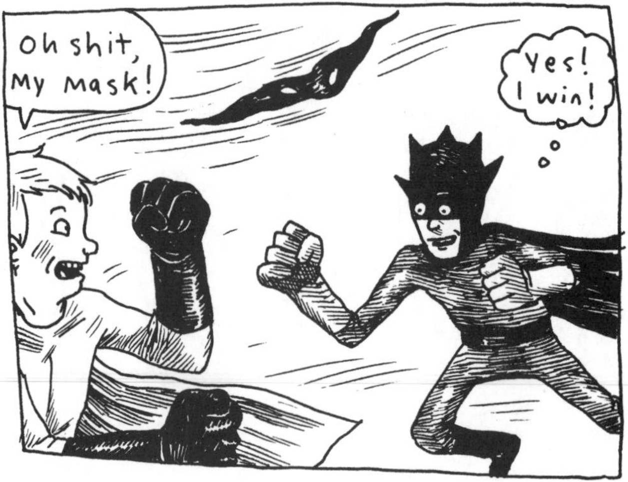
Oh shit, My mask!
Yes! I win!

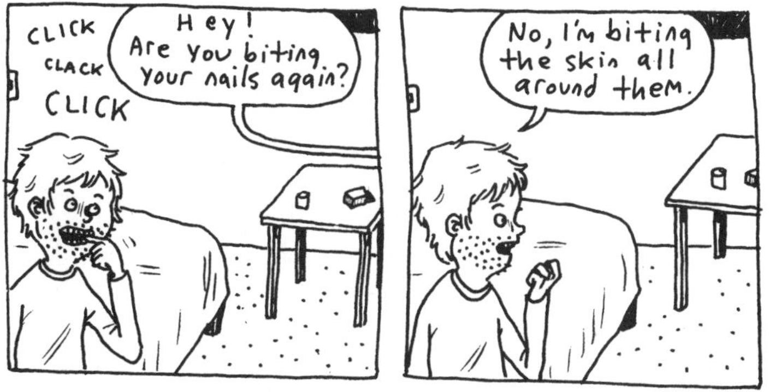
CLICK
CLACK
CLICK
Hey!
Are you biting your nails again?
No, I'm biting the skin all around them.

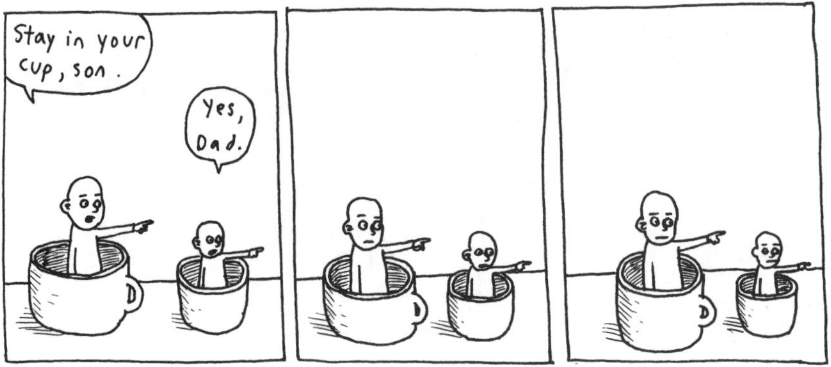
Stay in your cup, son.
Yes, Dad.

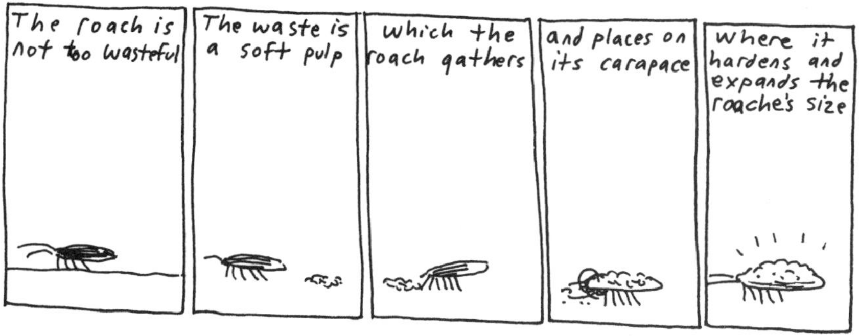
The roach is not too wasteful
The waste is a soft pulp
which the roach gathers
and places on its carapace
where it hardens and expands the roache's size

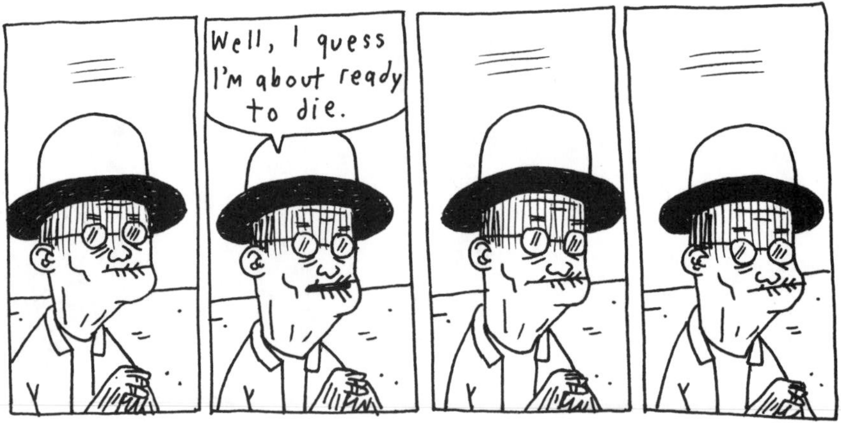
Well, I guess I'm about ready to die.

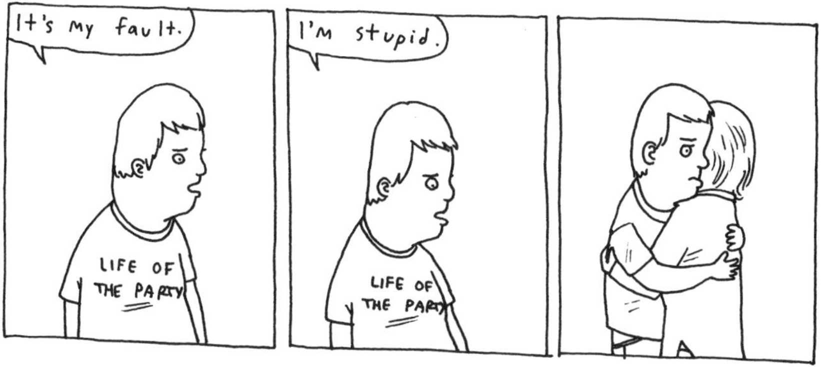
It's my fault.
LIFE OF THE PARTY
I'm stupid.
LIFE OF THE PARTY

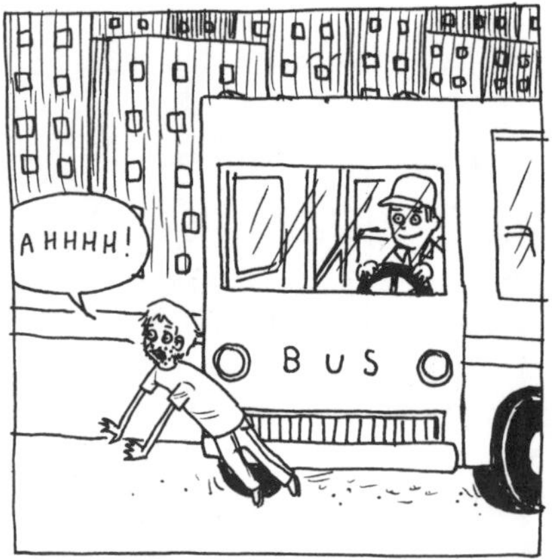
AHHHH!
BUS

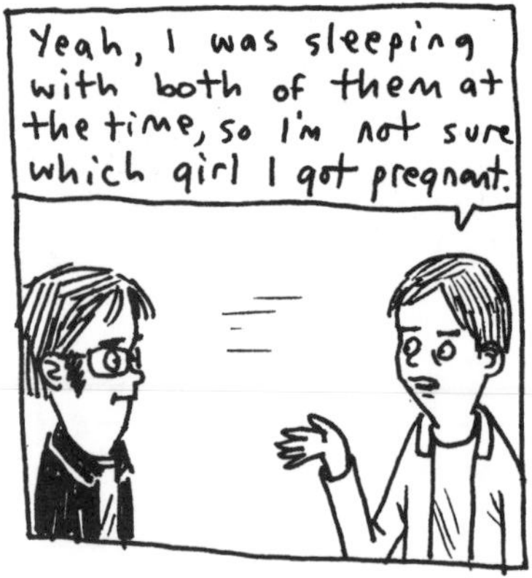
Yeah, I was sleeping with both of them at the time, so I'm not sure which girl I got pregnant.

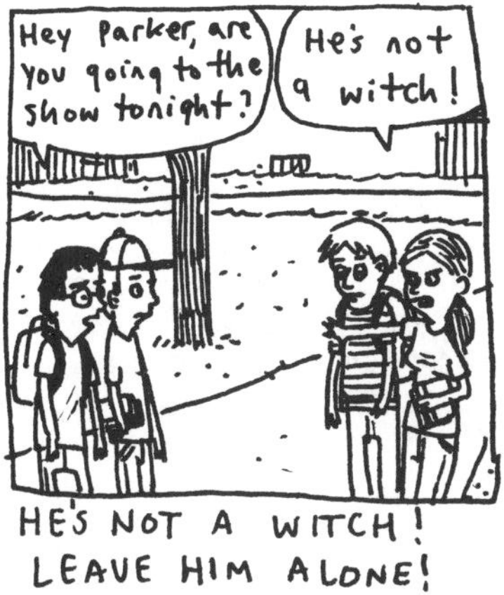
Hey Parker, are you going to the show tonight?
He's not a witch!
HE'S NOT A WITCH! LEAVE HIM ALONE!

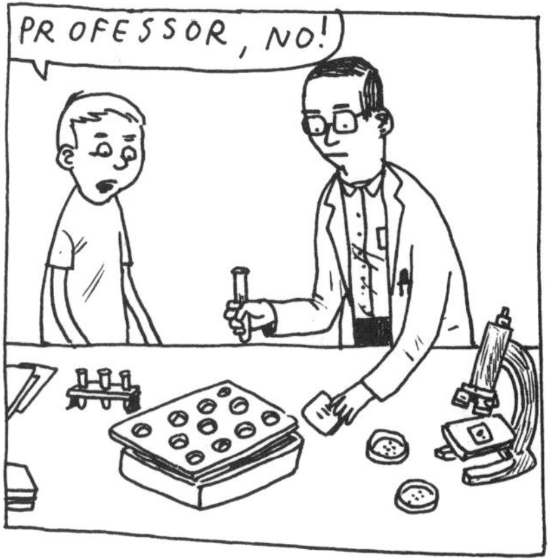
PROFESSOR, NO!

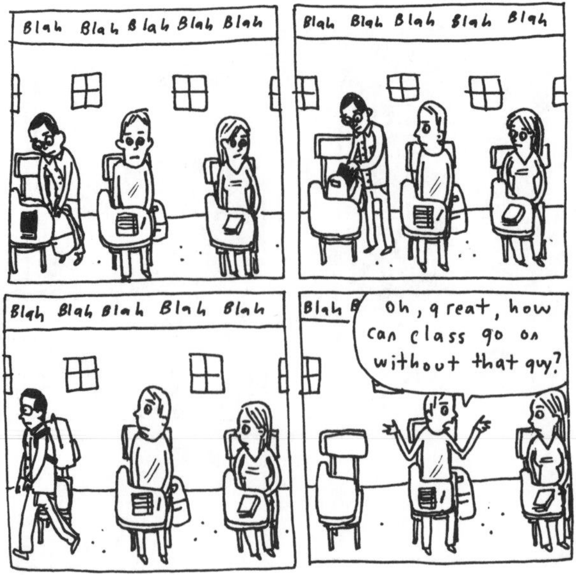
Blah Blah Blah Blah Blah
Blah Blah Blah Blah Blah
Blah Blah Blah Blah Blah
Blah
Oh, great, how can class go on without that guy?

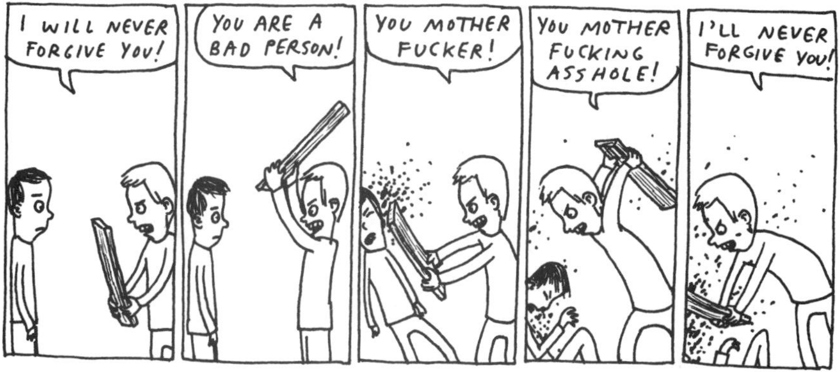
I WILL NEVER FORGIVE YOU!
YOU ARE A BAD PERSON!
YOU MOTHER FUCKER!
YOU MOTHER FUCKING ASSHOLE!
I'LL NEVER FORGIVE YOU!

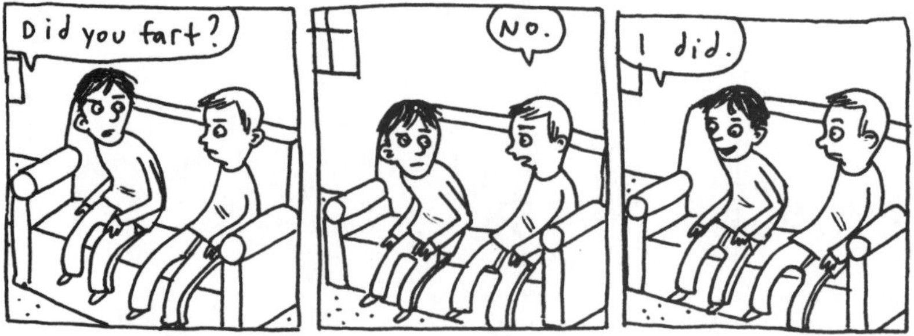
Did you fart?
No.
I did.

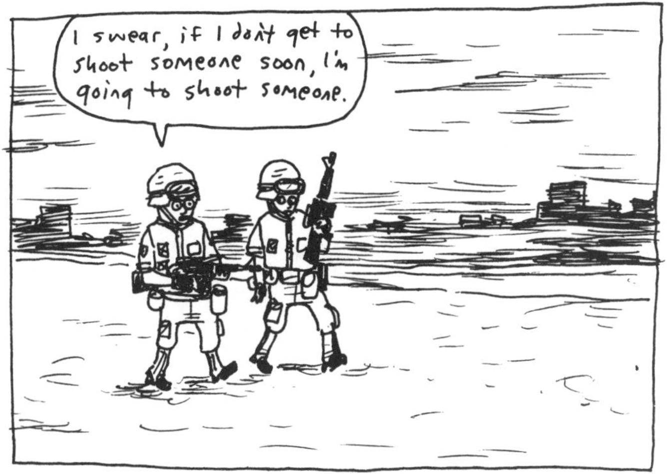
I swear, if I don't get to shoot someone soon, I'm going to shoot someone.

HOW TO END ARGUMENTS

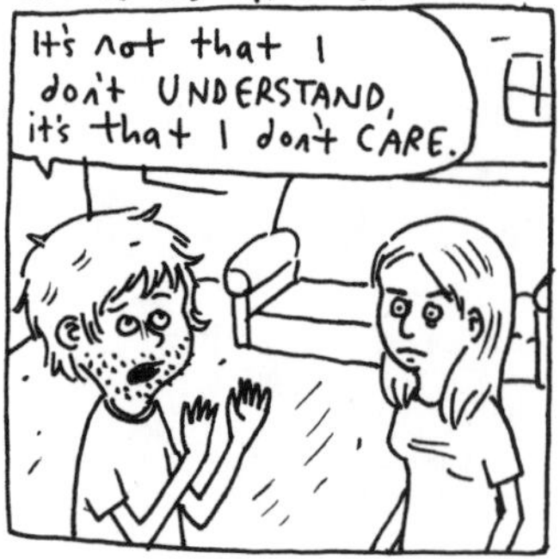
It's not that I don't UNDERSTAND, it's that I don't CARE.

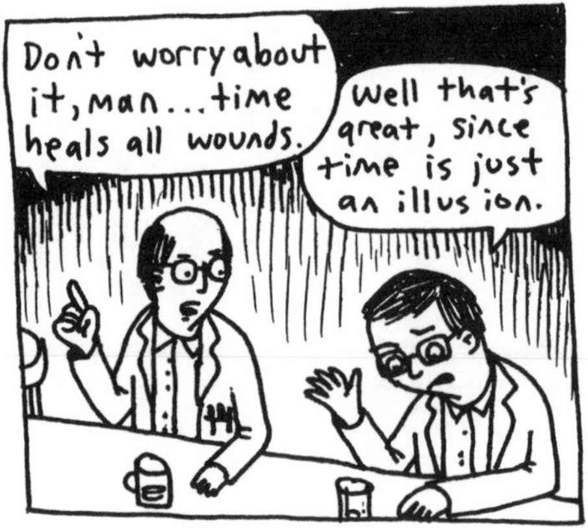
Don't worry about it, man... time heals all wounds.
Well that's great, since time is just an illusion.

BRRRAPPP
Thanks for turning your head when you burped, honey. That's very thoughtful.

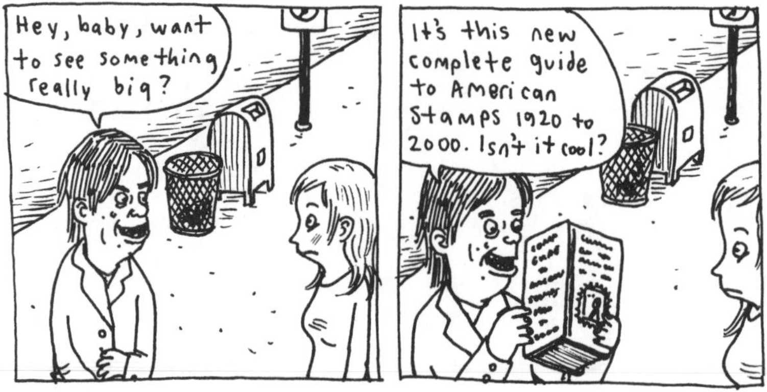
Hey, baby, want to see something really big?
It's this new complete guide to American Stamps 1920 to 2000. Isn't it cool?

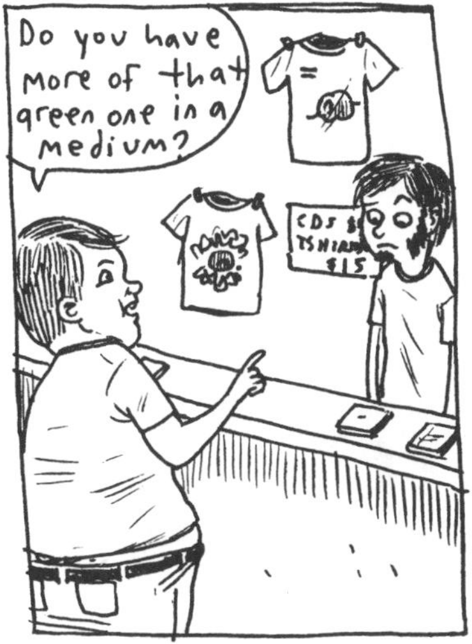
Do you have more of that green one in a medium?

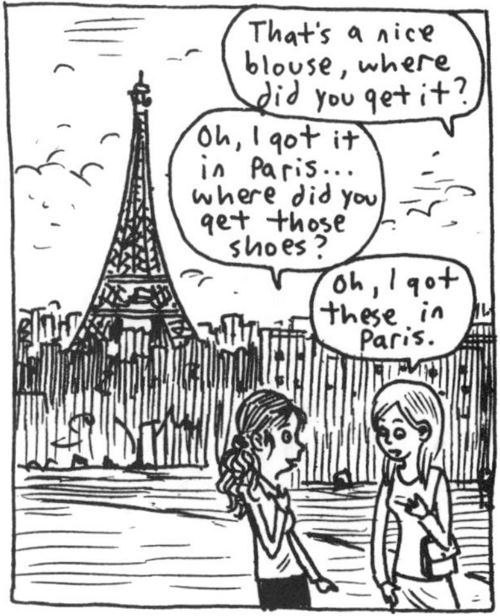
That's a nice blouse, where did you get it?
Oh, I got it in Paris... where did you get those shoes?
Oh, I got these in Paris.

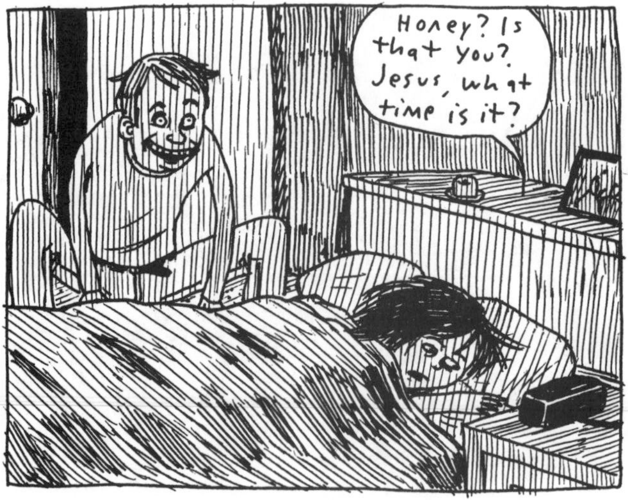
Honey? Is that you? Jesus, what time is it?

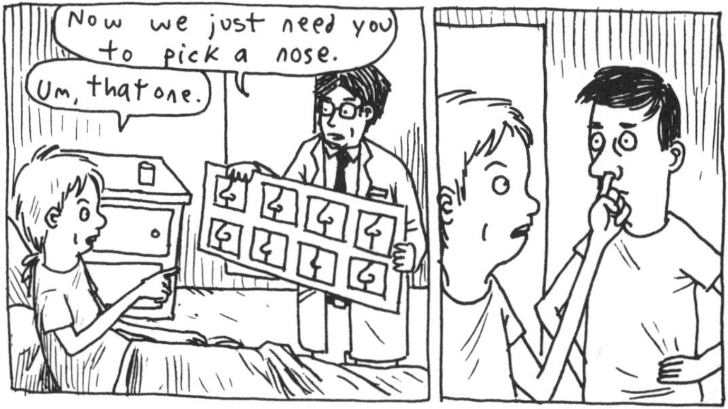
Now we just need you to pick a nose.
Um, that one.

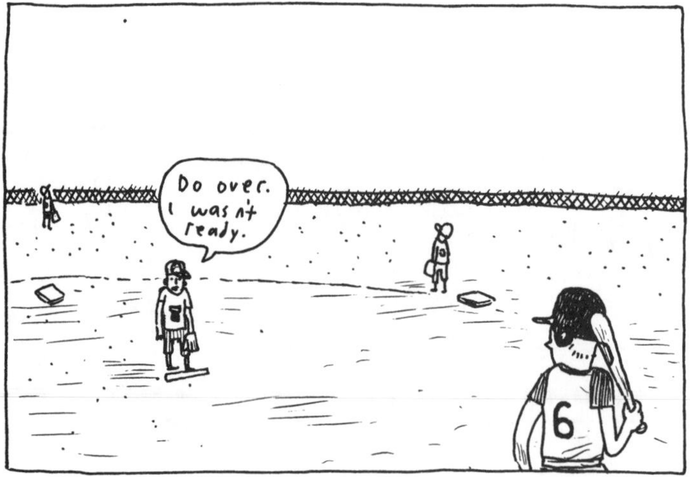
Do over. I wasn't ready.

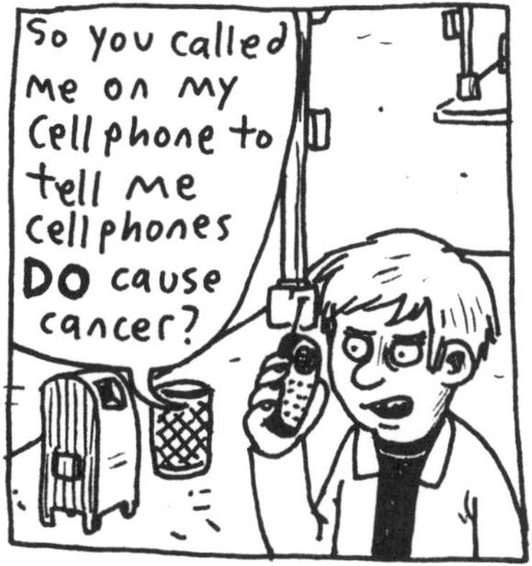
So you called me on my Cellphone to tell me cellphones DO cause cancer?

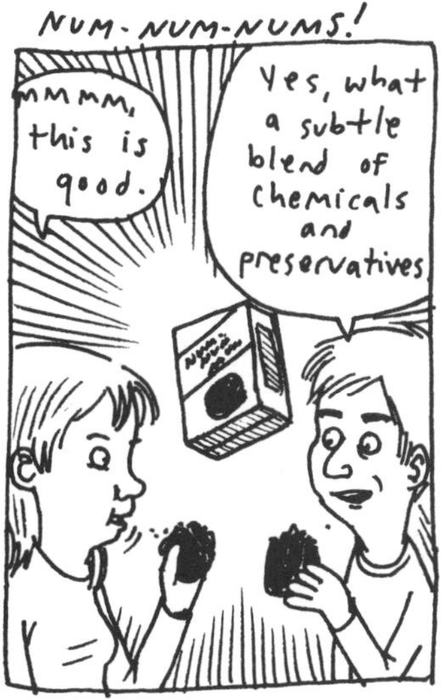
NUM-NUM-NUMS!
MMMM, this is good.
Yes, what a subtle blend of Chemicals and preservatives

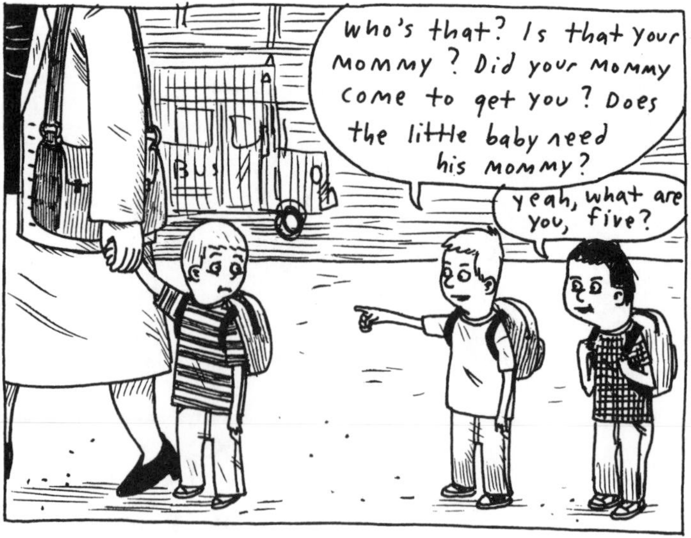

Who's that? Is that your MOMMY? Did your MOMMY come to get you? Does the little baby need his MOMMY?
yeah, what are you, five?
BUS

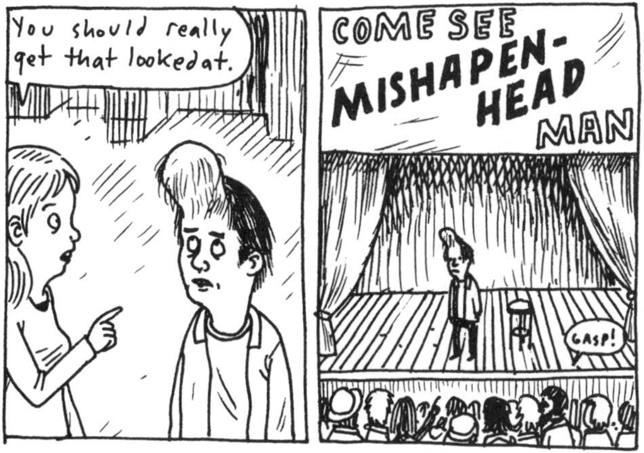
You should really get that lookedat.
COME SEE
MISHAPEN-HEAD
MAN
GASP!

HE IS ANGRY

C'MON, LADY, THIS IS A PARKING LOT NOT A PARKING SPACE!
JESUS CHRIST!
What are you doing?
I'm sulking.
Rewind that part. I want to see it again.

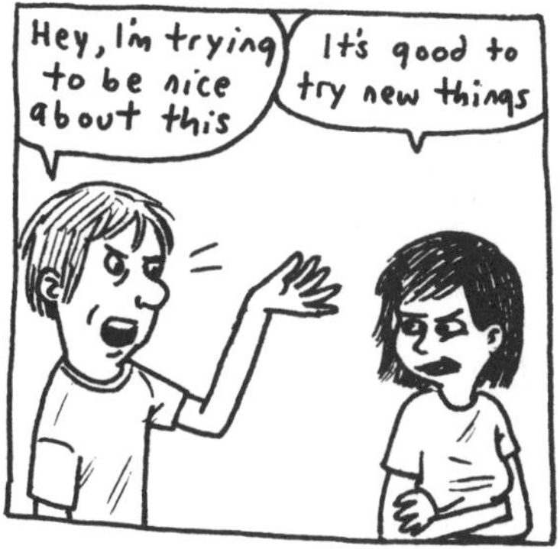
Hey, I'm trying to be nice about this
It's good to try new things

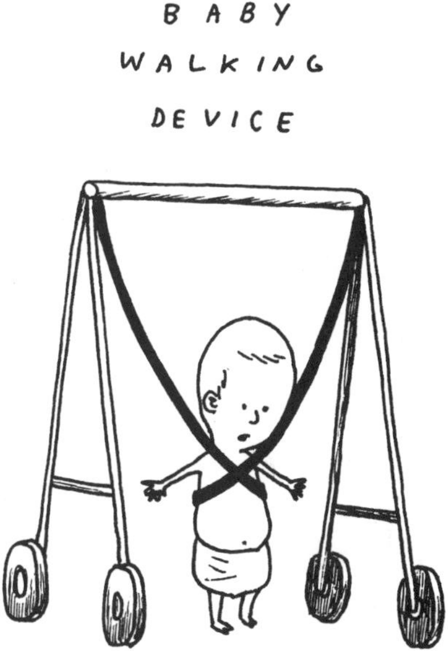
BABY WALKING DEVICE

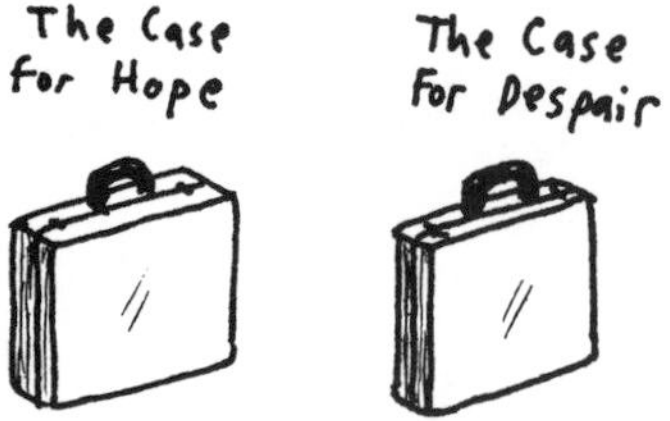
The Case
for Hope
The Case
For Despair

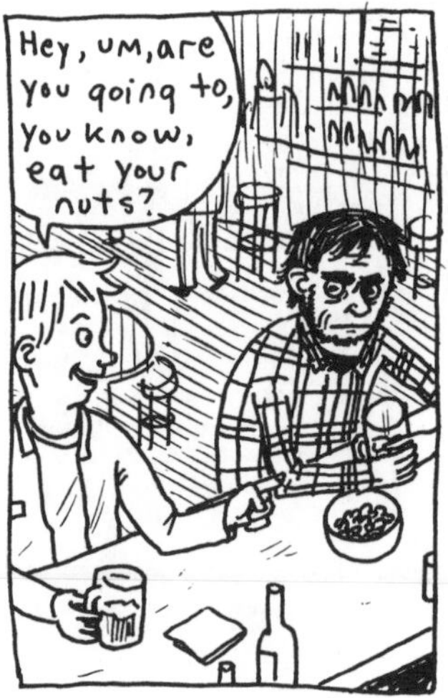
Hey, um, are you going to, you know, eat your nuts?

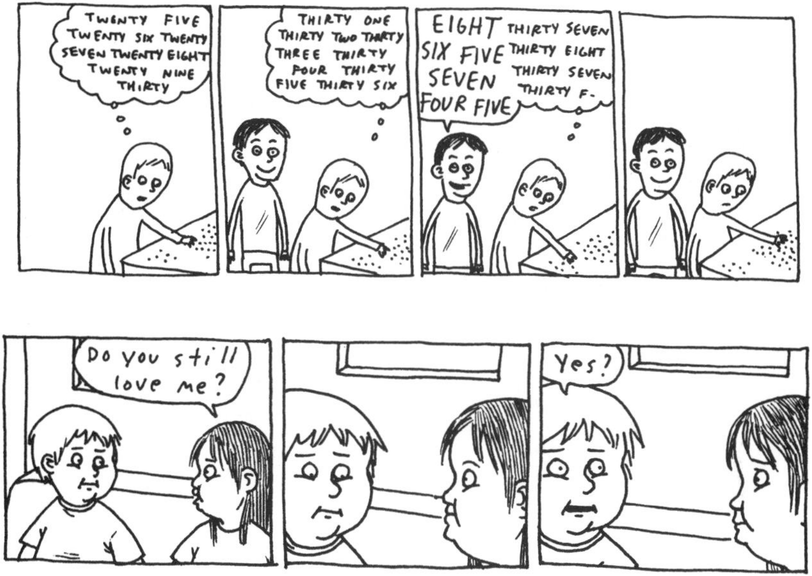
TWENTY FIVE TWENTY SIX TWENTY SEVEN TWENTY EIGHT TWENTY NINE THIRTY
THIRTY ONE THIRTY TWO THIRTY THREE THIRTY FOUR THIRTY FIVE THIRTY SIX
EIGHT SIX FIVE SEVEN FOUR FIVE
THIRTY SEVEN THIRTY EIGHT THIRTY SEVEN THIRTY F-
Do you still love me?
Yes?

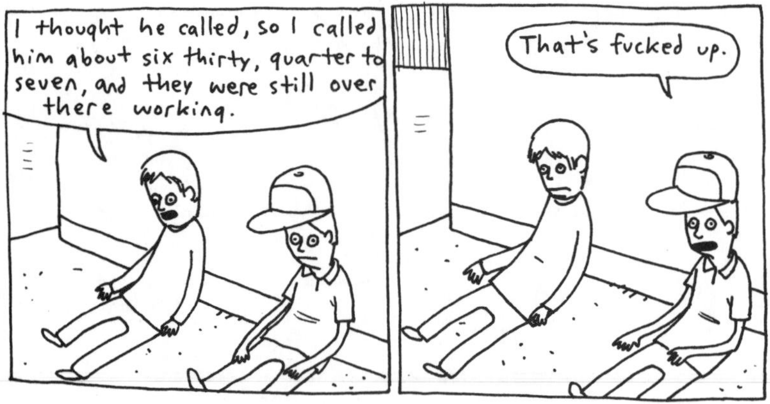
I thought he called, so I called him about six thirty, quarter to seven, and they were still over there working.
That's fucked up.

WAR STORIES

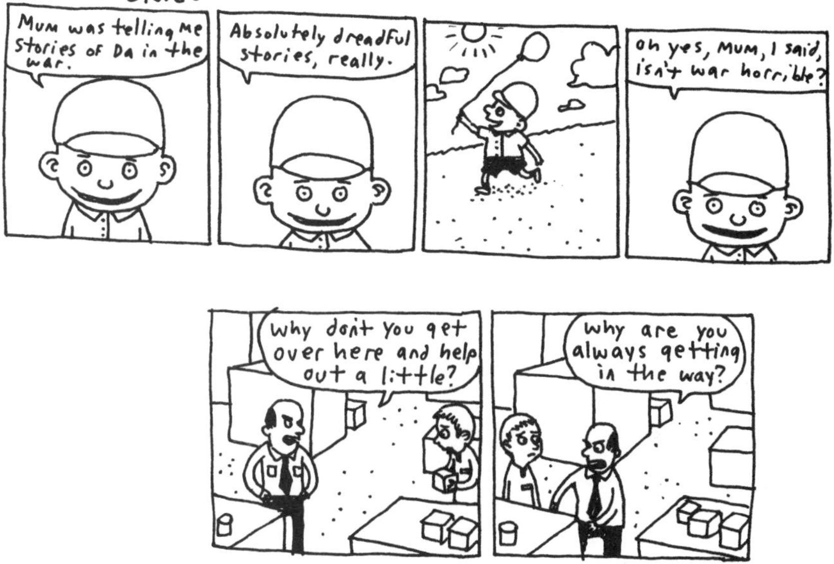
Mum was telling me stories of Da in the war.
Absolutely dreadful stories, really.
Oh yes, Mum, I said, isn't war horrible?
why don't you get over here and help out a little?
why are you always getting in the way?

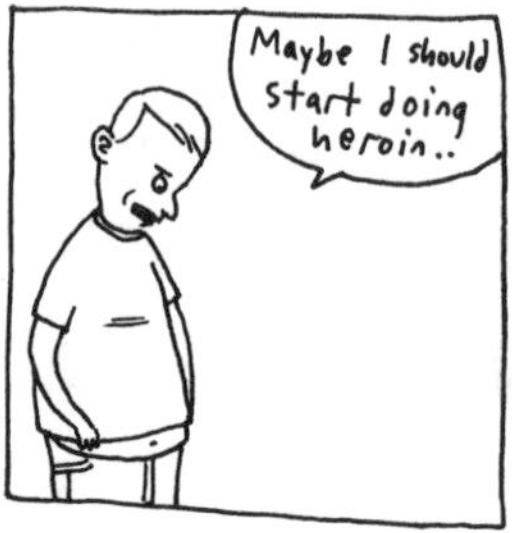
Maybe I should start doing heroin..

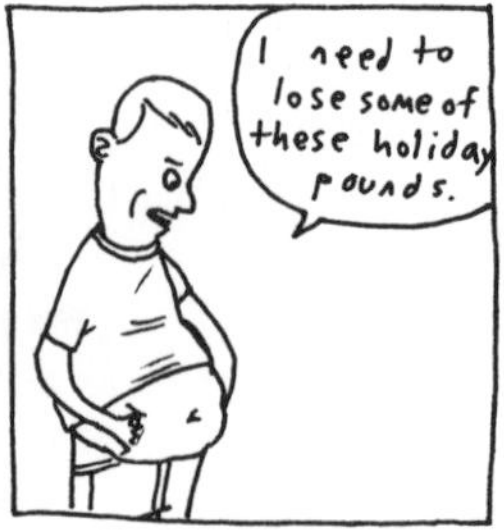
I need to lose some of these holiday pounds.

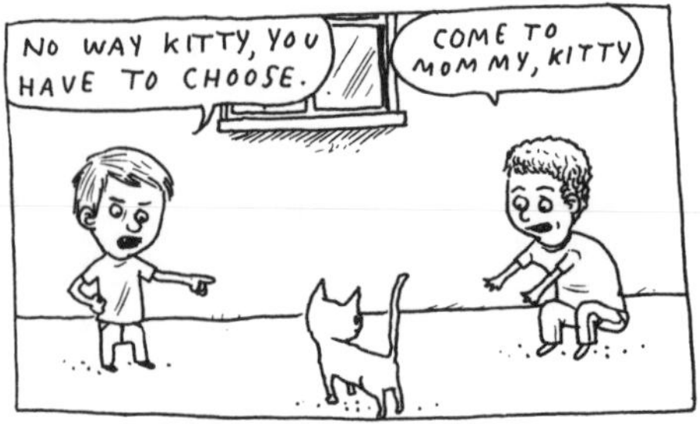
NO WAY KITTY, YOU HAVE TO CHOOSE.
COME TO MOMMY, KITTY

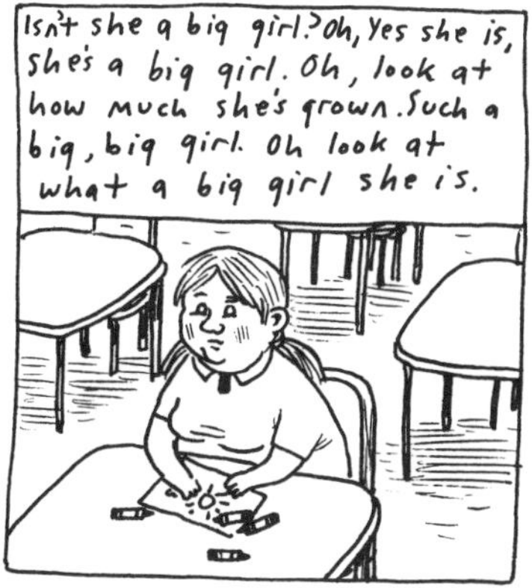
Isn't she a big girl? Oh, yes she is, she's a big girl. Oh, look at how much she's grown. Such a big, big girl. Oh look at what a big girl she is.

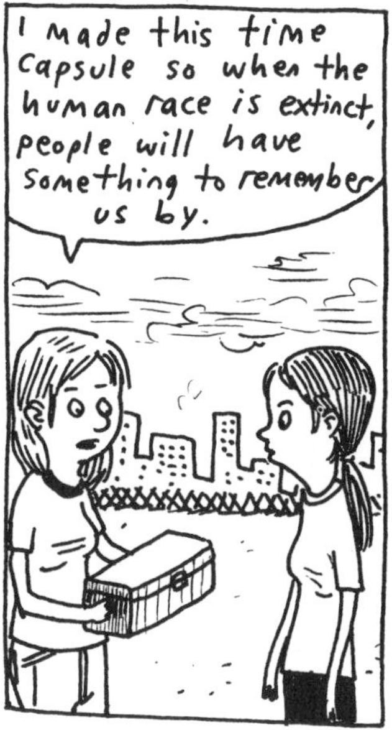
I made this time capsule so when the human race is extinct, people will have something to remember us by.

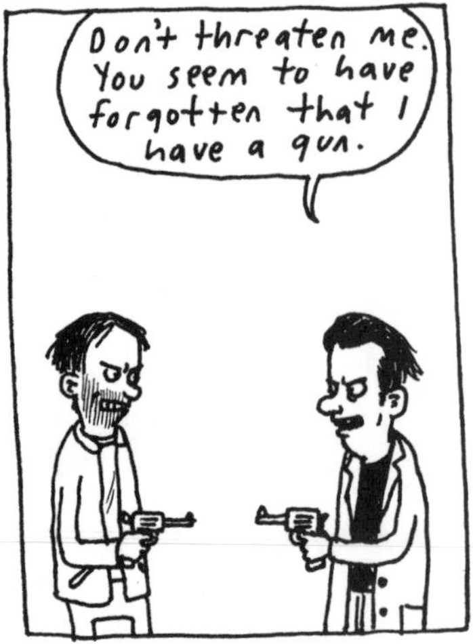
Don't threaten me. You seem to have forgotten that I have a gun.

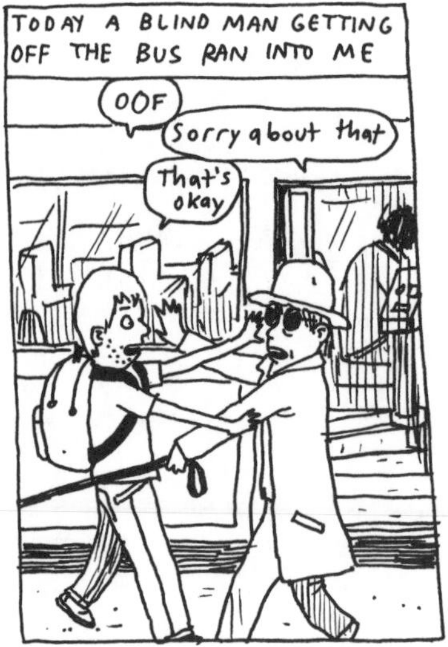
TODAY A BLIND MAN GETTING OFF THE BUS RAN INTO ME
OOF
Sorry about that
That's okay

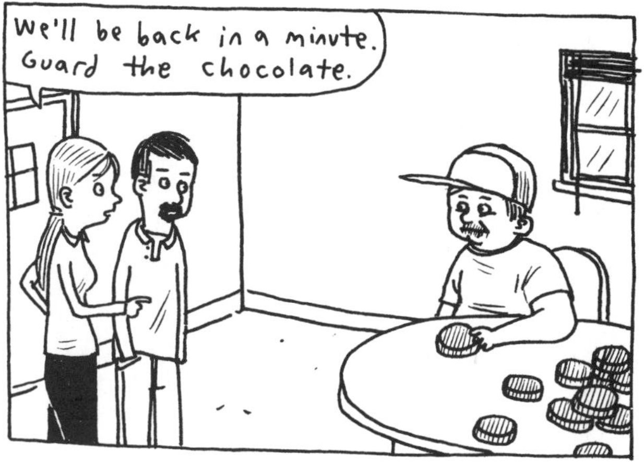
We'll be back in a minute. Guard the chocolate.

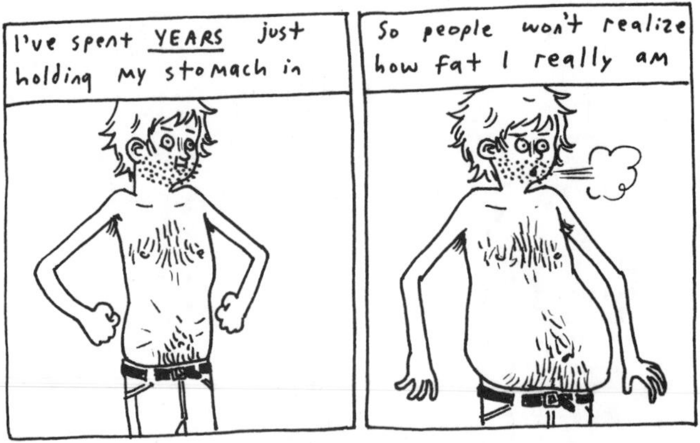
I've spent YEARS just holding my stomach in
So people won't realize how fat I really am

DO YOU KNOW WHAT A GUITAR IS?

Do you know what a guitar is?
So, what, I'm not allowed to even look at some beautiful thing?
No.

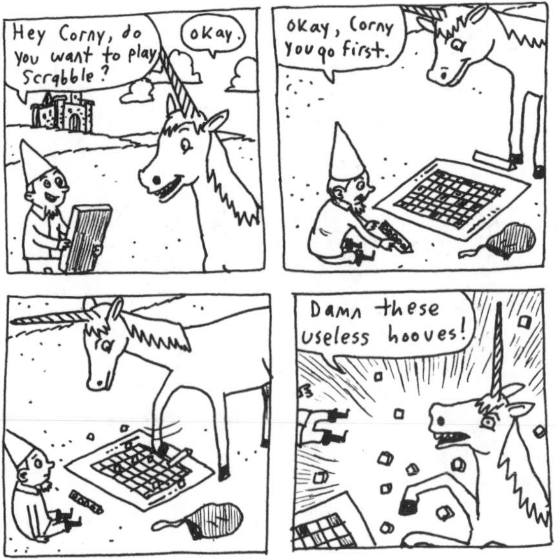
Hey Corny, do you want to play Scrabble?
okay.
okay, Corny you go first.
Damn these useless hooves!

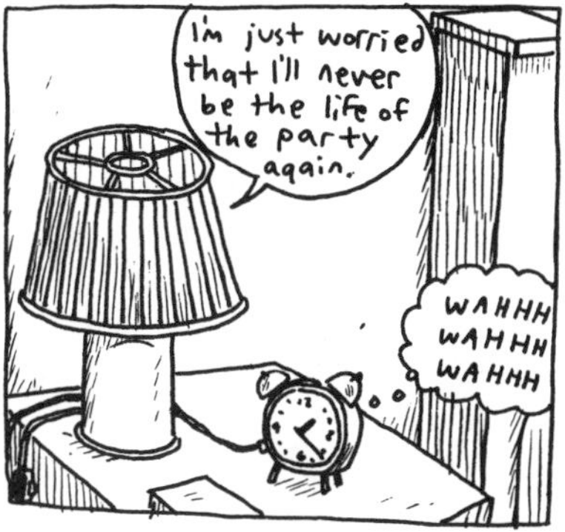
I'm just worried that I'll never be the life of the party again.
WAHHH WAHHH WAHHH

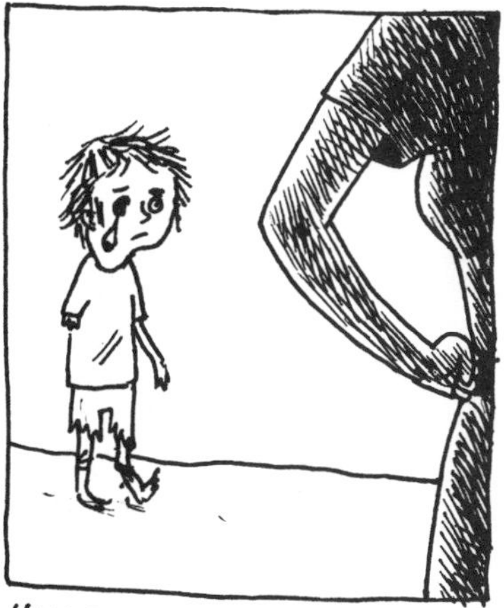

"NOW WHAT DID YOU GET INTO?"

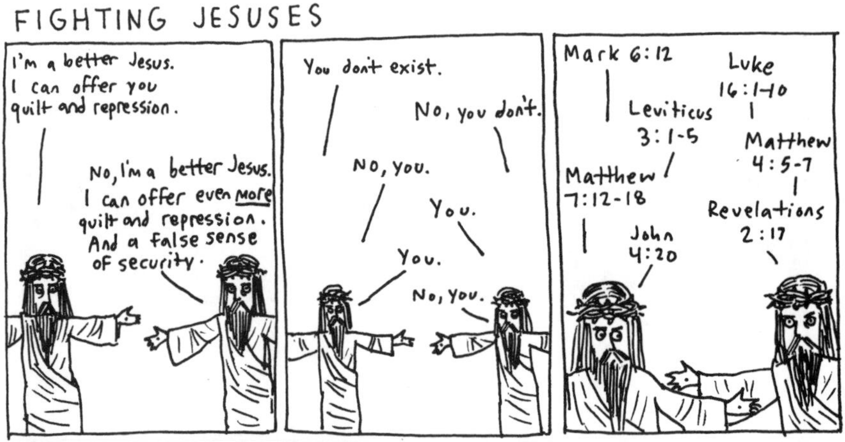
FIGHTING JESUSES
I'm a better Jesus. I can offer you quilt and repression.
No, I'm a better Jesus. I can offer even MORE quilt and repression. And a false sense of security.
You don't exist.
No, you don't.
No, you.
You.
You.
No, you.
Mark 6:12
Luke 16:1-10
Leviticus 3:1-5
Matthew 4:5-7
Matthew 7:12-18
Revelations 2:17
John 4:20

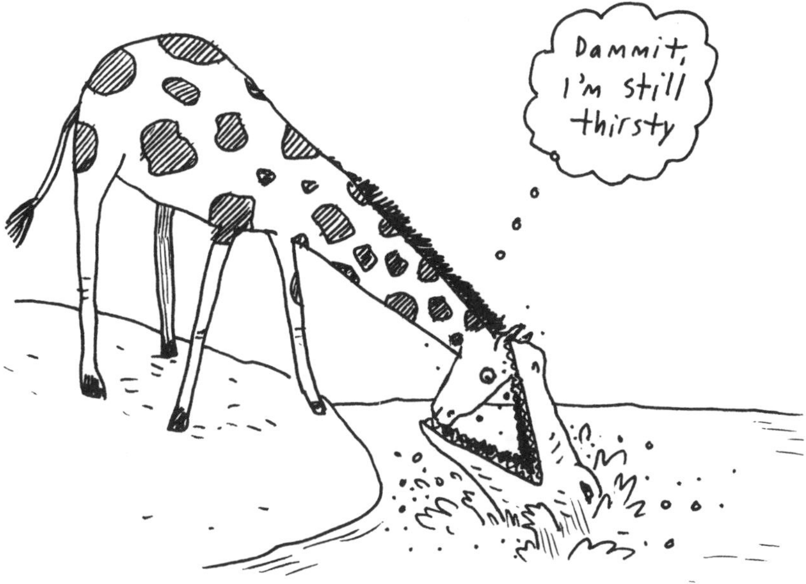
Dammit, I'm still thirsty

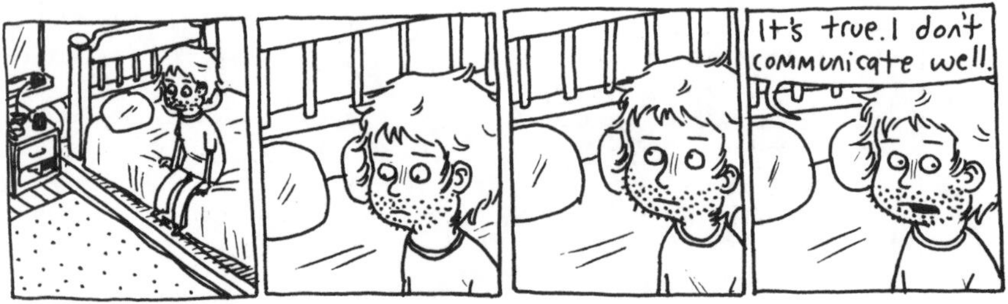
It's true. I don't communicate well.

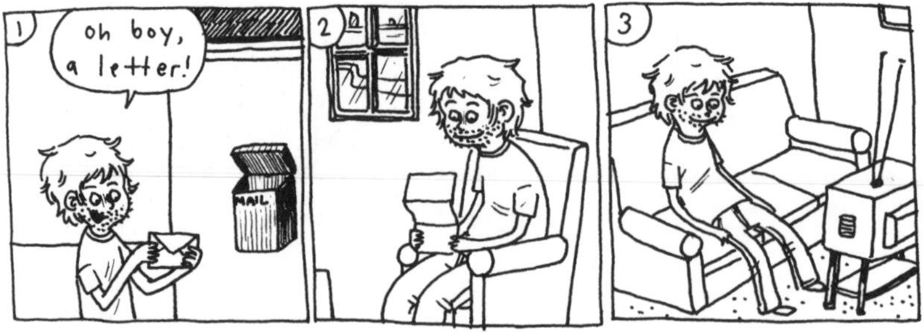
1
oh boy, a letter!
MAIL
2
3

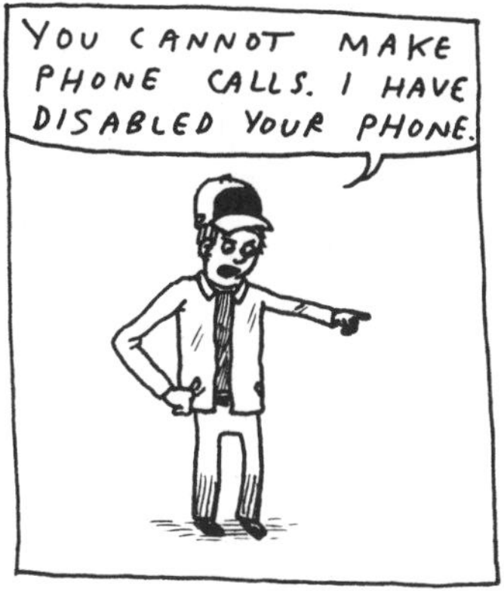
YOU CANNOT MAKE PHONE CALLS. I HAVE DISABLED YOUR PHONE.

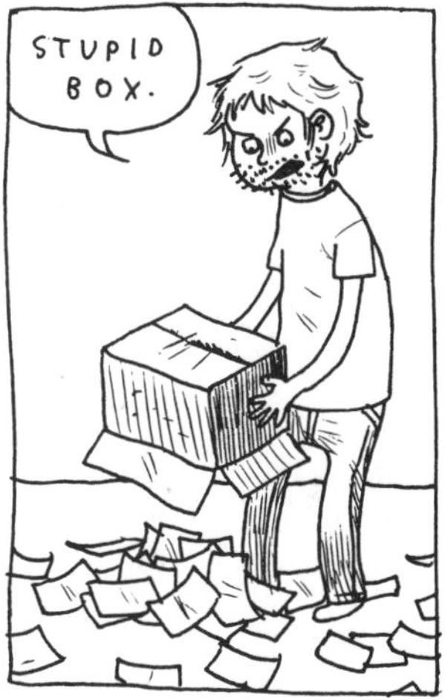
STUPID BOX.

Shhhhh! Quiet! This is my favorite part!
Ha ha ha ha! I love that part.
!
POW
Tell... tell everyone that I love them..
Except that bastard who shot me..

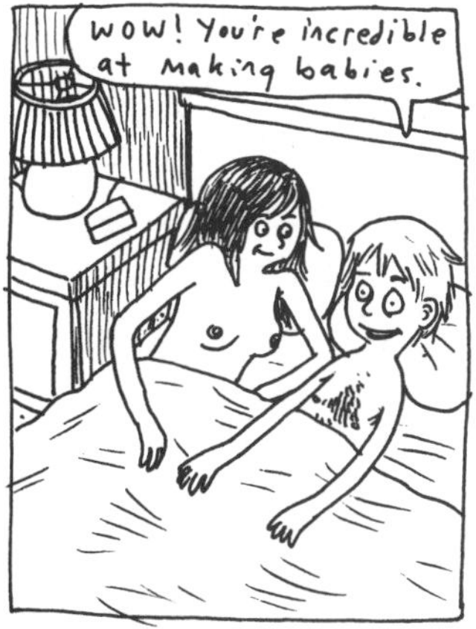
WOW! You're incredible at making babies.

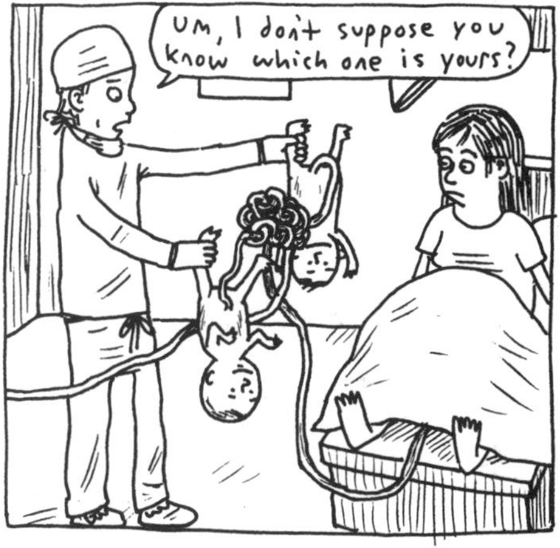
Um, I don't suppose you know which one is yours?

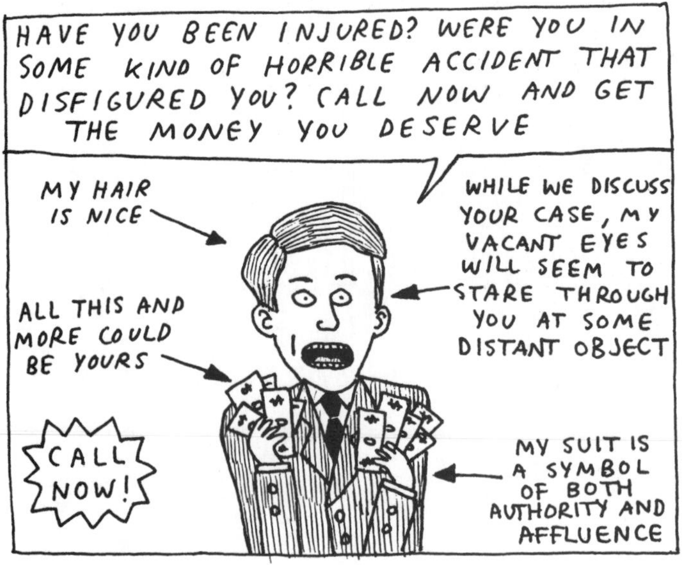
HAVE YOU BEEN INJURED? WERE YOU IN SOME KIND OF HORRIBLE ACCIDENT THAT DISFIGURED YOU? CALL NOW AND GET THE MONEY YOU DESERVE
MY HAIR IS NICE
WHILE WE DISCUSS YOUR CASE, MY VACANT EYES WILL SEEM TO STARE THROUGH YOU AT SOME DISTANT OBJECT
ALL THIS AND MORE COULD BE YOURS
CALL NOW!
MY SUIT IS A SYMBOL OF BOTH AUTHORITY AND AFFLUENCE

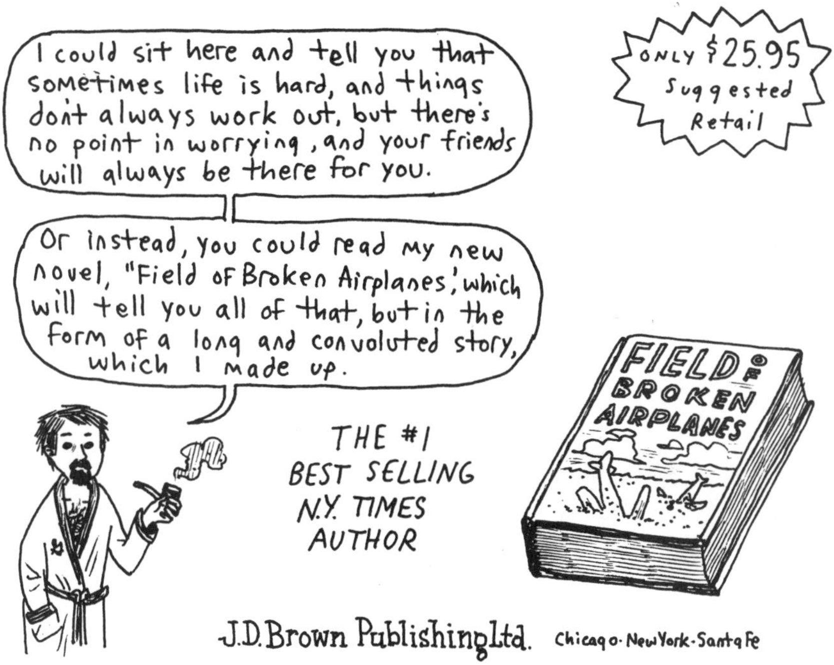
I could sit here and tell you that sometimes life is hard, and things don't always work out, but there's no point in worrying, and your friends will always be there for you.
Or instead, you could read my new novel, "Field of Broken Airplanes," which will tell you all of that, but in the form of a long and convoluted story, which I made up.
ONLY $25.95 Suggested Retail
FIELD OF BROKEN AIRPLANES
THE #1 BEST SELLING N.Y. TIMES AUTHOR
J.D. Brown Publishing Ltd.
Chicago · New York · Santa Fe

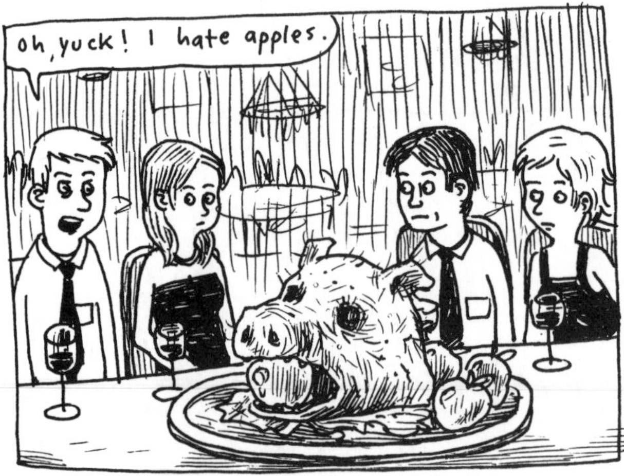
oh, yuck! I hate apples.

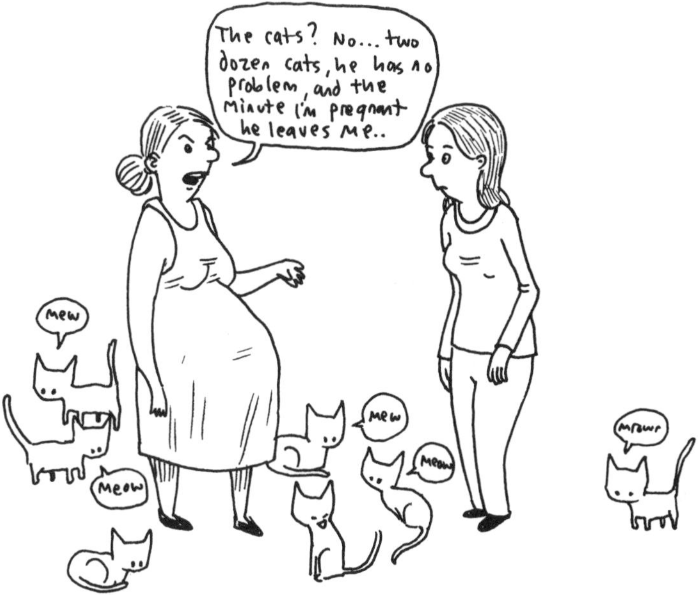
The cats? No... two dozen cats, he has no problem, and the minute I'm pregnant he leaves me..
mew
mew
meow
meow
mrowr

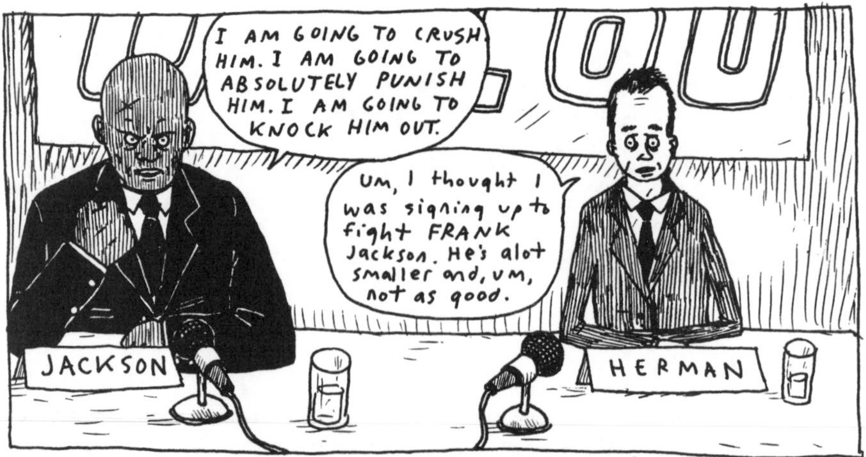
I AM GOING TO CRUSH HIM. I AM GOING TO ABSOLUTELY PUNISH HIM. I AM GOING TO KNOCK HIM OUT.
Um, I thought I was signing up to fight FRANK Jackson. He's alot smaller and, um, not as good.
JACKSON
HERMAN

AT THE ULTIMATE FIGHTING CHAMPIONSHIP PRESS CONFERENCE

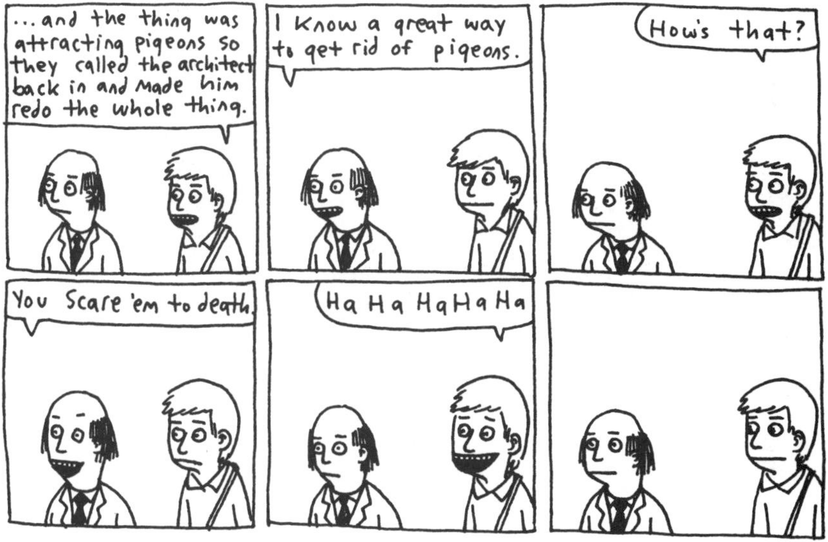
...and the thing was attracting pigeons so they called the architect back in and made him redo the whole thing.
I know a great way to get rid of pigeons.
How's that?
You scare 'em to death.
Ha Ha HaHaHa

THIS IS MY MUG!

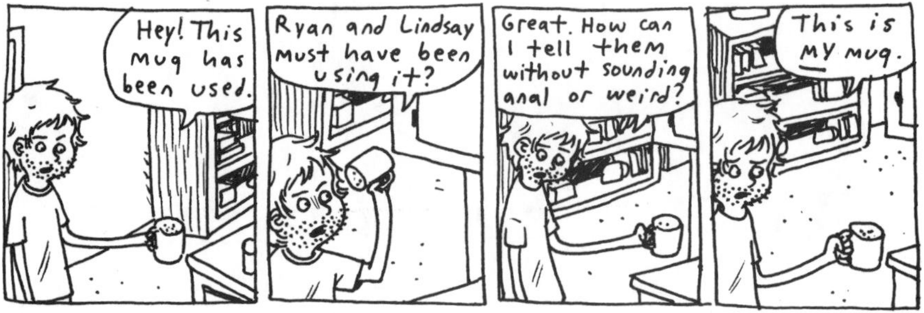
Hey! This mug has been used.
Ryan and Lindsay must have been using it?
Great. How can I tell them without sounding anal or weird?
This is MY mug.

True Stories

True Stories

Hey Jacquee
what?
Is everyone jealous of my rock star hair?
I think so.

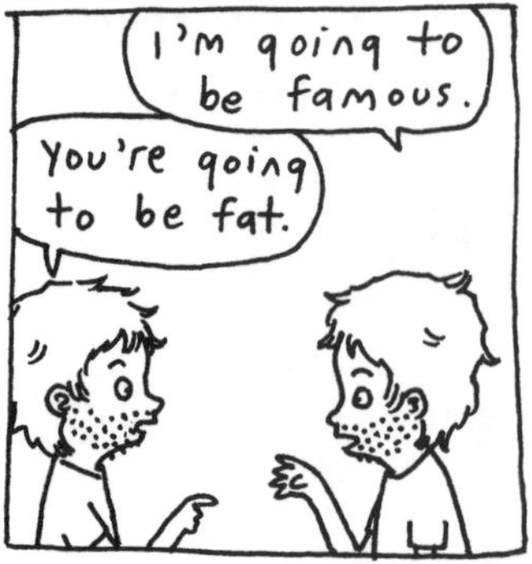
I'm going to be famous.
You're going to be fat.

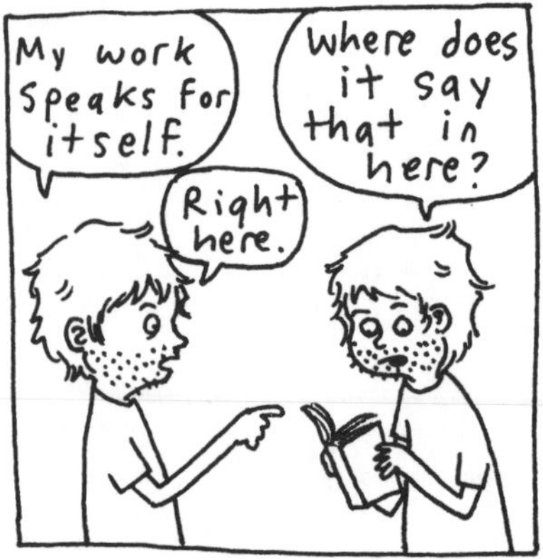
My work speaks for itself.
Where does it say that in here?
Right here.

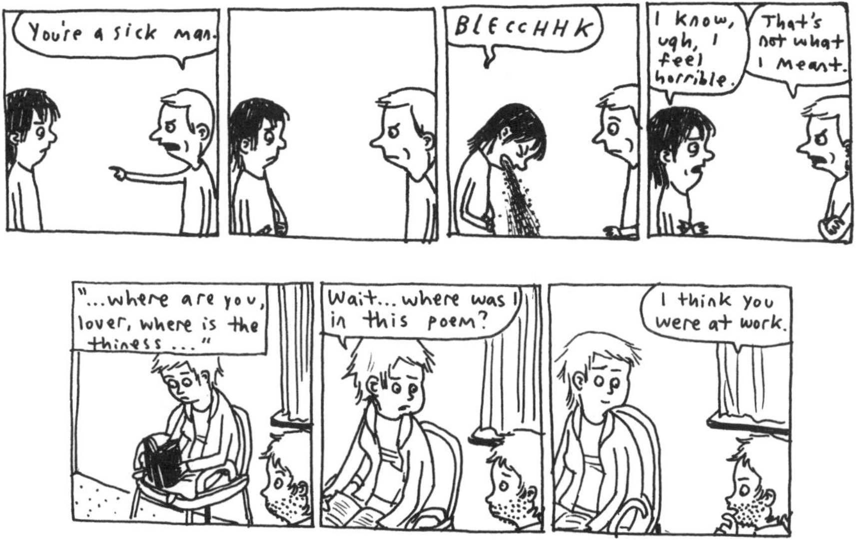
You're a sick man.
BLECCHHK
I know, ugh, I feel horrible.
That's not what I meant.
"...where are you, lover, where is the thiness ..."
Wait... where was I in this poem?
I think you were at work.

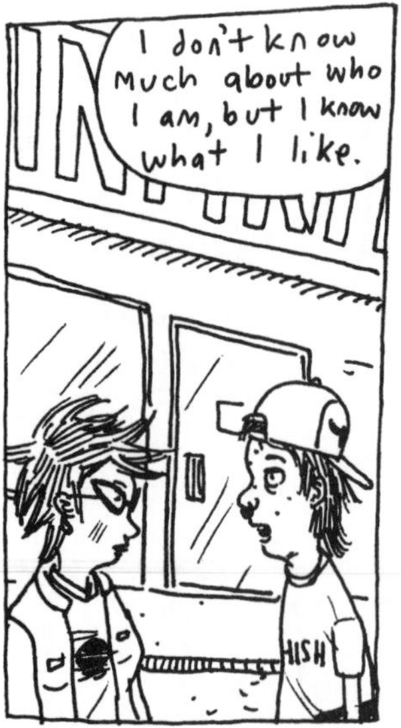
I don't know much about who I am, but I know what I like.

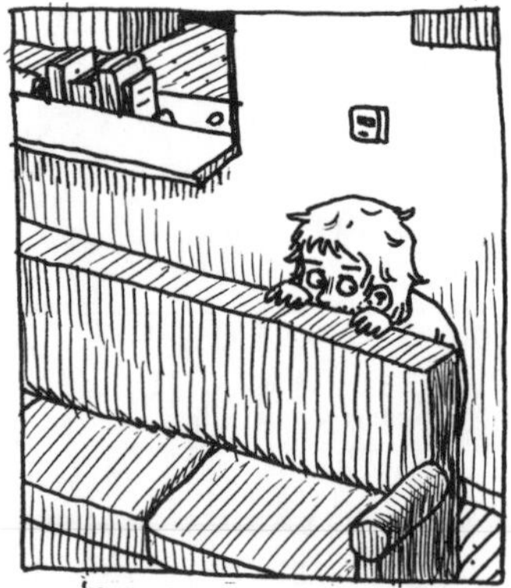

IF I'M SO PARANOID, WHY ARE YOU LOOKING AT ME LIKE THAT?

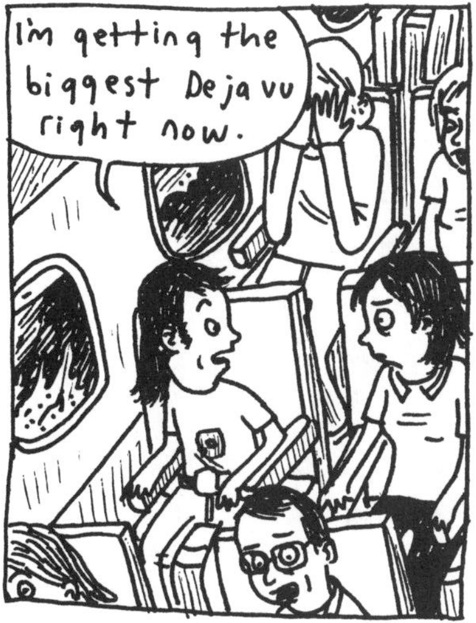
I'm getting the biggest Deja vu right now.

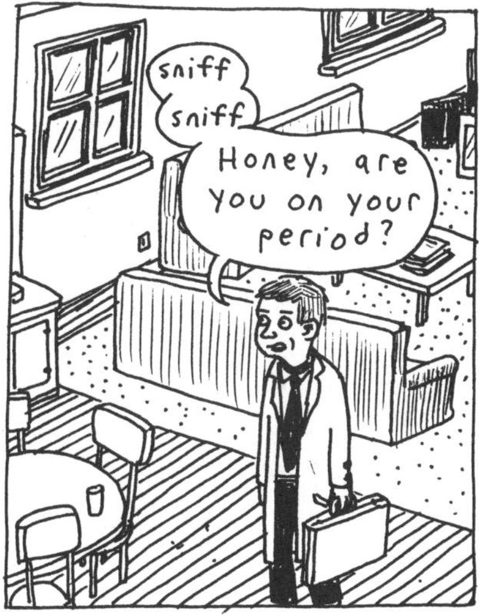
sniff
sniff
Honey, are you on your period?

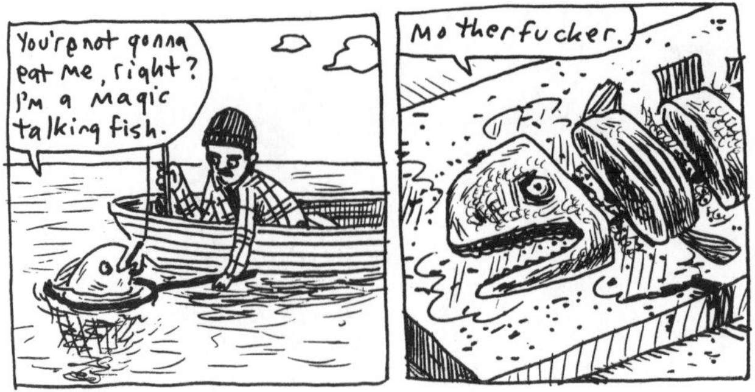
You're not gonna eat me, right? I'm a magic talking fish.
Motherfucker.

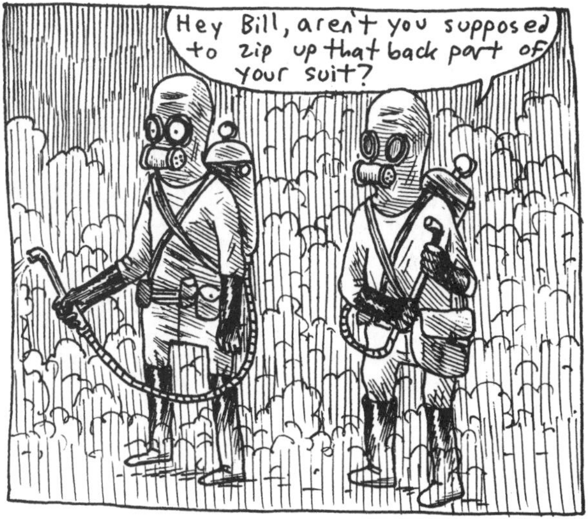
Hey Bill, aren't you supposed to zip up that back part of your suit?

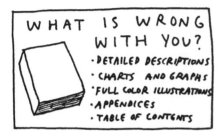

WHAT IS WRONG WITH YOU?
- DETAILED DESCRIPTIONS
- CHARTS AND GRAPHS
- FULL COLOR ILLUSTRATIONS
- APPENDICES
- TABLE OF CONTENTS

"I'VE BEEN LIVING ON SCREWDRIVERS AND HOPE FOR TOO LONG."

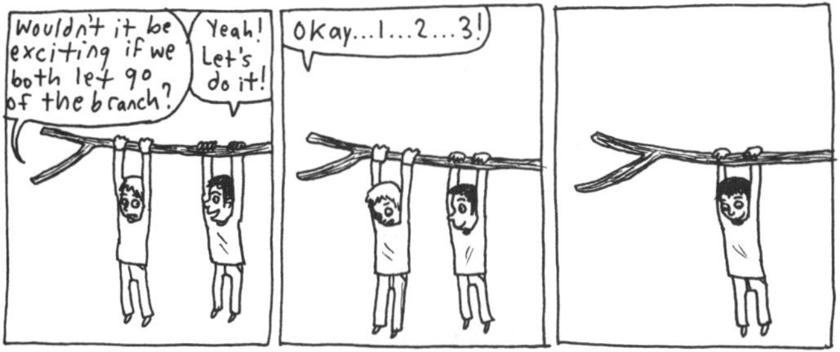
Wouldn't it be exciting if we both let go of the branch?
Yeah! Let's do it!
Okay...1...2...3!

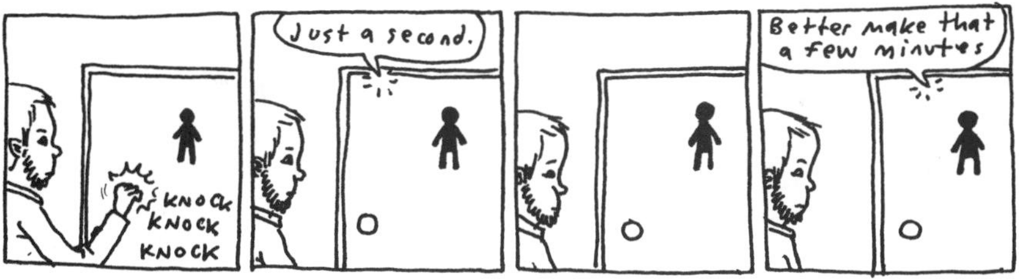
KNOCK KNOCK KNOCK
Just a second.
Better make that a few minutes

Walstore

Posterboard?
Hell, you need an umbrella
Look at that.
Just makes one little poster.

Did you ever watch that show "Silver spoons"?
No, I don't think I ever heard of it.
I'm dating myself, aren't I?
I guess.
Well, I liked that show.
Thanks, honey

RUN, FATTY... RUN

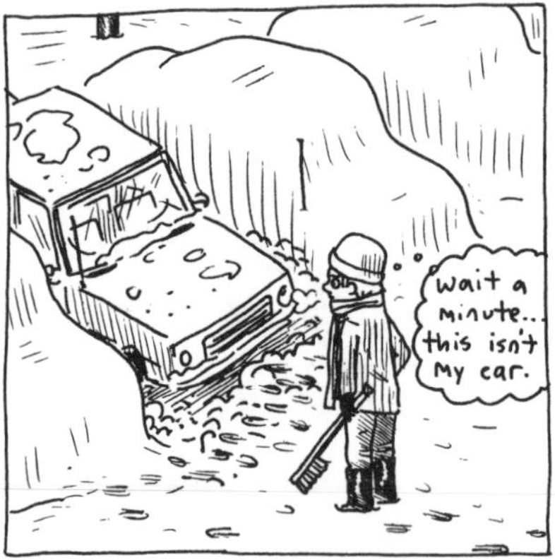
wait a minute... this isn't my car.

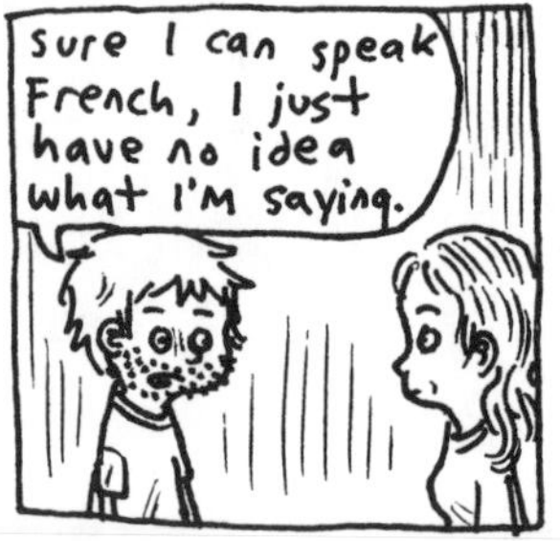
Sure I can speak French, I just have no idea what I'm saying.

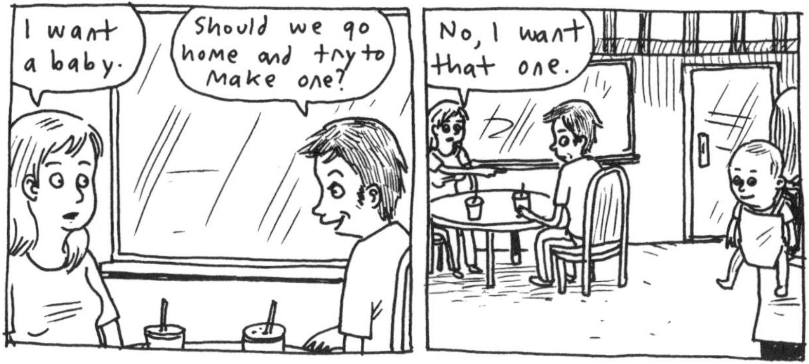
I want a baby.
Should we go home and try to make one?
No, I want that one.

...and she's having all these mood swings, it's driving me crazy. I thought you said being pregnant would be like she's having no periods for nine months.
?
No, I said it's like she's on her period for nine months.

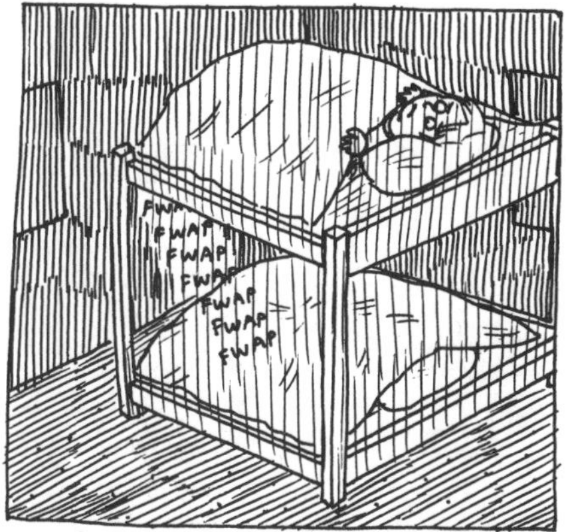
FWA
FWAP
FWAP
FWAP
FWAP
FWAP
FWAP

Self awareness and self conciousness are two different things

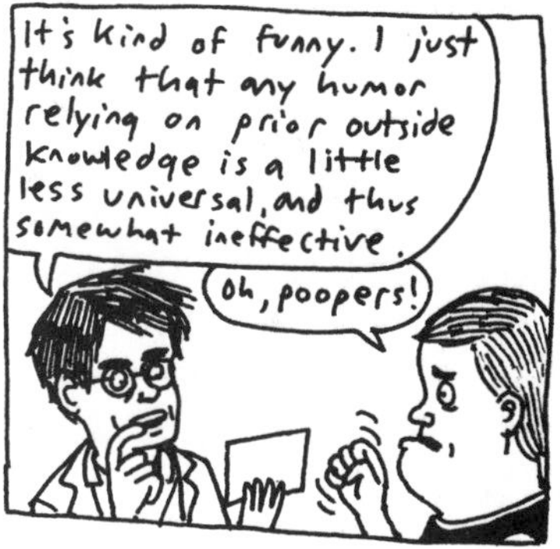
It's kind of funny. I just think that any humor relying on prior outside knowledge is a little less universal, and thus somewhat ineffective.
Oh, poopers!

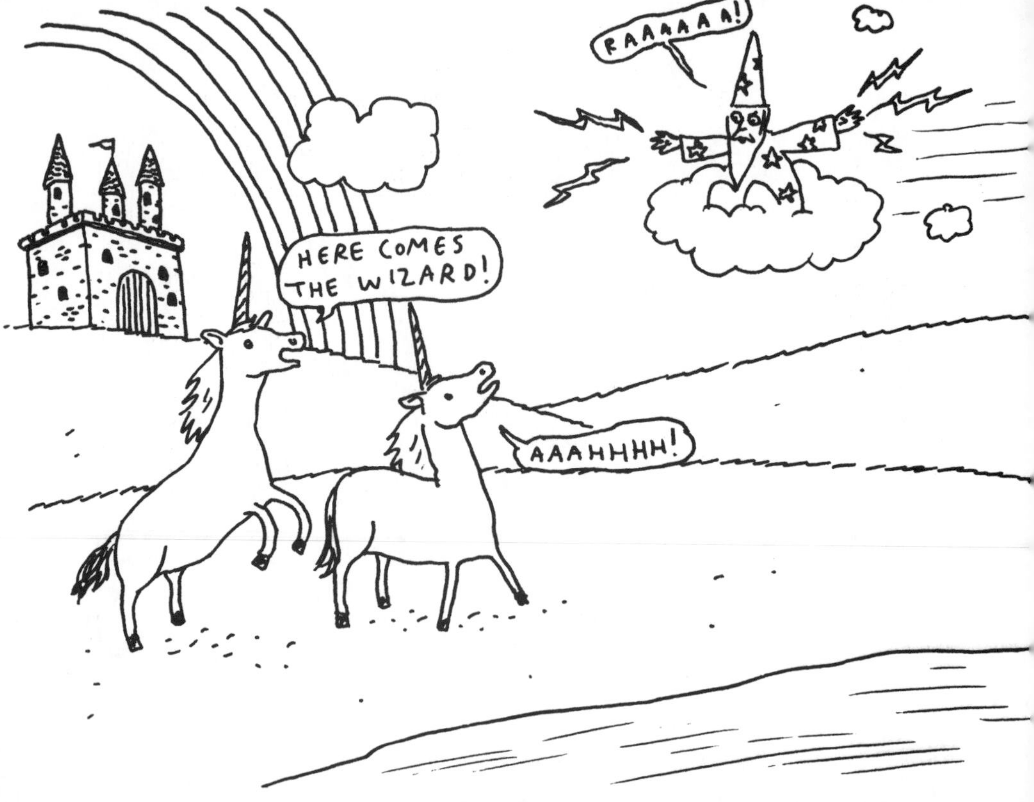
RAAAAAAA!
HERE COMES THE WIZARD!
AAAHHHH!

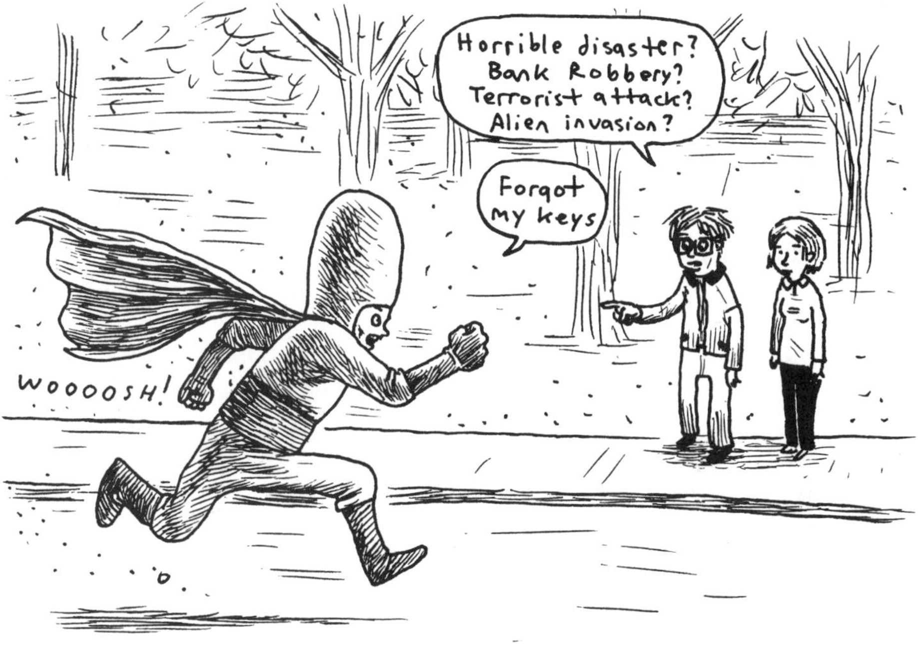
Horrible disaster? Bank Robbery? Terrorist attack? Alien invasion?
Forgot my keys
WOOOOOSH!

It's my finest work!
It sucks.
Well, I'm not very good.

...and I will grant you three wishes.
Okay, first I want to be rich... and I want a beautiful wife... and
C'mon, dude, I'm a frog. Be realistic.

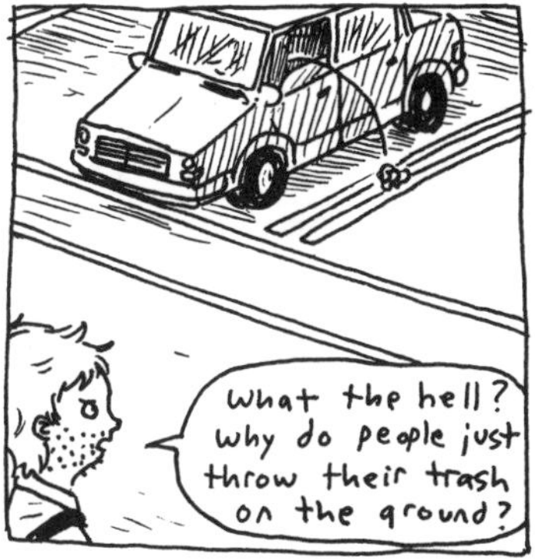
what the hell? why do people just throw their trash on the ground?

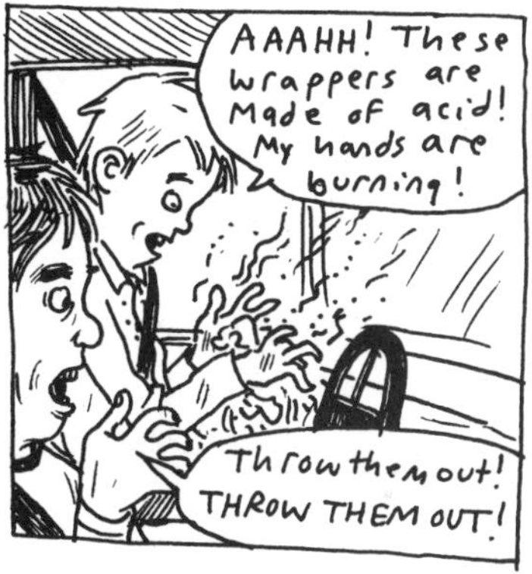
AAAHH! These wrappers are made of acid! My hands are burning!
Throw them out! THROW THEM OUT!

I love you.
But I'm not IN love with you.
I just don't understand why you don't want to hold hands.

What are you thinking about?
I was just thinking about how the human population has already surpassed the level of sustainability on this planet.

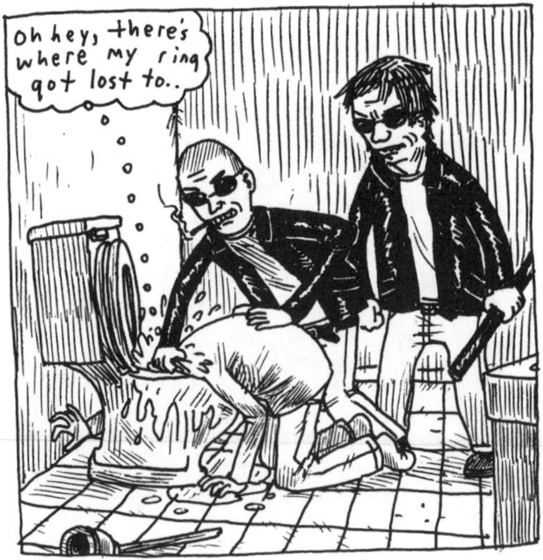
Oh hey, there's where my ring got lost to..

Well, here at Christian Solutions, we believe abstinence is the only sexual education we should be giving to our children.
Are those all of your children?
No, those are all my illegitimate grandkids.

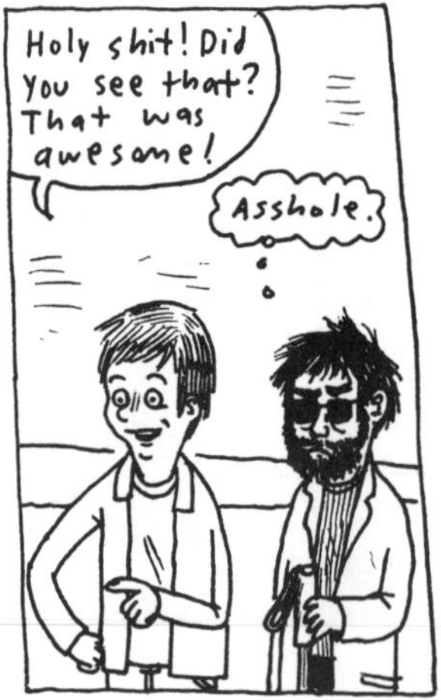
Holy shit! Did you see that? That was awesome!
Asshole.

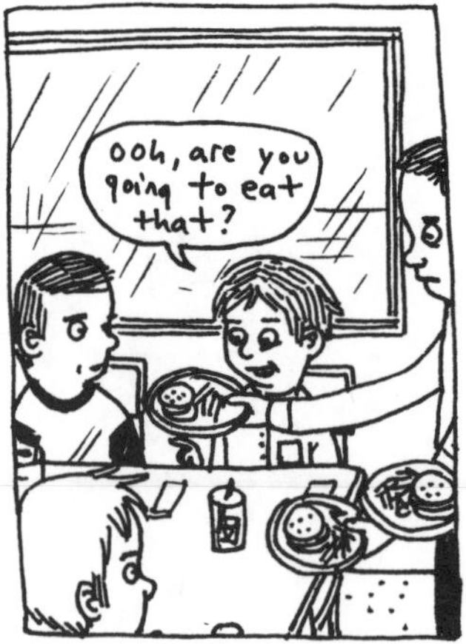
Ooh, are you going to eat that?

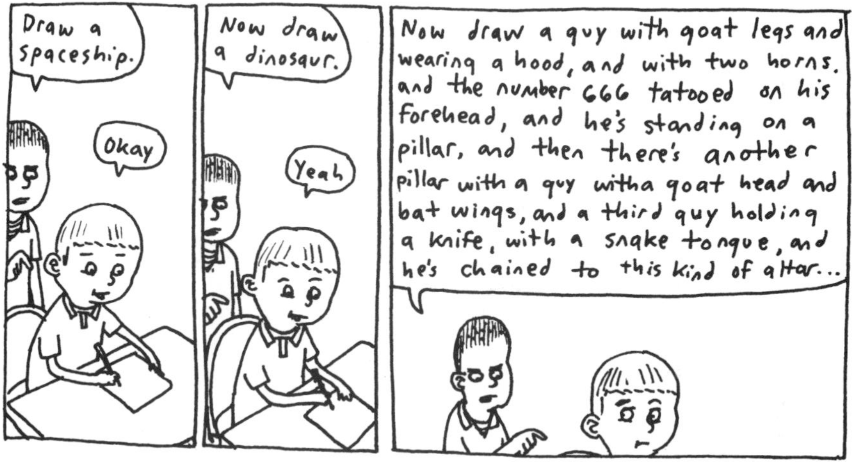
Draw a spaceship.
Okay
Now draw a dinosaur.
Yeah
Now draw a guy with goat legs and wearing a hood, and with two horns. and the number 666 tatooed on his forehead, and he's standing on a pillar, and then there's another pillar with a guy witha goat head and bat wings, and a third guy holding a knife, with a snake tongue, and he's chained to this kind of altar...

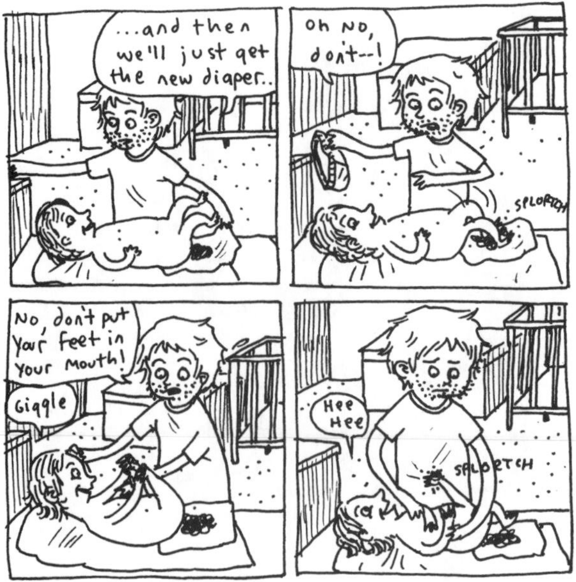
...and then we'll just get the new diaper..
Oh NO, don't--!
SPLORTCH
No, don't put your feet in your Mouth!
Giggle
Hee Hee
SPLORTCH

True Story

C'mon, guys!

I'M TOO GOOD FOR HIM, YOU BITCH
YOUR FACE ISN'T SO PRETTY NOW
SMACK
He is so over you.
Nice PURSE.

YOU'RE FIRED, JONES!
You can't fire Jones, sir, he's the best burger man we got. If he goes, I quit too!

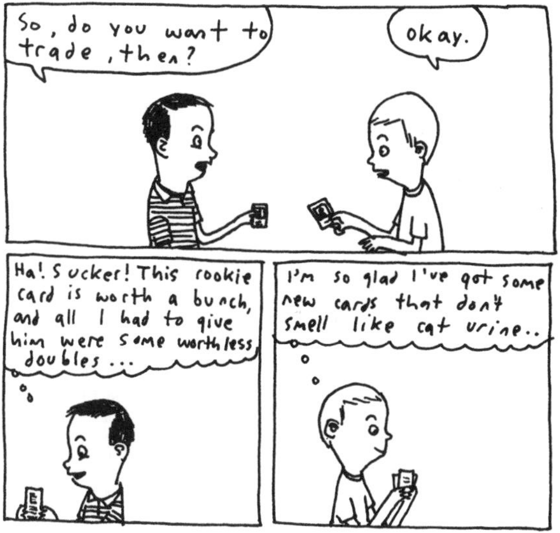
So, do you want to trade, then?
okay.
Ha! Sucker! This rookie card is worth a bunch, and all I had to give him were some worthless doubles...
I'm so glad I've got some new cards that don't smell like cat urine..

ELEMENTARY SCHOOL QUIZ GAME

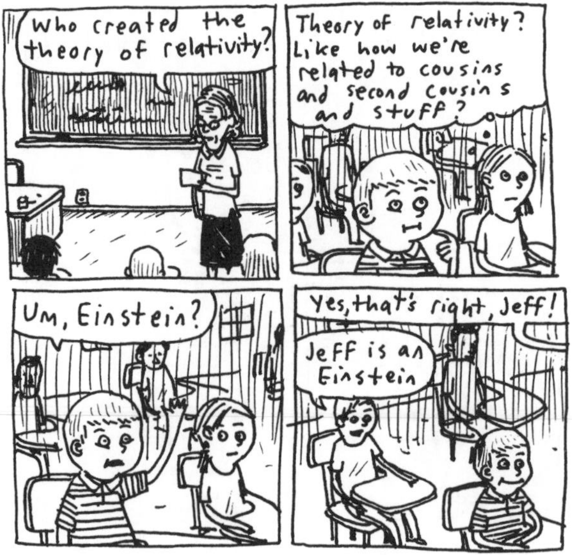

Who created the theory of relativity?
Theory of relativity? Like how we're related to cousins and second cousins and stuff?
Um, Einstein?
Yes, that's right, Jeff!
Jeff is an Einstein

CHEESEY PLATE

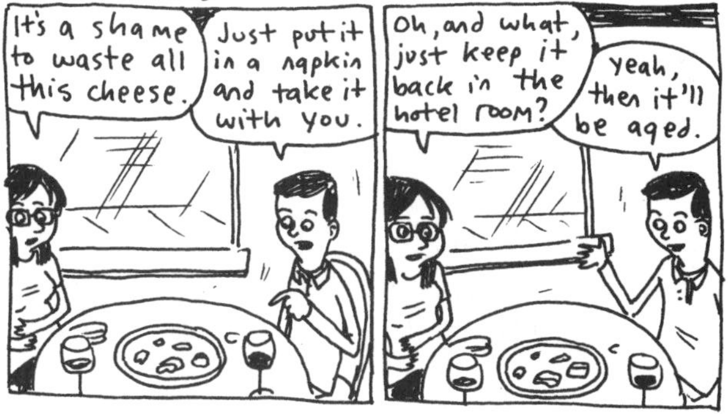
It's a shame to waste all this cheese.
Just put it in a napkin and take it with you.
Oh, and what, just keep it back in the hotel room?
yeah, then it'll be aged.

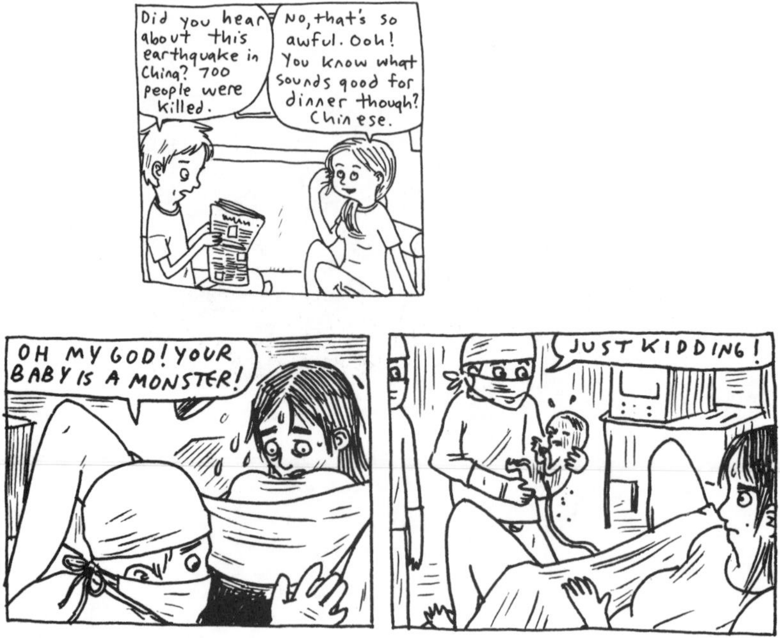
Did you hear about this earthquake in China? 700 people were killed.
No, that's so awful. Ooh! You know what sounds good for dinner though? Chinese.
OH MY GOD! YOUR BABY IS A MONSTER!
JUST KIDDING!

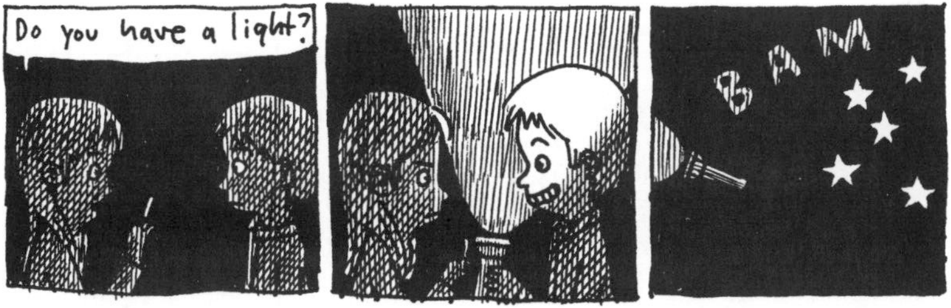
Do you have a light?
BAM

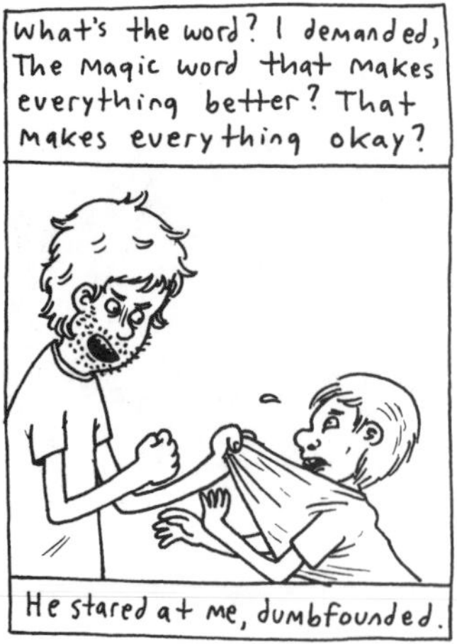
What's the word? I demanded, The magic word that makes everything better? That makes everything okay?
He stared at me, dumbfounded.

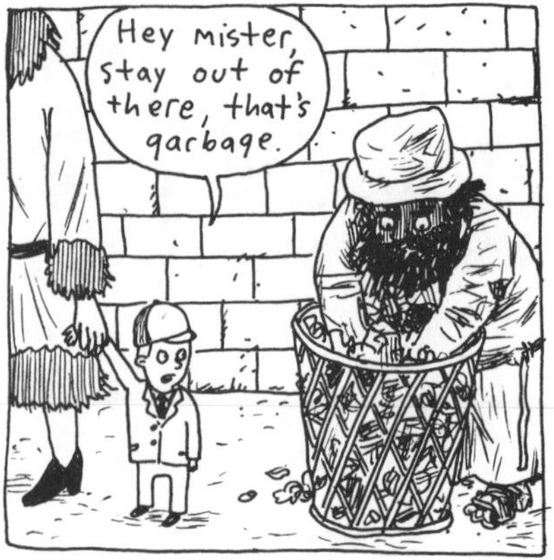
Hey mister, stay out of there, that's garbage.

Not tonight...
I've got a headache.
SEX
Here's some Tylenol...
DRUGS
Can you turn the music down? It's making my head hurt worse.
ROCK AND ROLL

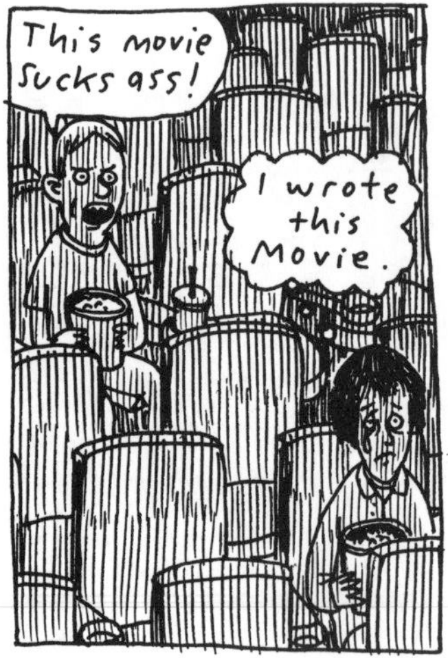
This movie sucks ass!
I wrote this movie.

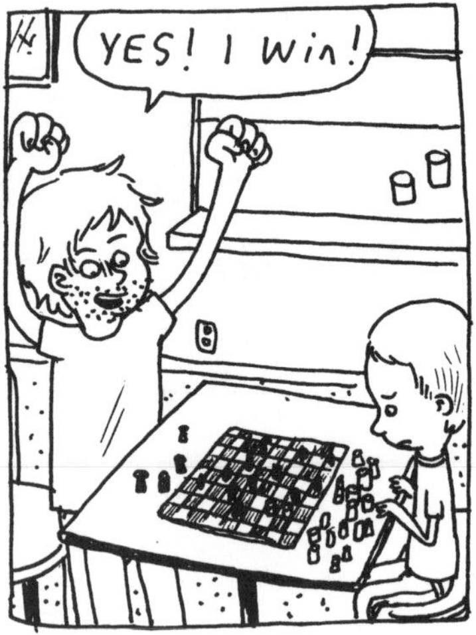
YES! I win!

BRAPPPPP!
FWUMP
Dude, you made him fart on me

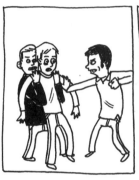

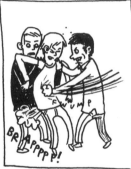

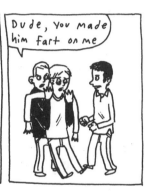

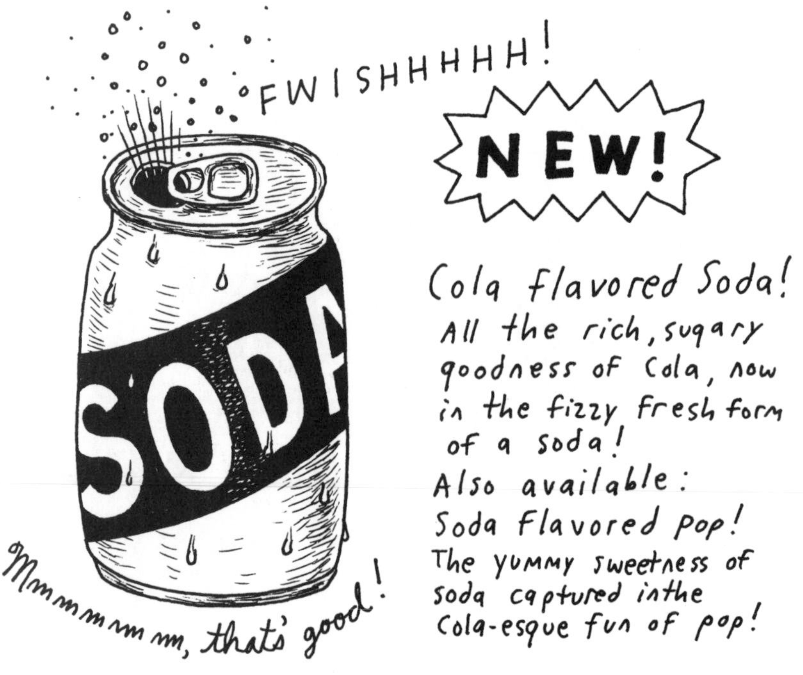
FWISHHHHHH!
SODA
NEW!
Cola flavored Soda!
All the rich, sugary goodness of Cola, now in the fizzy fresh form of a soda!
Also available:
Soda Flavored pop!
The yummy sweetness of soda captured inthe Cola-esque fun of pop!
Mmmmmmmm, that's good!

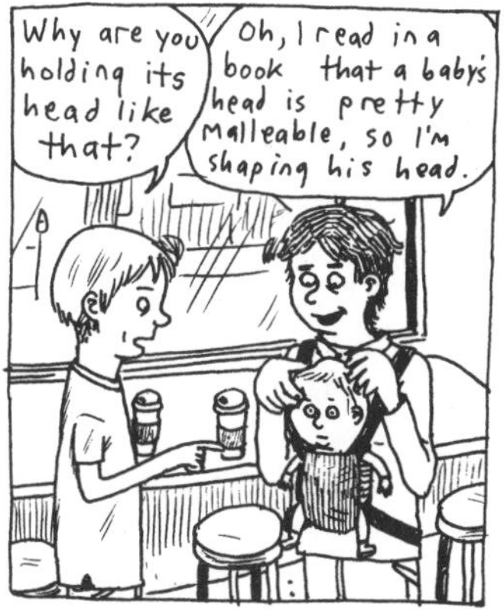
Why are you holding its head like that?
Oh, I read in a book that a baby's head is pretty malleable, so I'm shaping his head.

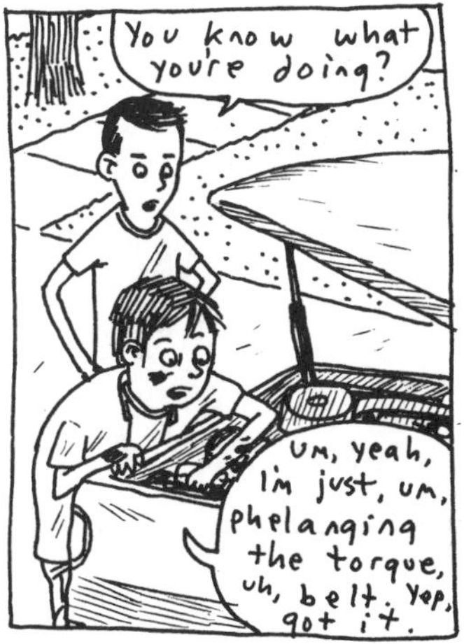
You know what you're doing?
Um, yeah, I'm just, um, phelanging the torque, uh, belt. Yep, got it.

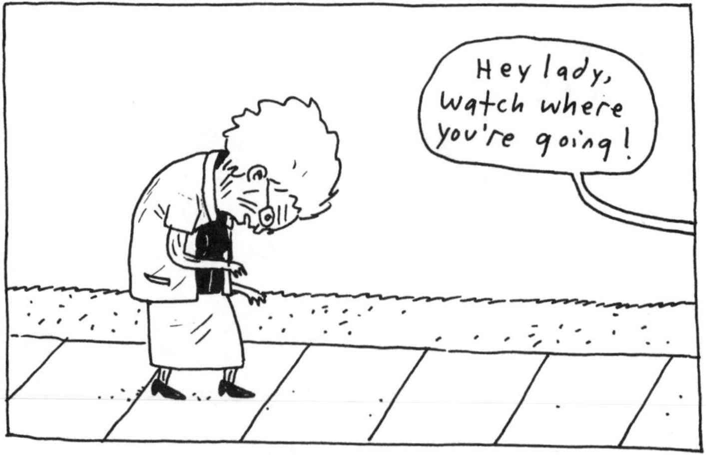
Hey lady, watch where you're going!

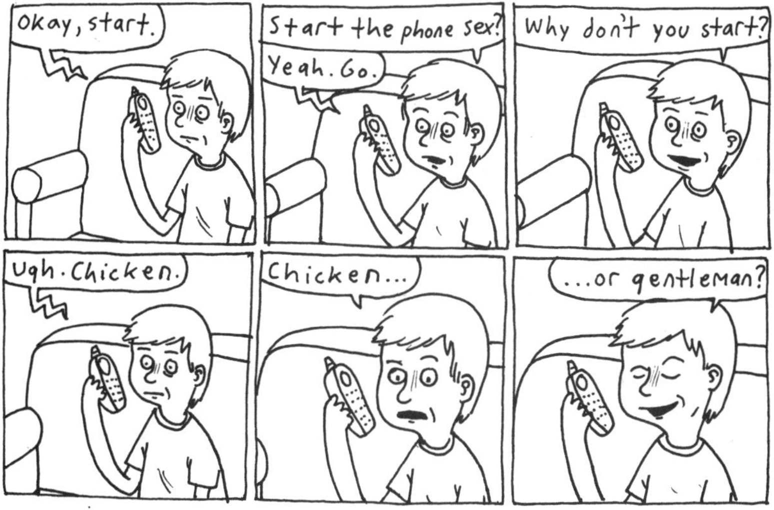
Okay, start.
Start the phone sex?
Yeah. Go.
Why don't you start?
Ugh. Chicken.
Chicken...
...or gentleman?

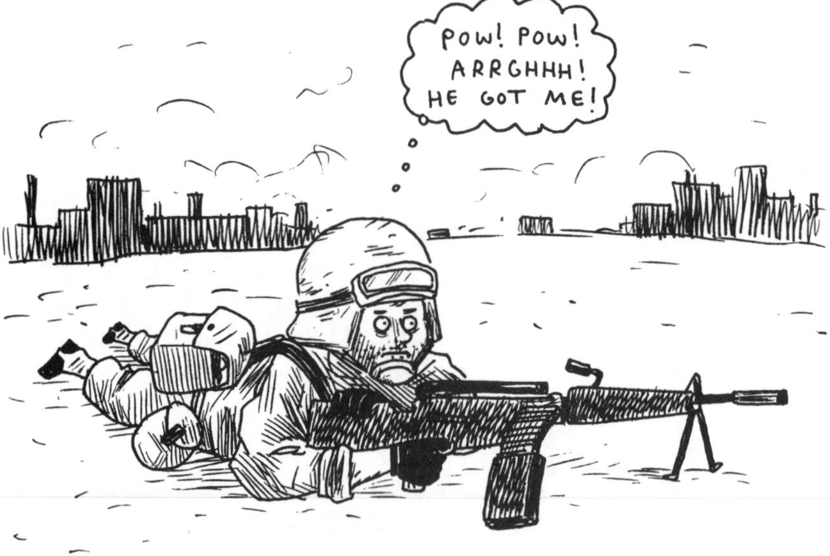
POW! POW!
ARRGHHH!
HE GOT ME!

DRAGNUT

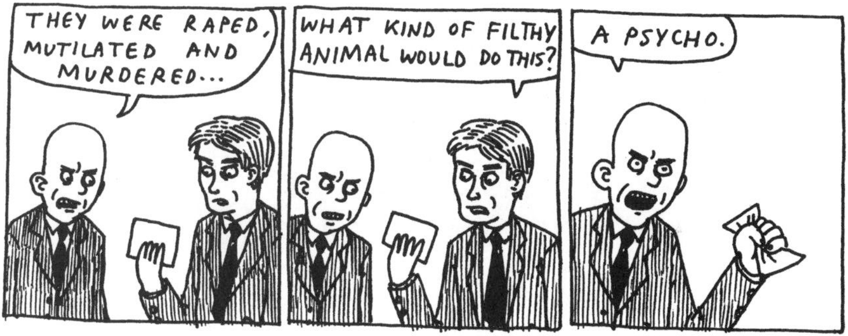
THEY WERE RAPED, MUTILATED AND MURDERED...
WHAT KIND OF FILTHY ANIMAL WOULD DO THIS?
A PSYCHO.

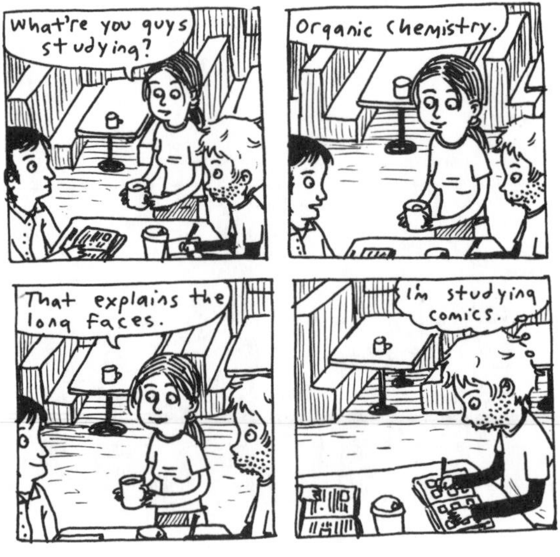
What're you guys studying?
Organic chemistry.
That explains the long faces.
I'm studying comics.

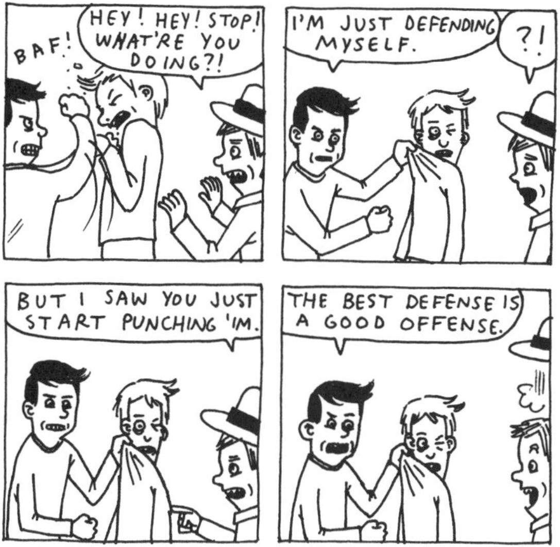
BAF!
HEY! HEY! STOP! WHAT'RE YOU DOING?!
I'M JUST DEFENDING MYSELF.
?!
BUT I SAW YOU JUST START PUNCHING 'IM.
THE BEST DEFENSE IS A GOOD OFFENSE.

THIS AMERICAN LIFE

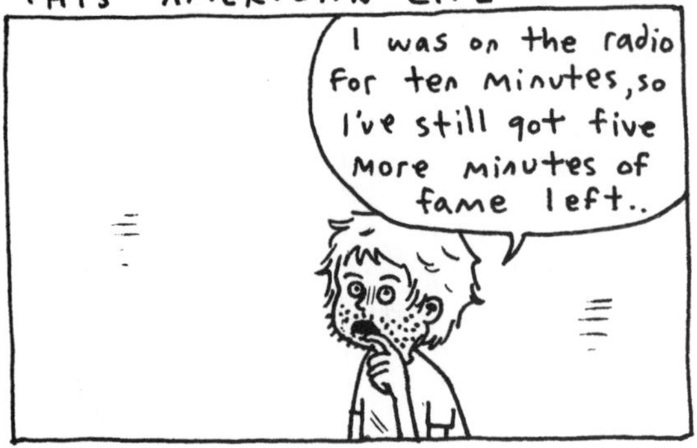
I was on the radio for ten minutes, so I've still got five more minutes of fame left..

SHAMELESS NAME-DROPPING/SELF-PROMOTING COMIC

CONGRATULATIONS ON YOUR NOMINATION FOR THE 'BEST COLORIST' AWARD

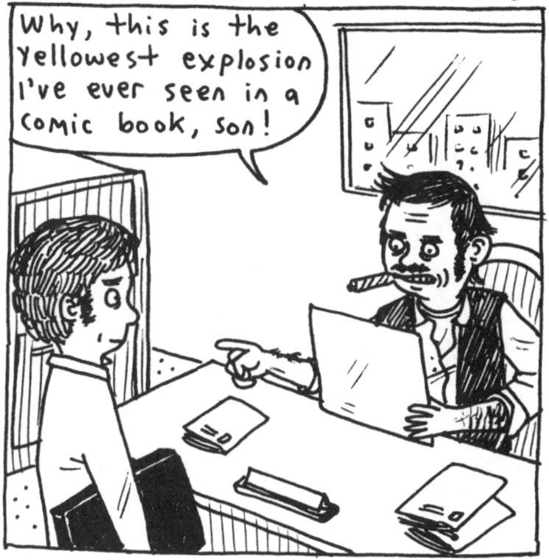
Why, this is the yellowest explosion I've ever seen in a comic book, son!

PRINT

My meth dealer is the dreamiest.
Three fifty Three sixty Three Seventy Okay, there you go
Thanks Chuck
So chuck, what are you doing tonight?
None of your damn business.
Sigh
Oh Chuck, I love you
Did you get her phone number?
um... no.
Aw, Man, I'm going to shoot you!
Pow!
Pow!
Pow!

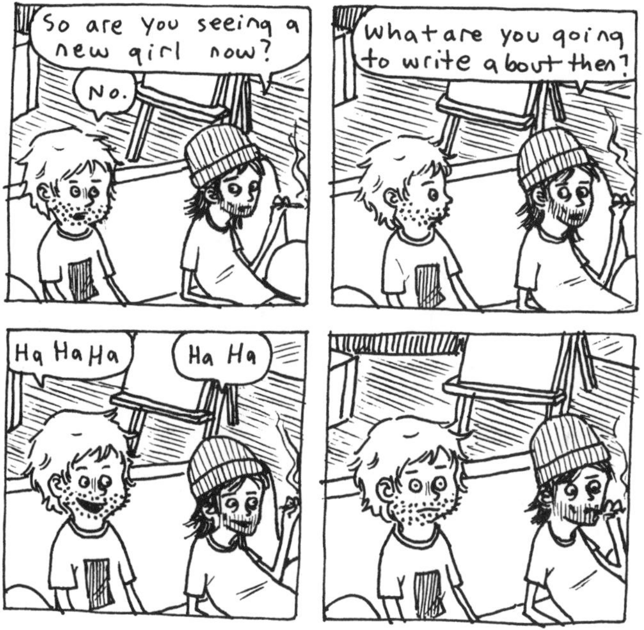
So are you seeing a new girl now?
No.
What are you going to write about then?
Ha Ha Ha
Ha Ha

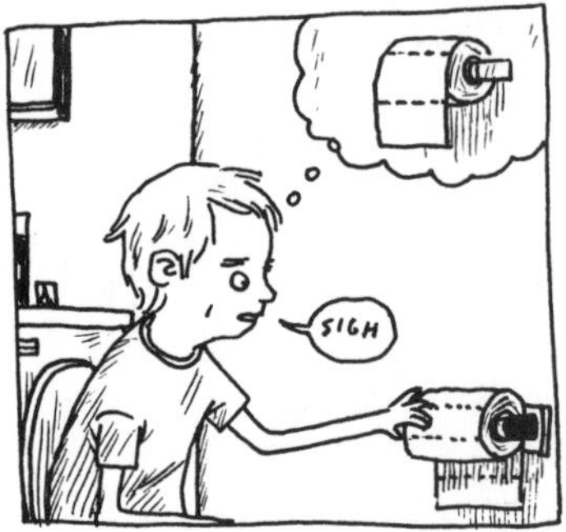
SIGH

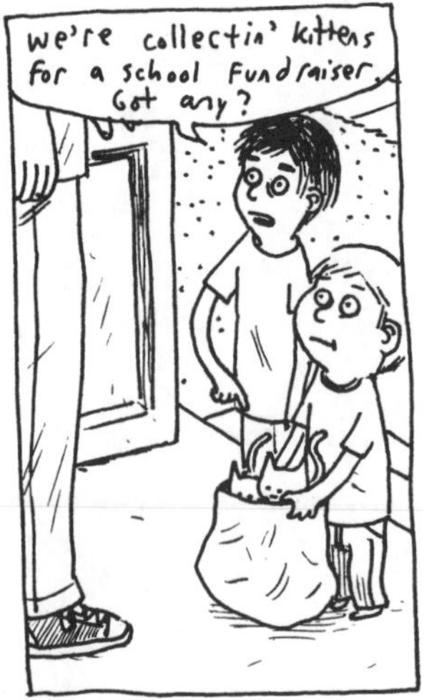
We're collectin' kittens for a school fundraiser. Got any?

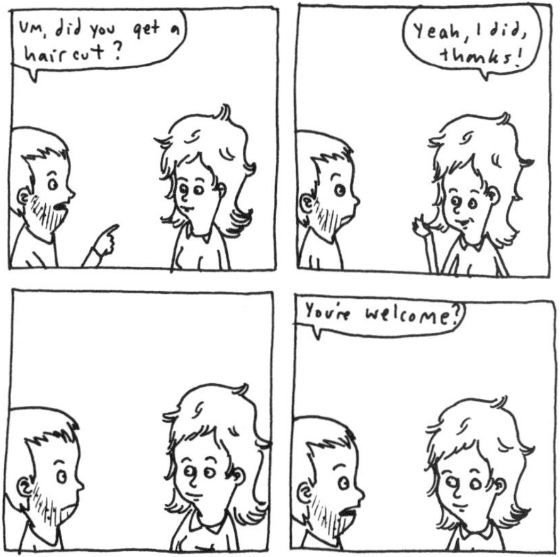
Um, did you get a haircut?
Yeah, I did, thanks!
You're welcome?

I WILL OVERPOWER YOU!

I will overpower you. You stand little chance. All you can know now is that once we step into the Octagon my only thought is of destroying you. You will be like a schoolbus of children and I will be like an angry evil bus driver who is driving you into a lake where you will drown and all your screams of protest will find you helpless against my authority. For that is the authority of my will in the Octagon. How many ways can I destroy you? It would take days for me to list them. I will choke you until your head droops in unconciousness. I will bend your arm in half the wrong way. I will break your legs. I will pound your face into such a bloody mess that when people later tell of my destroying you, the word 'pulp' will be frequently used. Do you remember the video of the kitties stuck in the drain pipe and the firemen had to come and cut them out, barely saving them just in time? Well, you are a puny mewing kitty but I am not a fireman. I am a drainpipe and there are no firemen. Do you know what it is that you are feeling now? It is fear.

Dad, do we have a pencil sharpener?
Yeah, we do. Going to do some drawing?
I want to give myself claw hands.

I'm worried about you.
Why?
I think you worry too much.

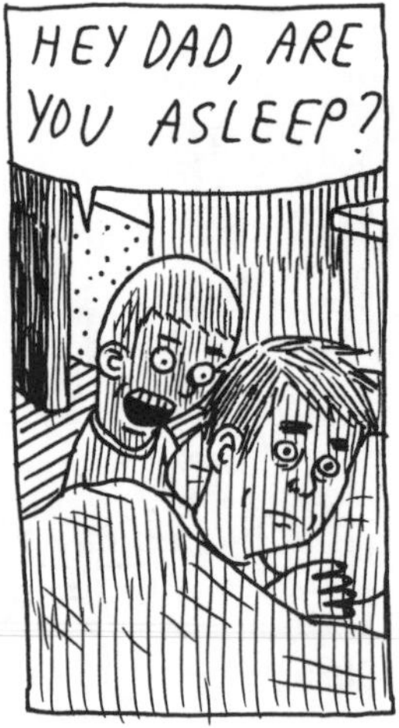
HEY DAD, ARE YOU ASLEEP?

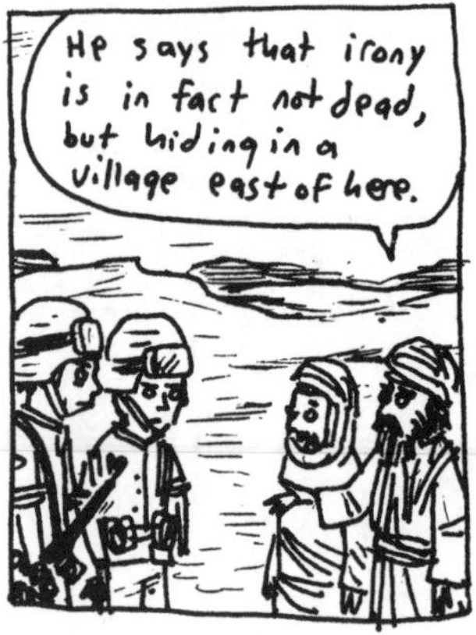
He says that irony is in fact not dead, but hiding in a village east of here.

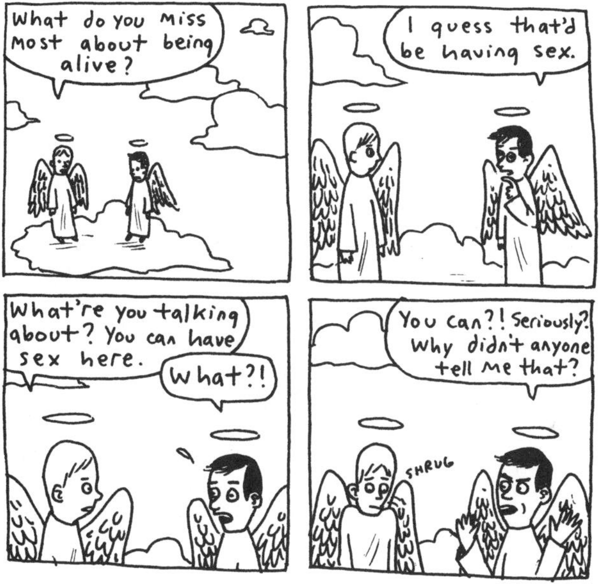
What do you miss most about being alive?
I guess that'd be having sex.
What're you talking about? You can have sex here.
What?!
SHRUG
You can?! Seriously? Why didn't anyone tell me that?

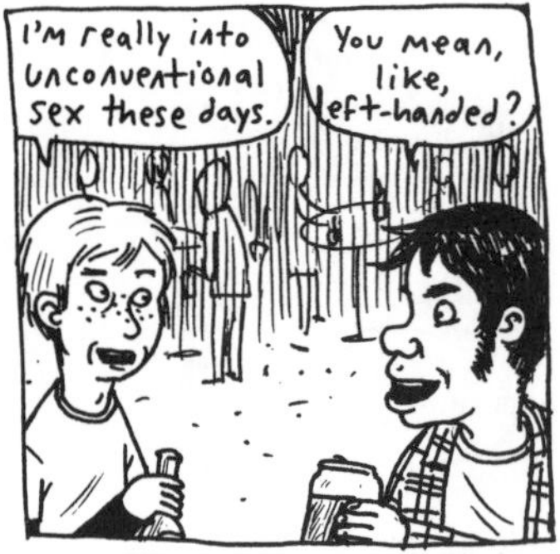
I'm really into unconventional sex these days.
You mean, like, left-handed?

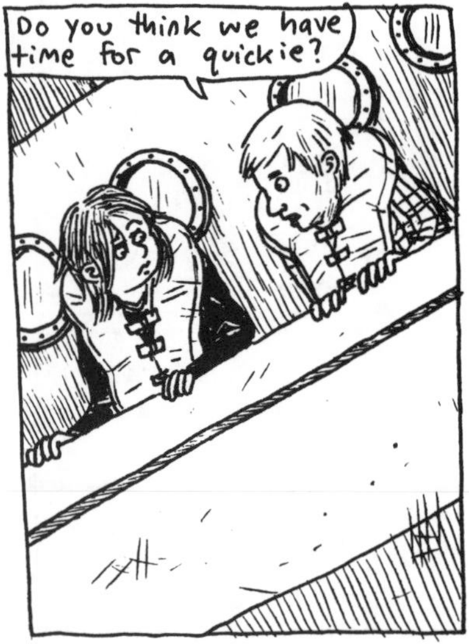
Do you think we have time for a quickie?

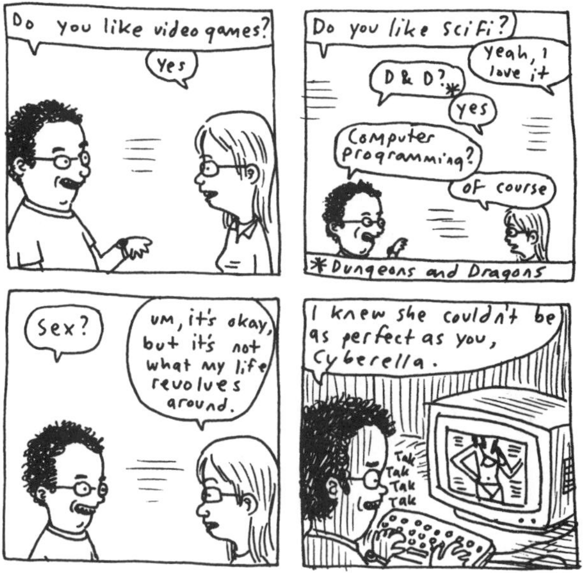

Do you like video games?
yes
Do you like scifi?
yeah, I love it
D & D?*
yes
Computer programming?
of course
* Dungeons and Dragons
Sex?
um, it's okay, but it's not what my life revolves around.
I knew she couldn't be as perfect as you, Cyberella.
Tak Tak Tak Tak

oh, hey I love this movie! Have you seen it before? The ending is so brilliant, you know, where it turns out the roomate is the killer, I mean, younever suspect that, and, hey, are those pretzels, can I have some? Thanks.

OUR DAD WAS A MINISTER

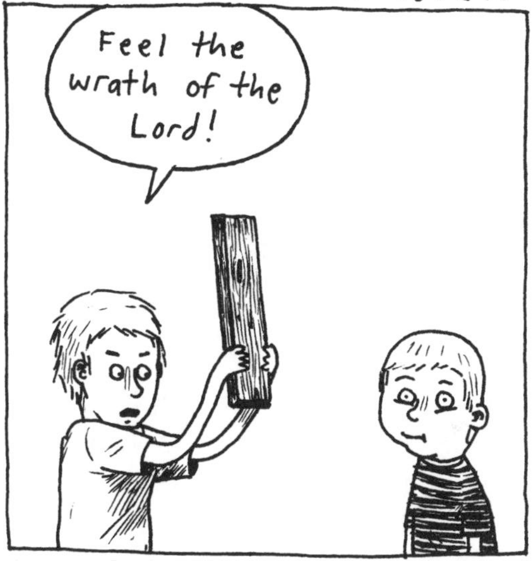
Feel the wrath of the Lord!

MY BROTHERS AND I USED TO PLAY GOD WHEN WE WERE KIDS

I can't remember. Are we supposed to START things with a bang, or END things with a bang?
. . .

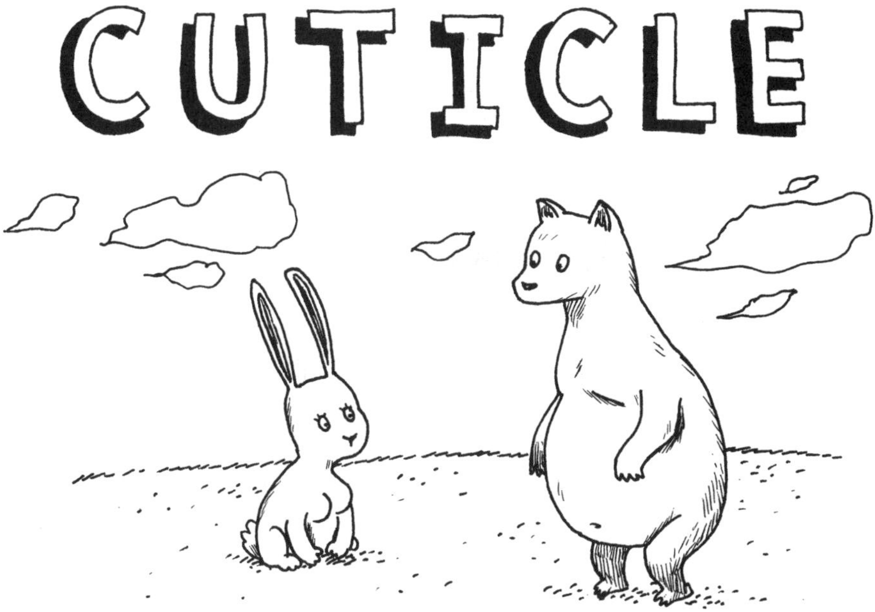
CUTICLE

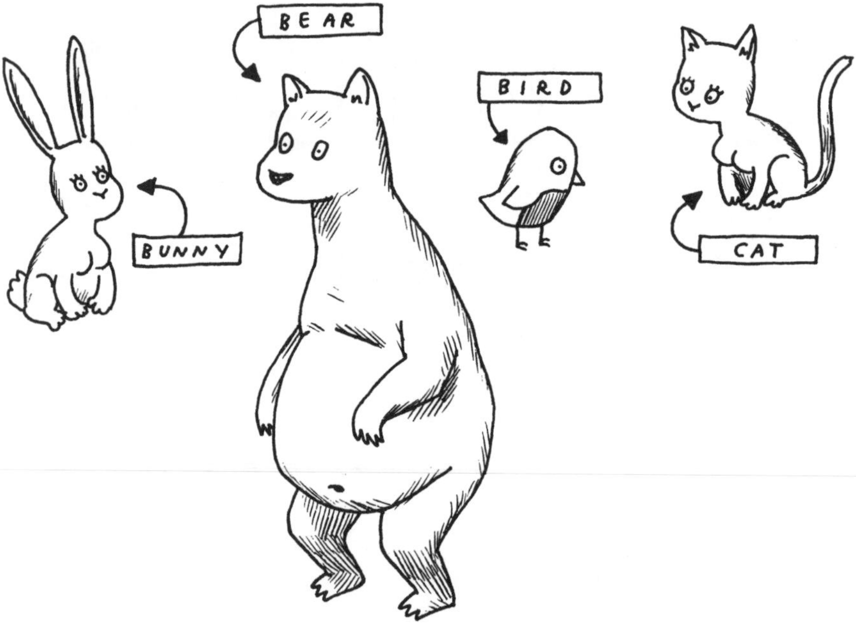
BEAR
BIRD
BUNNY
CAT

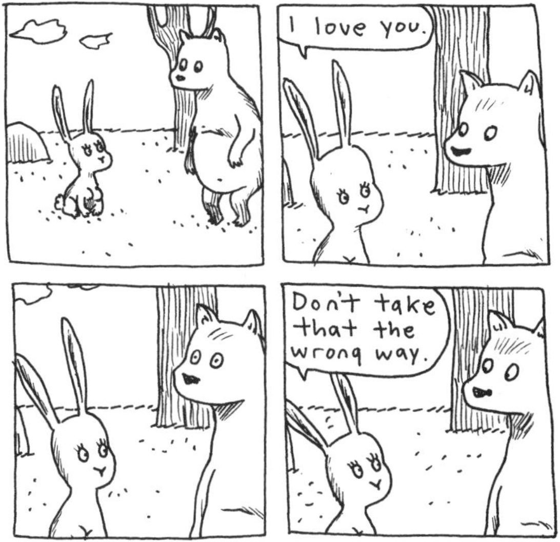
I love you.
Don't take that the wrong way.

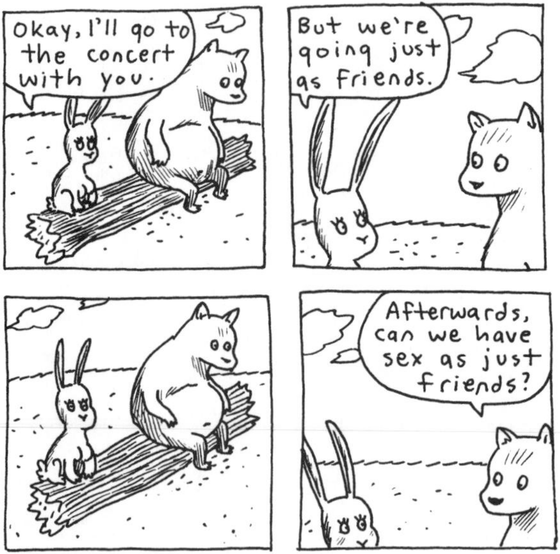
Okay, I'll go to the concert with you.
But we're going just as friends.
Afterwards, can we have sex as just friends?

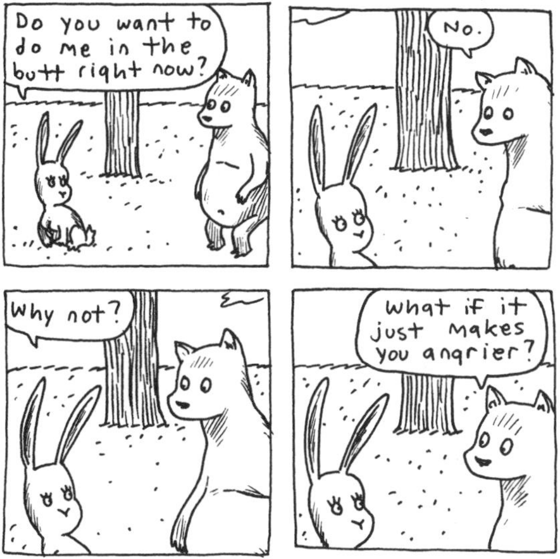
Do you want to do me in the butt right now?
No.
Why not?
What if it just makes you angrier?

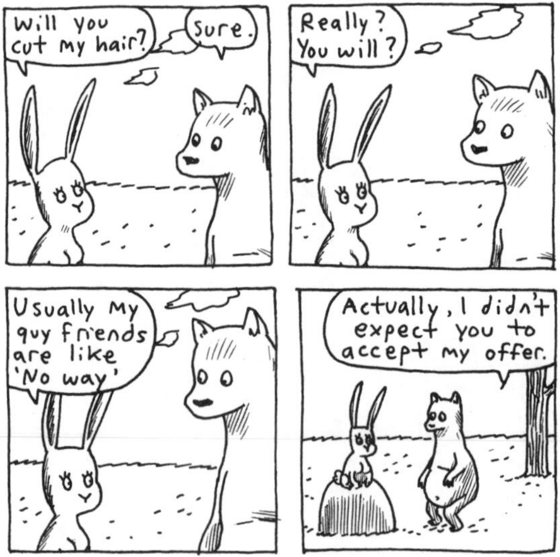
Will you cut my hair?
Sure.
Really? You will?
Usually my guy friends are like 'No way'
Actually, I didn't expect you to accept my offer.

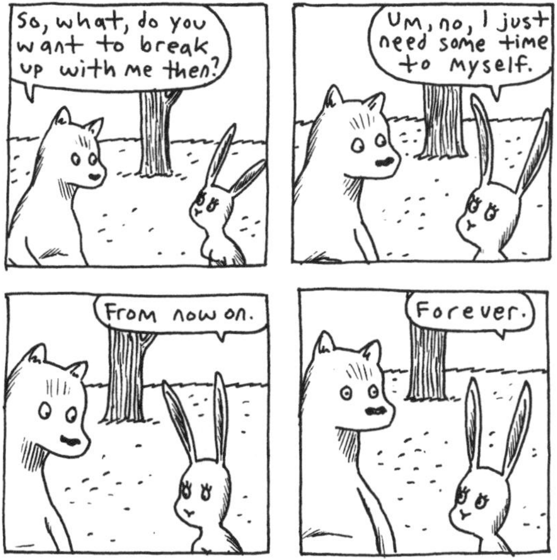
So, what, do you want to break up with me then?
Um, no, I just need some time to myself.
From now on.
Forever.

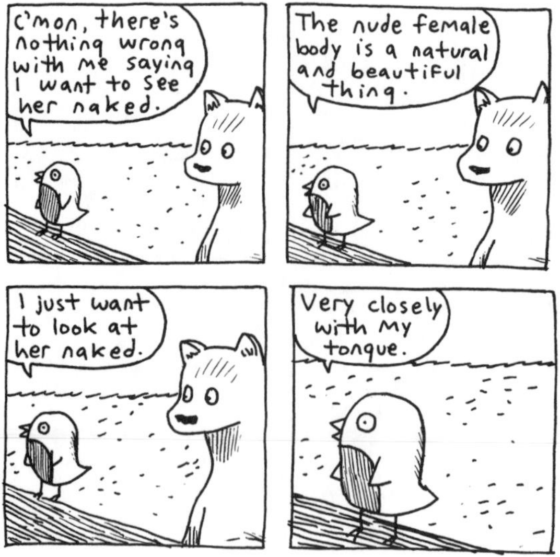
C'mon, there's nothing wrong with me saying I want to see her naked.
The nude female body is a natural and beautiful thing.
I just want to look at her naked.
Very closely with my tongue.

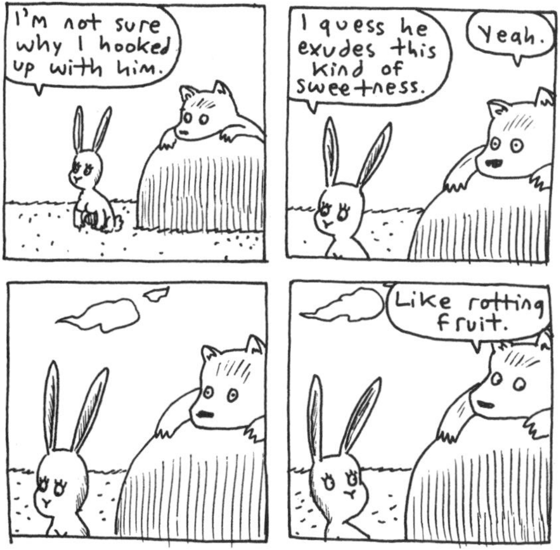
I'm not sure why I hooked up with him.
I guess he exudes this kind of sweetness.
Yeah.
Like rotting fruit.

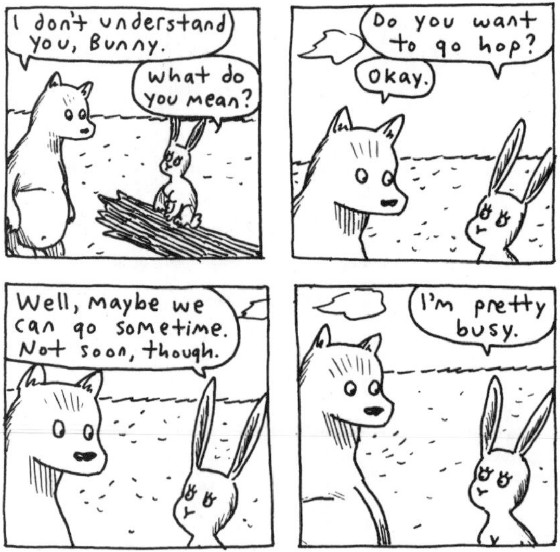
I don't understand you, Bunny.
what do you mean?
Do you want to go hop?
Okay.
Well, maybe we can go sometime. Not soon, though.
I'm pretty busy.

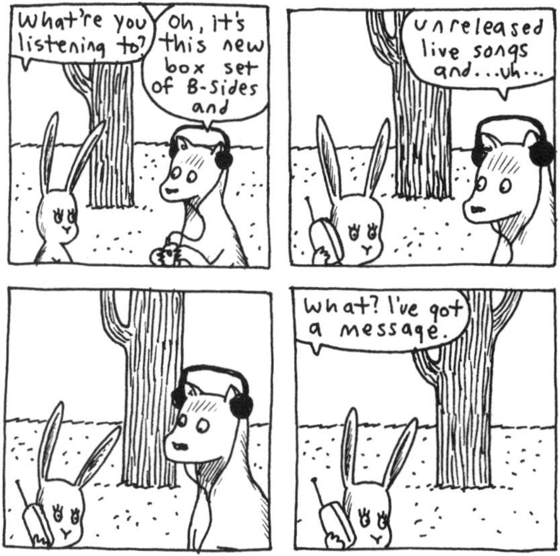
What're you listening to?
Oh, it's this new box set of B-sides and
unreleased live songs and...uh...
What? I've got a message.

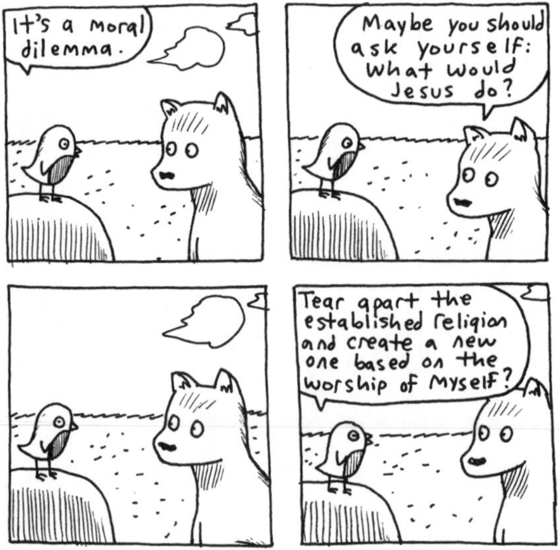
It's a moral dilemma.
Maybe you should ask yourself: What would Jesus do?
Tear apart the established religion and create a new one based on the worship of Myself?

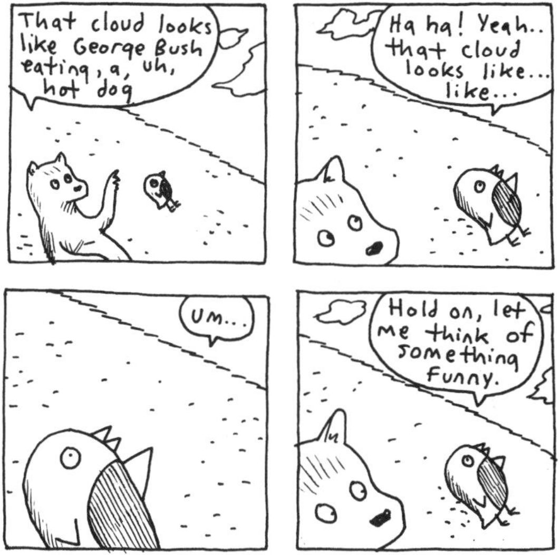
That cloud looks like George Bush eating, a, uh, hot dog
Ha ha! Yeah.. that cloud looks like... like...
Um...
Hold on, let me think of something funny.

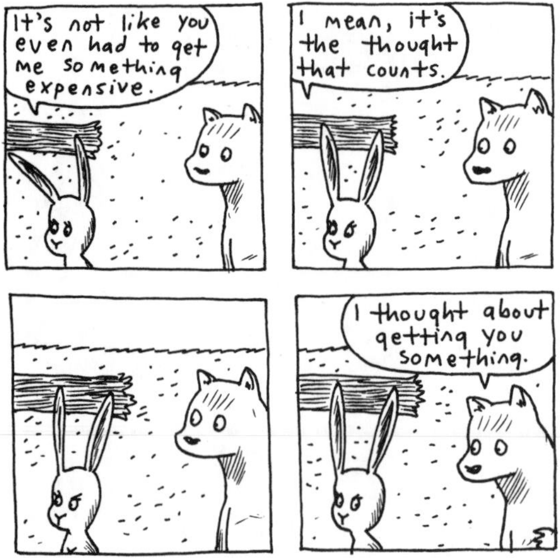
It's not like you even had to get me something expensive.
I mean, it's the thought that counts.
I thought about getting you something.

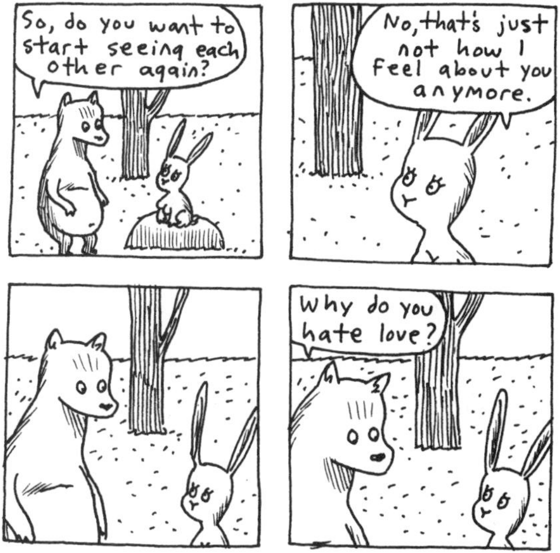
So, do you want to start seeing each other again?
No, that's just not how I feel about you anymore.
Why do you hate love?

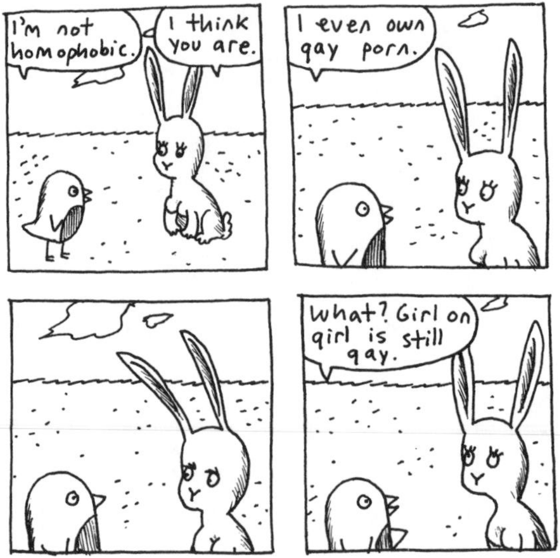
I'm not homophobic.
I think you are.
I even own gay porn.
What? Girl on girl is still gay.

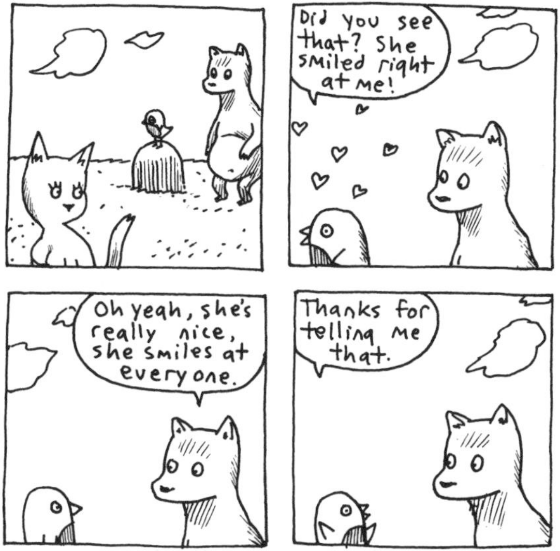
Did you see that? She smiled right at me!
Oh yeah, she's really nice, she smiles at everyone.
Thanks for telling me that.

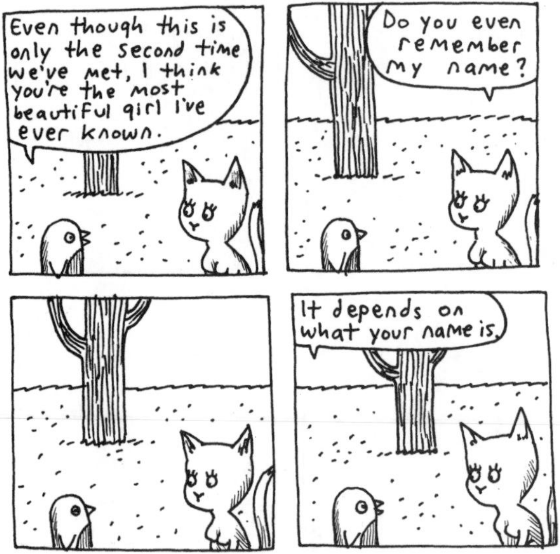
Even though this is only the second time we've met, I think you're the most beautiful girl I've ever known.
Do you even remember my name?
It depends on what your name is.

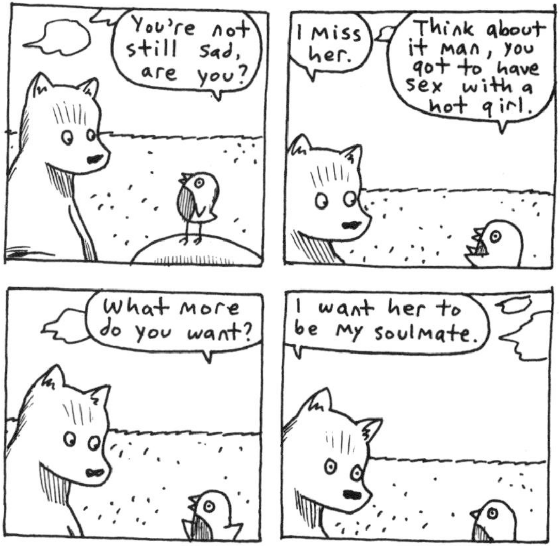
You're not still sad, are you?
I miss her.
Think about it man, you got to have sex with a hot girl.
What more do you want?
I want her to be my soulmate.

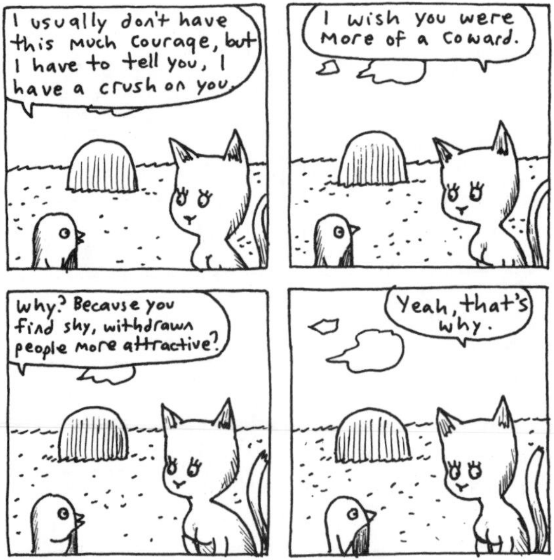
I usually don't have this much courage, but I have to tell you, I have a crush on you.
I wish you were more of a coward.
Why? Because you find shy, withdrawn people more attractive?
Yeah, that's why.

... and she says, well, do you have your receipt and I'm like no, I don't have my receipt, I mean
It's like, I don't see what the big problem is, I just need to get a a new one that's not broken, so I look at her and I say, look
Stop boring me.

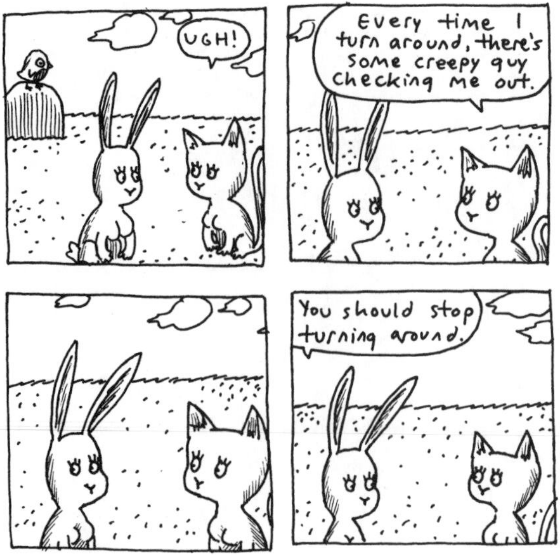
UGH!
Every time I turn around, there's some creepy guy checking me out.
You should stop turning around.

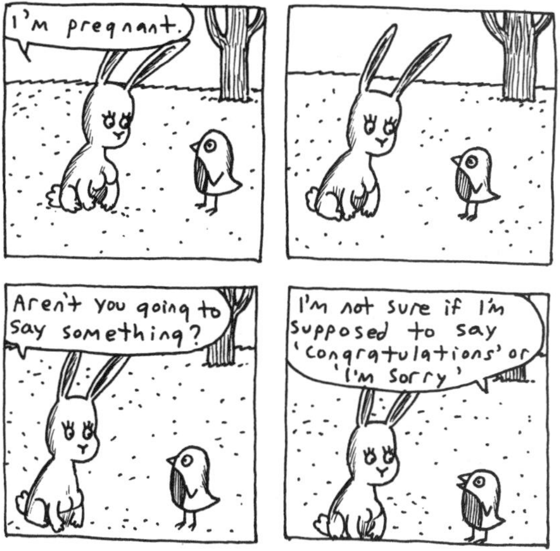
I'm pregnant.
Aren't you going to say something?
I'm not sure if I'm supposed to say 'congratulations' or 'I'm sorry'

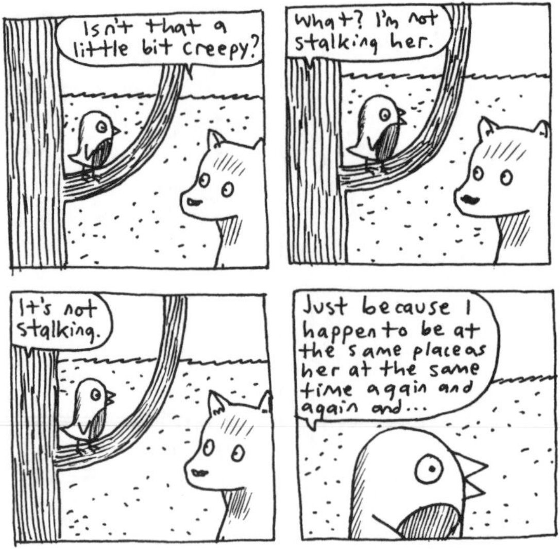
Isn't that a little bit creepy?
What? I'm not stalking her.
It's not stalking.
Just because I happen to be at the same place as her at the same time again and again and...

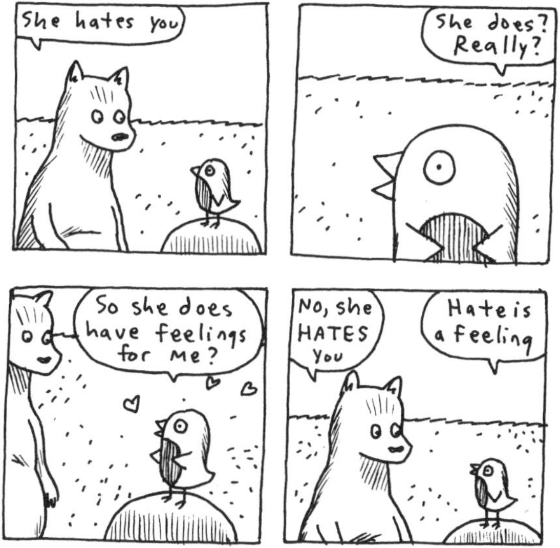
She hates you
She does? Really?
So she does have feelings for me?
No, she HATES you
Hate is a feeling

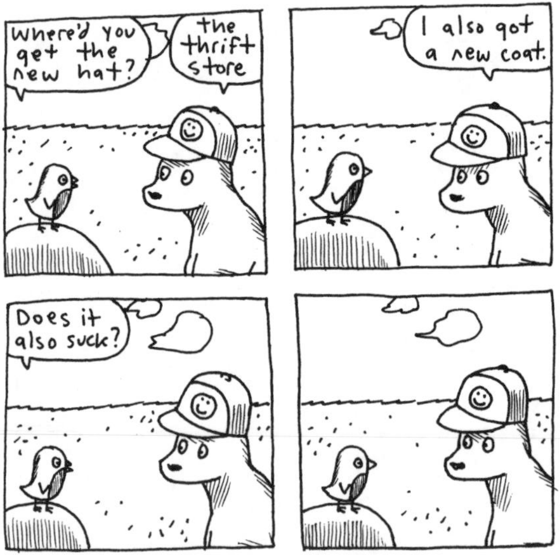
where'd you get the new hat?
the thrift store
I also got a new coat.
Does it also suck?

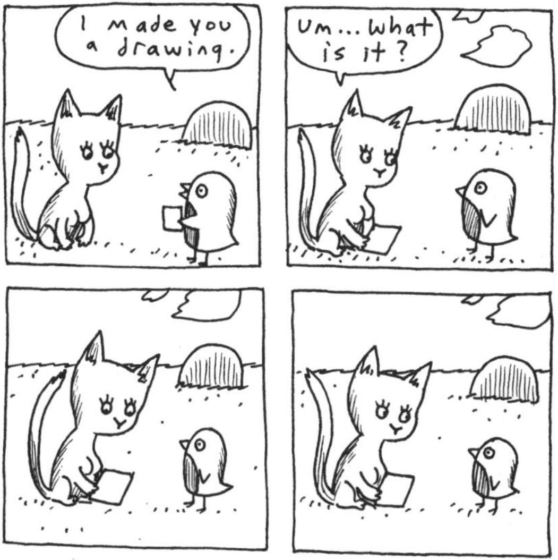
I made you a drawing.
Um... what is it?

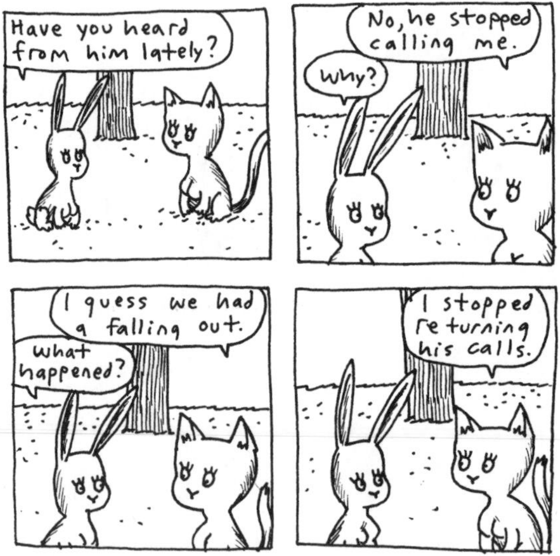
Have you heard from him lately?
No, he stopped calling me.
Why?
I guess we had a falling out.
What happened?
I stopped returning his calls.

Look, accept it. I'm never going to make out with you.
Okay?
So we'll never know the feeling of our soft lips pressed against each other, moist tongues gently probing--
Hey!
Stop fantasizing in front of me.

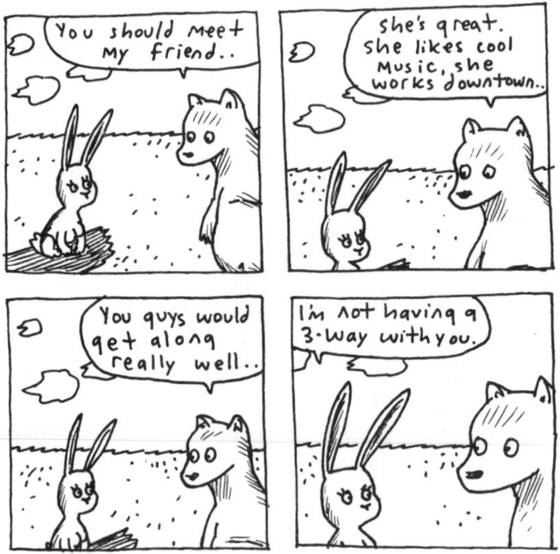
You should meet my friend..
She's great. She likes cool music, she works downtown..
You guys would get along really well..
I'm not having a 3-way with you.

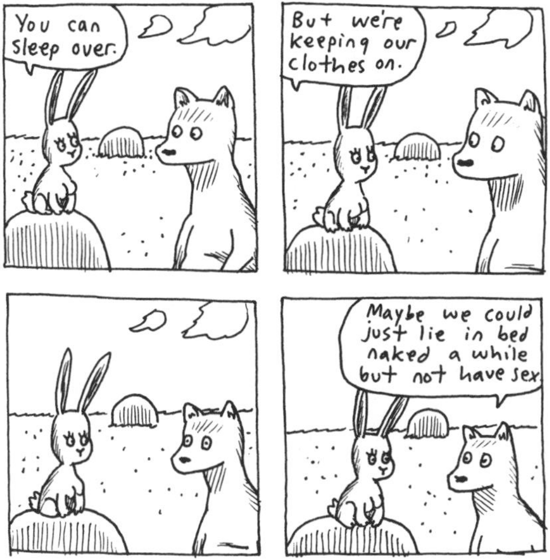
You can sleep over.
But we're keeping our clothes on.
Maybe we could just lie in bed naked a while but not have sex.

You missed a great party last night.
What happened?
I don't remember.
You don't remember?
That's how I know it was great.

Hey, give me five bucks.
Sure, what do you need five bucks for?
Uhhhh... never mind.

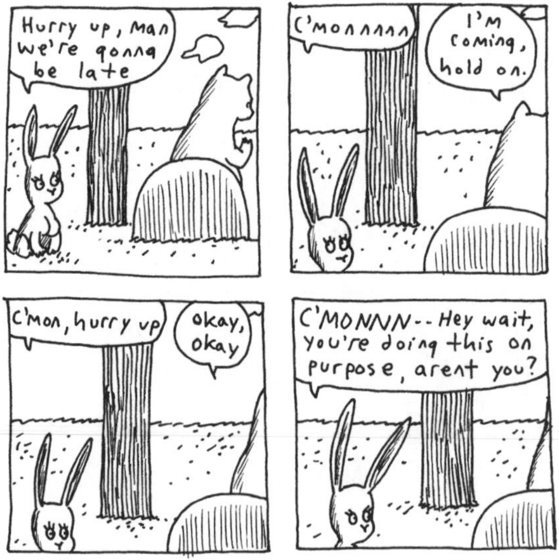
Hurry up, man we're gonna be late
C'MONNNNN
I'M coming, hold on.
C'mon, hurry up
okay, okay
C'MONNN-- Hey wait, you're doing this on purpose, arent you?

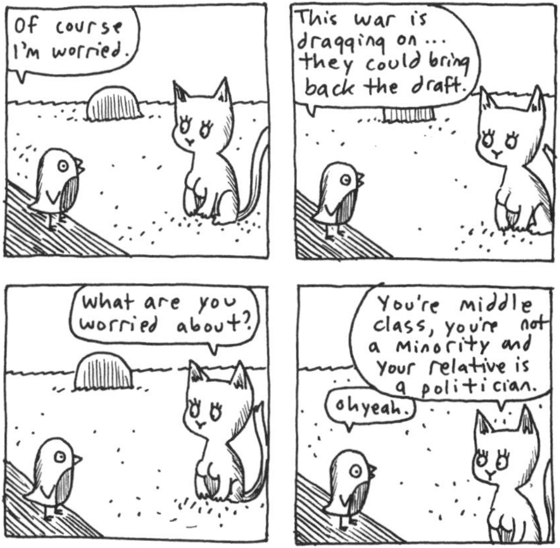
Of course I'm worried.
This war is dragging on... they could bring back the draft.
What are you worried about?
You're middle class, you're not a minority and your relative is a politician.
oh yeah.

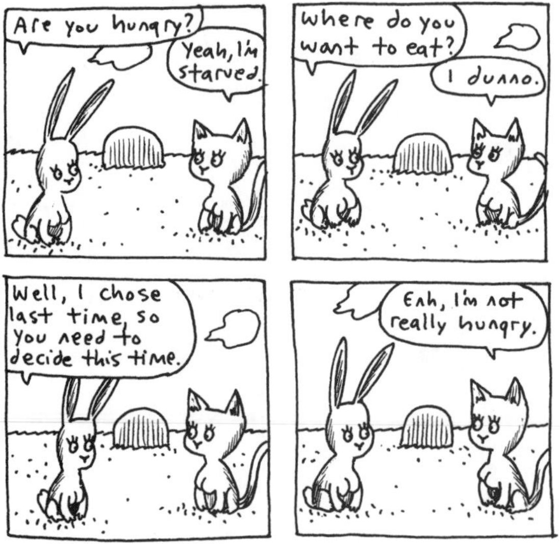
Are you hungry?
Yeah, I'm starved.
Where do you want to eat?
I dunno.
Well, I chose last time, so you need to decide this time.
Enh, I'm not really hungry.

Hey, have you been working out?
Yeah, I have actually.
Really? Because you can't really tell.

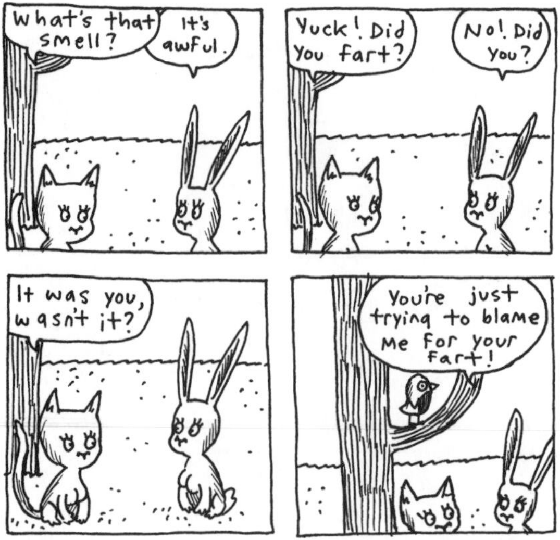
What's that smell?
It's awful.
Yuck! Did you fart?
No! Did you?
It was you, wasn't it?
You're just trying to blame me for your fart!

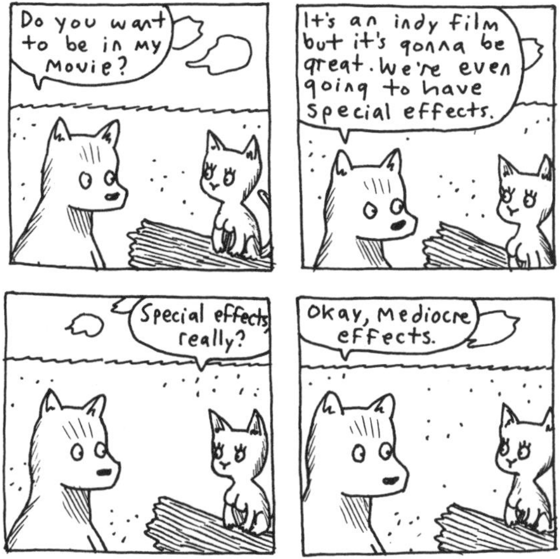
Do you want to be in my movie?
It's an indy film but it's gonna be great. We're even going to have special effects.
Special effects really?
Okay, mediocre effects.

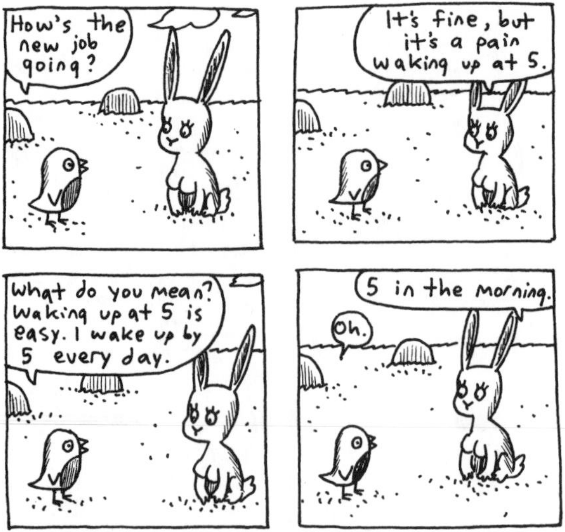
How's the new job going?
It's fine, but it's a pain waking up at 5.
What do you mean? Waking up at 5 is easy. I wake up by 5 every day.
5 in the morning.
Oh.

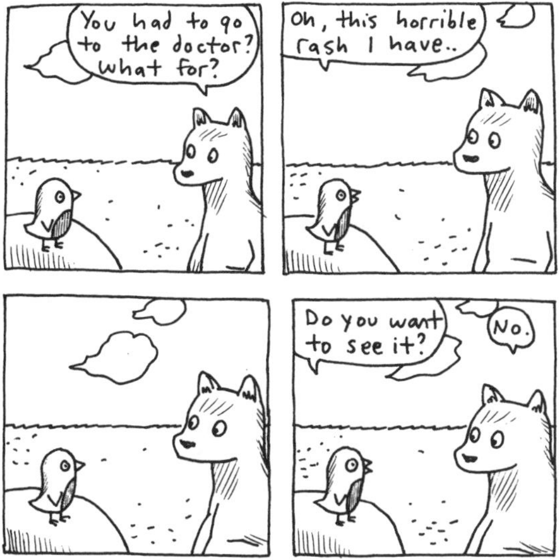
You had to go to the doctor? what for?
Oh, this horrible rash I have..
Do you want to see it?
No.

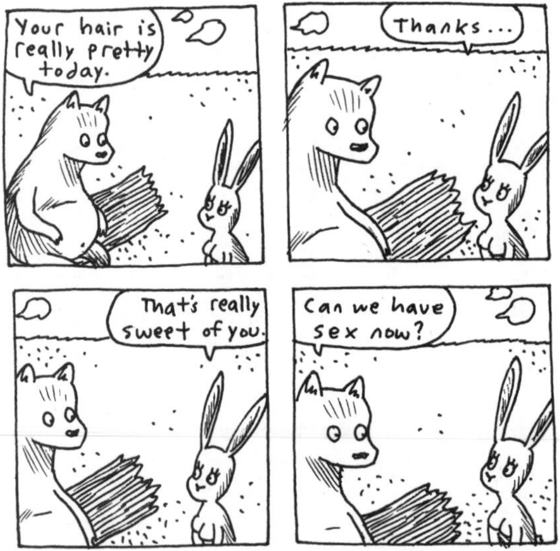
Your hair is really pretty today.
Thanks...
That's really sweet of you.
Can we have sex now?

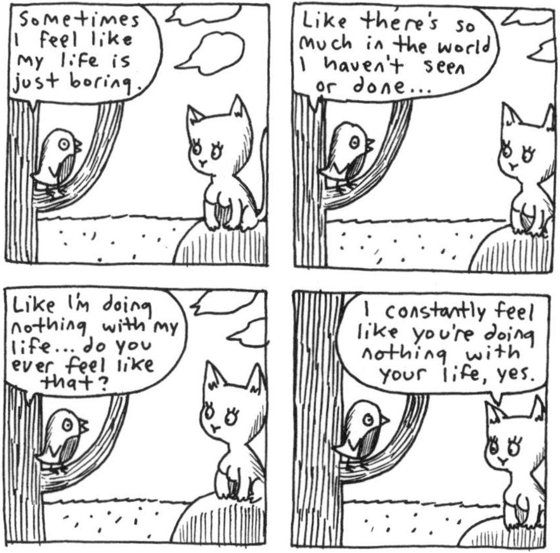
Sometimes I feel like my life is just boring.
Like there's so much in the world I haven't seen or done...
Like I'm doing nothing with my life... do you ever feel like that?
I constantly feel like you're doing nothing with your life, yes.

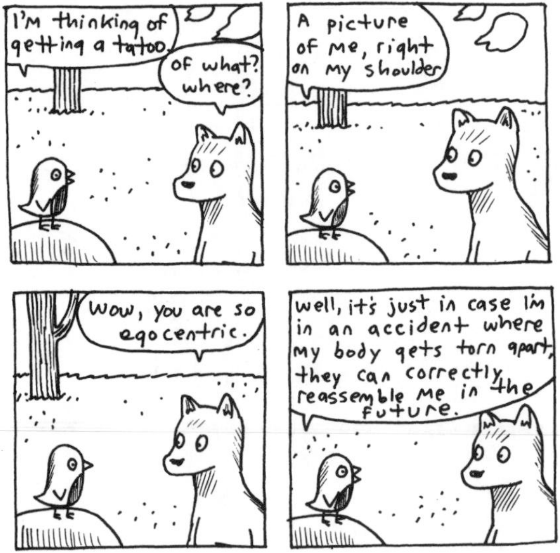
I'm thinking of getting a tatoo.
Of what? where?
A picture of me, right on my shoulder
Wow, you are so egocentric.
well, it's just in case I'm in an accident where my body gets torn apart, they can correctly reassemble me in the future.

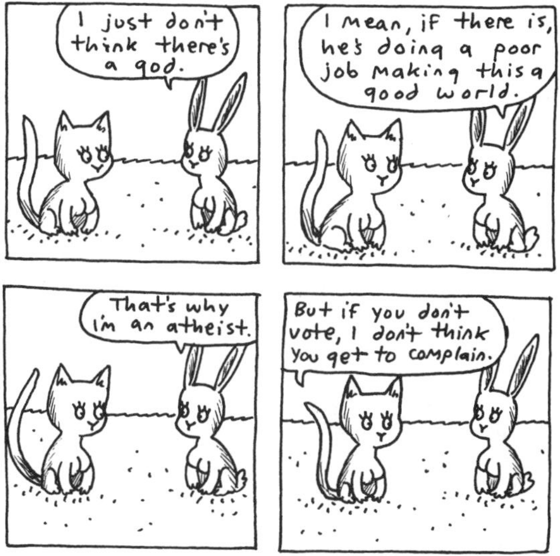
I just don't think there's a god.
I mean, if there is, he's doing a poor job making this a good world.
That's why I'm an atheist.
But if you don't vote, I don't think you get to complain.

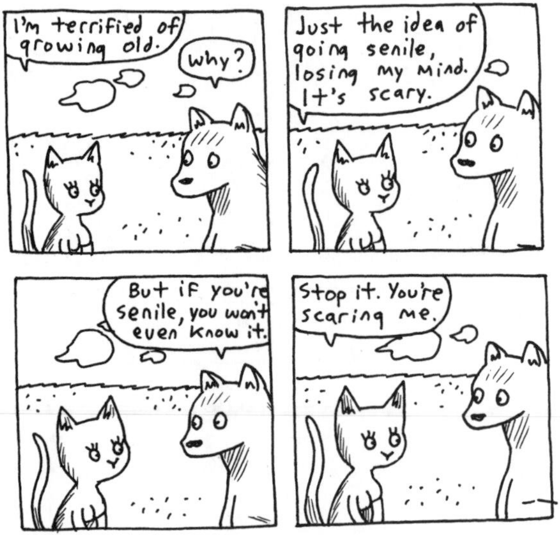
I'm terrified of growing old.
Why?
Just the idea of going senile, losing my mind. It's scary.
But if you're senile, you won't even know it.
Stop it. You're scaring me.

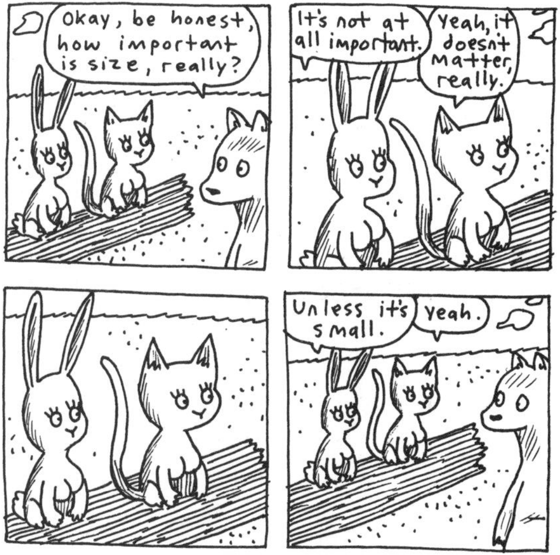
Okay, be honest, how important is size, really?
It's not at all important.
Yeah, it doesn't matter, really.
Unless it's small.
Yeah.

I could really use a massage.
I--
A PROFESSIONAL massage.
I profess to you my desire to give you a massage.

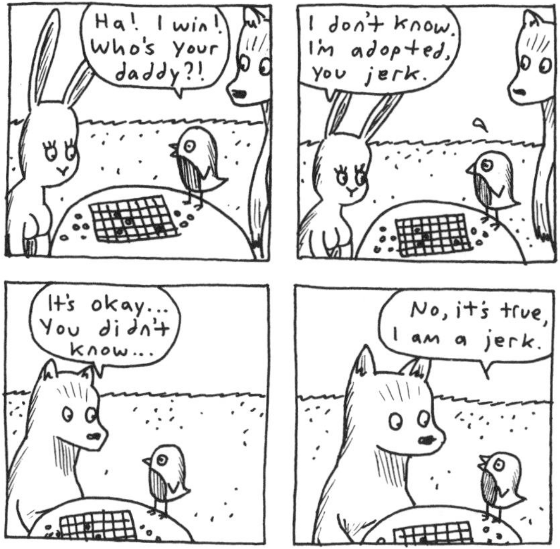
Ha! I win! Who's your daddy?!
I don't know. I'm adopted, you jerk.
It's okay... You didn't know...
No, it's true, I am a jerk.

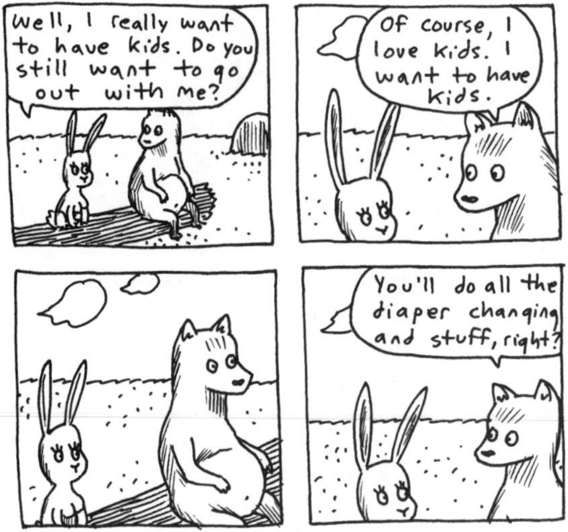
Well, I really want to have kids. Do you still want to go out with me?
Of course, I love kids. I want to have kids.
You'll do all the diaper changing and stuff, right?

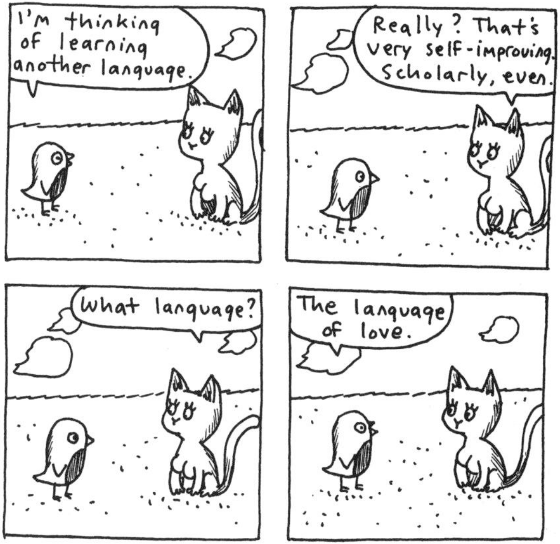
I'm thinking of learning another language.
Really? That's very self-improving. Scholarly, even.
What language?
The language of love.

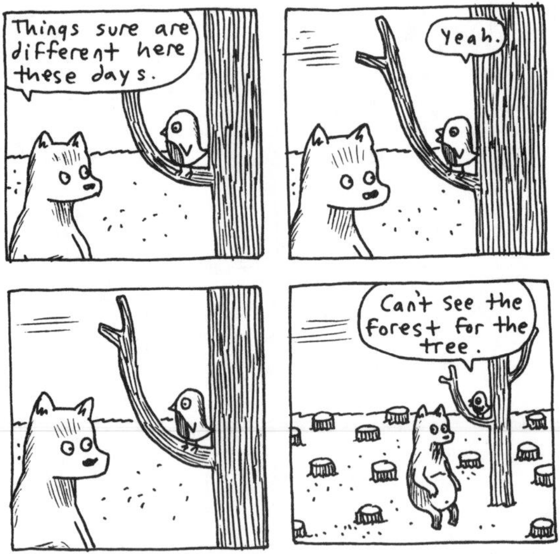
Things sure are different here these days.
Yeah.
Can't see the forest for the tree.

* except for the 'blank page' starburst **
** and these asterices

JEFFREY BROWN was born in 1975, and then started drawing comics. Then he stopped drawing comics, but later, he started drawing comics again, and then he started publishing them. The End---?

MORE FUNNY BOOKS FROM JEFFREY BROWN:

 **CLUMSY**
Unconvincing and confusing portrait of romance.

UNLIKELY
More autobiography exploiting a past relationship.

ANY EASY INTIMACY
You can't even tell what's happening with this relationship.

 **EVERY GIRL IS THE END OF THE WORLD FOR ME**
Hopefully the end of every girl book that Jeffrey Brown keeps writing and obsessing about.

 MINIATURE SULK
A funny collection of shorts, although one must wonder if they were intended to be funny.

 BE A MAN
An odd self parody, but at least it's funnier than 'Clumsy.'

 BIGHEAD
Superhero parody, full of clichés and predictable punchlines.

CONVERSATION #2
Thankfully co-authored by James Kochalka.

ALL THESE AND MORE AVAILABLE AT www.topshelfcomix.com

PLEASE WRITE TO JEFFREY BROWN WITH
A FEW ENCOURAGING WORDS FROM THE
HEART. HE IS OBVIOUSLY A LITTLE PATHETIC.
jeffreybrownrq@hotmail.com
or
P.O. BOX 120 DEERFIELD IL 60015-0120 USA

ALSO PLEASE SPEND A FEW HOURS VISITING:

www.theholyconsumption.com

THEN CAREFULLY CHOOSE SOME ORIGINAL
ARTWORK TO PURCHASE FOR YOUR HOME FROM:

www.bequiling.com